A Calculating People

A
Calculating
People

The Spread of Numeracy
in Early America

Patricia Cline Cohen

The University of Chicago Press

Chicago and London

The University of Chicago Press, Chicago 60637
The University of Chicago Press, Ltd., London

Library of Congress Cataloging in Publication Data

Cohen, Patricia Cline.
  A calculating people.

Includes index.
  1. Numeracy—United States—History.   2. United
States—Civilization—To 1783.   3. United States—
Civilization—1783–1865.   4. United States—Statistical
services—History.   I. Title.
QA27.U5C63   306′.42   82-7089
ISBN 0-226-11283-7

PATRICIA CLINE COHEN is assistant professor of history at the
University of California, Santa Barbara

To my parents, Laura and Jack Cline

Contents

Acknowledgments

The inspiration for this study was sparked by a seemingly simple question put to me by Winthrop D. Jordan back in my graduate-school days: Why the sudden popularity of numbers and statistics in Jacksonian America? It is a question more likely to occur to a nonquantifying historian, which Professor Jordan is by constitution; he could appreciate that the predilection for numbers was an oddity calling for explanation. But it is also a question best tackled by someone who partakes of the mentality and can therefore understand its appeal; I count myself in that camp. Now that the thesis has become a book, I am grateful that Professor Jordan encouraged me to take up a big and virtually untouched subject, although there were times along the way when I was less than grateful and wished for a topic with foreordained, definite boundaries.

Several friends and colleagues have been generous with their time and advice. At an early point, Philip Fertik minutely dissected the argument of the book and compelled me to rethink its entire conceptual framework. Although I have not satisfied all of his criticisms, the book is far better for its exposure to his intellectual conscience. Carl V. Harris followed the manuscript through several drafts and always offered thoughtful comments that resulted in greater clarity. Charles G. Sellers alerted me early to the significance of gender in my study. Martha T. Blauvelt, Christine Heyrman, Ronald Walters, J. Sears McGee, Margo Conk, Jonathan Dewald, and Hal Saunders all read parts of the manuscript at various stages and gave me the benefit of their diverse areas of expertise, ranging from American, English, and

ix

European history to high-school mathematics. None of these friends is accountable, of course, for the flaws that still remain.

Financial assistance for research and writing came from the Fred Harris Daniels fund of the American Antiquarian Society, the American Council of Learned Societies, the Newberry Library, and the University of California Faculty Development Award program. Chapter 5 appeared, in somewhat altered form, in the *William and Mary Quarterly* in January, 1981, and I am grateful to its editors for permission to republish it here. In chapter 4 I quote from Catharine Beecher's "First School Closing Address" to the girls who attended her Hartford Seminary. For permission to quote this material I thank the Schlesinger Library at Radcliffe College and the Stowe-Day Foundation, Hartford, Connecticut.

Both this project and my son, Jeremy, were conceived in the same year, and in infancy they each competed for my attention. No doubt the child impeded the book in the beginning, but that changed as both matured. Observing Jeremy acquire the rudiments of numeracy and develop into a child with a genuine talent for numbers greatly enhanced my understanding of how calculating people come into being. Benjamin Cohen has lived with the project over the long haul, a special trial known only to spouses of authors. He has been a sounding board for ideas and a stern critic of my prose; his moral support and his sharing of family responsibilities contributed immeasurably to the final product.

A Calculating People

Introduction

When Alexis de Tocqueville visited the United States in 1830, he found a people intent on material acquisition and an atmosphere permeated by an anxious spirit of gain. The young Frenchman observed that commerce stirred the Americans' passions more than anything else; they looked at the world with the trader's eye and brought a market mentality into their social and political relations. Tocqueville thought this a peculiarly American disposition and attributed it to the egalitarian social order, which, he believed, fueled a desire for economic betterment and insured everlasting discontent with one's present status. Americans were always calculating how to improve their lot. Unceasingly they weighed risks, computed advantages, and gauged the utility of any particular course of action. "Their minds," Tocqueville said, were "accustomed to definite calculations."[1]

In Jacksonian America the habit of calculation was endorsed by educators, moralists, politicians, and patriotic boosters. William Alcott, whose book *The Young Man's Guide* was a leading prototype of advice literature for ambitious young men, stressed that calculation was indispensable for the moral and profitable life. "Live within your income," he warned; "to this end you must calculate." Alcott demonstrated the proper technique by figuring the cost of the indolent habit of staying up until eleven o'clock at night and rising two hours past daybreak: the bill for candles would run to $182.50 in fifty years. Arithmetic was a crucial study for Alcott's ideal young man. Everyone learned the fundamentals in school, he said, but it was essential to practice it endlessly: "Seize on every circumstance . . . where reckoning

3

is required." News of a shipwreck, for example, should spur the enterprising lad to compute the numbers saved and lost, thus sharpening his numerical skills.[2]

"We are a travelling and a calculating people," said Ohio booster James Hall in his book *Statistics of the West*, with evident satisfaction. "Arithmetic I presume comes by instinct among this guessing, reckoning, expecting and calculating people," said English traveler Thomas Hamilton, with evident distaste. Each man attached a different value to the idea, but both agreed that Americans in the 1830s had some sort of innate reckoning skill that set them apart from Europeans.[3] What they may not have realized is that this skill also differentiated Jacksonians from their own grandfathers, for numeracy did not become widespread in America until the early decades of the nineteenth century.

This book traces the development of numeracy in America from its English origins in the seventeenth century to its diffusion and acceptance in the first half of the nineteenth century. My research for it, which began some time ago, was undertaken to answer what at first seemed a small question: Why was it that in the 1820s and 1830s there suddenly appeared many types of quantitative materials and documents that previously had been quite rare? Not only government agencies but private associations and individuals were eagerly counting, measuring, and churning out data. Antebellum reform sentiment alone could not account for it, for temperance and abolitionist societies had powerful moral arguments at their disposal well before they turned to quantitative facts to prove the justice of their cause. Nor could a faith in progress alone account for it, although that faith certainly inspired many of the statistically backed boasts of the period. The widening circle of commerce was somehow implicated in the origins of the new propensity to count, but the link was unclear until I recast the question in this form: What was it, before the 1820s, that prevented statistics and numbers from being part of the ordinary discourse of Americans? In this light, my subject became the history of the diffusion of a skill, numeracy.

The word "numeracy" is a relatively recent addition to the English language. It has the awkwardness of a concocted word not yet weathered to smoothness through frequent use. The 1976 supplement to the *Oxford English Dictionary* has leanly defined it as "ability with or knowledge of numbers" and locates its origins in a 1959 report on English education that contrasted illiterate scientists with innumerate humanists. The word was intended to be the analogue of "literacy." It reflected the late 1950s concern that the humanities and the sciences were diverging into two cultures, each unable to comprehend the other because of the extent to which knowledge had become esoteric. In this context, "illiterate" did not mean "unable to read," nor did "innumerate" mean "unable to add"; rather, the words referred to an unspecified degree of deficiency at high levels that hindered communication among scholars.

Concern over a divergence of two cultures has somewhat abated now, two decades later, partly because we more readily accept the necessity of specialization of knowledge but largely because numeracy is no longer the distinct preserve of science. The computer revolution of our time has pulled increasing numbers of people into daily familiarity with numbers and statistics. Not only scientists but business managers, college administrators, and public servants need to know enough arithmetic and statistics to interpret the data that are now routinely used as a basis for rational decisionmaking. There is still a dividing line, an important boundary in the job market, that is defined by the possession of numerical skills. But it is no longer a question of humanist versus scientist, of opposed skills, numeracy and literacy, competing for dominance. Rather, numeracy looms now as the successor to literacy. Just as the possession of basic literacy once marked a significant dividing line in society, between the powerful and the powerless or between the priests and the people, so numeracy is now the basic skill that increasingly establishes a status boundary in the world of work.

But what exactly is numeracy? "An ability with or knowledge of numbers" does not quite say enough, since it does not specify what sort of ability or what level of knowledge constitutes mastery of numbers. Literacy is a similarly unspecific word, meaning a knowledge of the written symbols of language coupled with some sort of ability to manipulate them. To gain specificity, we ought to be able to describe and arrange the bundle of skills that are the component parts of numeracy and to identify the level of competence that meaningfully separates innumerate from numerate people. But these are not such easy tasks, for both a hierarchy of skills, arranged in order of increasing difficulty, and the meaning of functional innumeracy have changed greatly over the past three centuries. What might have been a superfluous skill for most Americans in the seventeenth century—say, an ability to do long division—would now be insufficient to warrant graduation from elementary school. Since this is the case, a history of numeracy must not only try to establish the level of numerical knowledge possessed by a particular society or by subgroups within it; it must also connect that level of knowledge to the uses to which numbers are put in that society.

Analogies drawn from the history of literacy can help clarify the meaning of a history of numeracy, for there are some parallels, as well as important differences, between the two that illuminate the way a historian can study them. Literacy and numeracy both involve cognitive skills, usually deliberately taught; we do not assume that children will pick up reading or arithmetic to any useful degree without some sort of intentional instruction, the way they pick up spoken language through imitation. This means that important clues to literacy and numeracy can be found in the history of education. Furthermore, each is easily thought of as a continuum, ranging from total illiteracy to lofty levels of literary talent, from innumeracy to mathematical sophistication. The batteries of achievement tests that claim to stratify students according to verbal and quantitative performance invite the view that these skills are logically related, fixed, hierarchical sequences. Just as individual persons progress along a path of development in each skill, so also have whole societies moved from the preliterate and prenumerate state toward our modern reliance on print and on quantification. Historians of literacy in the Western world have identified the sixteenth to eighteenth centuries as the critical period for the widespread diffusion of literacy; in this study of numeracy I have found that the seventeenth to nineteenth centuries were the critical years for the diffusion of basic numerical skills.[4]

Problems arise as soon as we try to become more specific about the exact nature of the continuums of literacy and numeracy. Is each simply a recapitulation of the way children learn reading and arithmetic today? Typically, children first learn the alphabet and then learn to recognize and write short familiar nouns, including their own names. Gradually they learn more words, some as spelling words and harder ones as recognition vocabulary. Later comes formal instruction in the rules of punctuation, grammar, and syntax. Literacy, as encountered in formal education, consists of an accumulation of skills in reading, writing, spelling, vocabulary, diction, and grammar, mapped out by professional educators in a prescribed course. Ideally, the endpoint of this continuum is the literate person, one who can comprehend written material, participate in the print culture of modern society, communicate in writing, and fix thoughts and events in records. The parallel development of numeracy begins with the child's introduction to the names of numbers and counting and progresses to learning about written numbers, the place system, and the four basic operations. Children practice manipulating ever-larger numbers, learning written techniques like borrowing and long division to facilitate computation. The sequence of mathematics instruction appears to move in an established path through elementary and high school education: addition comes before subtraction, fractions before percentages, algebra before trigonometry, geometry before calculus. Ideally, the endpoint of this continuum is the numerate person, one who can balance a checkbook, maintain financial records, understand economic indicators, and comprehend and even participate in the scientific and political cultures of our day that are so permeated by numbers and quantification.

The trouble with these two versions of the development of literacy and numeracy is that they are modern reconstructions. The order in which the various arithmetic skills are learned is in fact not immutable and has been surprisingly different in past times. In the eighteenth century, the few persons who studied arithmetic usually learned long division before they learned addition of decimal fractions; in the 1820s some students learned to add, subtract, multiply, and divide large numbers in their heads before they were ever taught written numbers and the place system of arabic numerals; in our own century, in the 1960s, the "new math" put simple set theory and geometry into the elementary grades. The teaching of language arts, too, has not always been the same as it now is. We teach reading and writing nearly simultaneously, but, up through the eighteenth century, there were many who learned to read without ever learning to write (which makes for an interesting wrinkle in literacy studies that depend on signatures as evidence). Furthermore, the order in which skills are taught does not guarantee that they will be learned in that order. Many a student today can read with a normal degree of comprehension but cannot spell even the simplest words.

An alternate way of thinking about literacy and numeracy—one that does not depend on assuming a fixed sequence of acquiring knowledge—is to separate each of them into types of abilities, like those used in constructing standardized aptitude tests. In a simplified scheme, memory might be one category, needed for spelling, vocabulary, rote computation, and application of memorized formulas. A second might be reasoning ability, both inductive and deductive, needed for understanding and constructing arguments and in solving word problems or constructing proofs in mathematics. Verbal analogies and spatial relations are other areas often treated as distinct abilities that contribute to literacy and numeracy. Such clusters of abilities do not easily lend themselves to an evolutionary view of skill development, but they can be quite useful, nonetheless, in a historical study of numeracy, for at various times some abilities have been more closely associated with mathematical skill than at others. For example, eighteenth-century arithmetic was largely conceived of as memory work, whereas nineteenth-century arithmetic was reformulated to rely on inductive reasoning. Failure to thrive in twentieth-century geometry is often blamed on poor ability in spatial relations, but those nineteenth-century educators who claimed that geometry was impossible for women to understand would never have assumed females to be deficient in spatial relations, for that would have been inconsistent with women's demonstrated talents in constructing garments out of flatgoods without benefit of patterns. Instead, they put the blame on insufficient abstract reasoning power, which women could develop only at the risk of losing their talent for dealing with the concrete and particular.

Both ways of viewing numeracy have their advantages, and fortunately it is not necessary to choose one to the exclusion of the other. The idea that numeracy is a continuum of knowledge is not negated by the discovery that the sequence in which numerical skills were learned may have been somewhat different in earlier times. All it means is that we must reconstruct what the particular sequence was at any given time and then see how far students progressed along it. That, historically, different clusters of abilities were seen to impinge on numerical talent and learning may in fact help to explain variations in the sequence in which skills were taught, i.e., the fact that memory and reasoning powers alternately come to the fore as predominant modes of instruction.

A further analogy between literacy and numeracy raises thorny problems. The essence of literacy is the manipulation and interpretation of *written* symbols; the most exalted speech in a Shakespearean play does not require literacy until it is written down and read. Literacy begins with the written word. Should the definition of numeracy be similarly restricted to the manipulation of written symbols? Or should it mean, more generally, the ability to manipulate numbers, whether written or not? Let us take each case, to see what happens to the meaning of *innumerate*.

If numeracy does not depend on written symbols, then the truly innumerate would be only those who completely lack a concept of number. Anyone who could add or subtract, using fingers, pebbles, beads, or the head, would be counted as numerate, however slightly. This would mean that most of the world's population over the age of five has always been numerate. For a time, Westerners harbored the notion that primitive peoples counted "one, two, many," but anthropological studies have demonstrated that most languages, even among primitives, have words expressing numbers into the hundreds, thousands, and more, building by tens, twelves, or twenties.[5] It is not unreasonable to assume that most humans easily learn to utilize numbers up to ten or twenty, perhaps aided by the tangible digits of the hands and feet, since the most basic of activities (economic exchange, food preparation, a sense of time) require some recourse to quantity. A definition of numeracy that is so general as to include any concept of number at all is not very useful, since only very small children would be innumerate.

We could repair this definition, still maintaining that numeracy can be mental as well as written, by raising the threshold of numeracy to the ability to manipulate numbers beyond twenty. The body itself suggests this threshold with its fingers and toes. It is a definition that, up to the eighteenth century, separates the many and unschooled from the few who were schooled. A scornful English mathematician dismissed Americans as a "barbarous" people in 1701 because most of them could "hardly reckon above twenty."[6] Although his scorn was unjustified, he was right about the Americans' low level of arithmetic knowledge, though it was quite sufficient for daily functioning in an agricultural and largely subsistence economy. Ciphering beyond twenty was a product of deliberate instruction, taught in response to perceived need. The innumerate, then, might be defined as those who have had no formal instruction in arithmetic and who manage to deal with quantities in life by wiggling their fingers or by piling up pebbles.

This might be one reasonable way to distinguish the threshold between numeracy and innumeracy, but it verges on a definition that features an ability to deal with written symbols as the essence of numeracy. Few people are sufficiently adept at mental calculation to carry out arithmetic problems with numbers above twenty without recourse to some symbolic representation of numbers; the brief span of short-term memory is the limiting factor. Even those extraordinary persons known as "mental calculators," who can do rapid computations with large numbers, rely on tricks and on facts stored in their long-term memory to shorten problems so that they will fit in the short-term memory's workspace. The rest of us reach for paper and pencil or an electronic calculator, and, with these, we are in the realm of the written symbol.

If we were to restrict numeracy to mean the ability to use written symbols for concepts of number, in strict parallel to literacy, then innumeracy would imply the absence of this ability. There is an appealing clarity about this definition, but a moment's reflection reveals that it raises problems. Is a society that calculates on an abacus innumerate? Is the *idiot-savant* who performs rapid mental calculations innumerate? Are roman numerals—surely a written symbol system—so very different from a condensed form of tally sticks? Suppose we tie numeracy to the use of arabic numerals, since they are the symbols that have the power of computing built into them. Should we then be forced to conclude that all the Greeks, Romans, and Renaissance Florentines were innumerate?

There are no easy answers to this dilemma. It certainly offends sensibilities to think that Plato, Pythagoras, and the Medici bankers had less of this thing called numeracy than a nineteenth-century schoolboy. Calculation by abacus can be every bit as swift and sure as the written manipulation of arabic numerals. And yet, the power and simplicity of arabic numerals have made quantification accessible to the masses and have turned Western society into the highly technical and mathematical world of today. Arithmetic without written arabic numerals is a rather more limited enterprise.

The fallacy at the heart of the definitions discussed so far lies in their insistence on defining a threshold. The argument of this book is that Anglo-American culture shifted from a prenumerate to a numerate state over the space of three centuries. The transition was gradual, occurring in many small stages. It is a mistake to think of numeracy as either wholly present or wholly absent. The exact point on the continuum at which an individual passes from being devoid of numeracy to possessing some dawning knowledge of the skill is not only hard to agree on and hard to identify; it is also rather meaningless. The same is true for literacy, but historians of that skill have been slow to recognize it, having been misled by the apparent simplicity of counting signatures versus x-marks and taking that as a measure of literacy. They surely know that kindergartners who can write their names are not literate in any meaningful sense, yet they persist in their measurements because the threshold of literacy is for them unambiguous (it begins with the written symbol), and one type of evidence for measuring it does exist. The historian of numeracy is spared that confusion: there are no recorded moments in the past when great numbers of typical citizens stepped forward and recited the multiplication table. (A statement of property valuation collected for a tax list or census might have been calculated by the assessor or enumerator, so it is not sure evidence of popular numeracy.) Ironic as it sounds, it has not proved possible to construct a quantitative measure of numeracy rates, both because of the indeterminate definition of the term and the lack of systematic historical evidence.

However, the fact that numeracy cannot be measured is less of a drawback than might be imagined. The most interesting question is not how crude numeracy rates have changed over time but rather how the domain of number has changed and expanded. There is, of course, a direct relation between the two: as the domain has become enlarged, more people have made an effort to become skillful with numbers. But even people with a rudimentary knowledge of numbers can, to some extent, participate in a quantitative society, just as illiterate people can participate in the world of letters by having others read to them.

All that is required when one enters into market exchange without understanding the arithmetic of the transaction is trust. Trust was the foundation of village-store transactions, where merchants made change or kept credit records for their less numerate clientele; trust was also a factor in the mills and factories of the early nineteenth century, where employers stated wage rates in shillings

per hour or per piece but paid in dollars per week. Trust necessitated by lack of skill (or energy) has not vanished today, for
who among us recalculates the terms of a thirty-year mortgage
to see that the bank's computer is charging the right monthly
payment? Who refigures the FICA deduction that appears on the
monthly paycheck? It is possible to live by the number without
always clearly knowing the derivation of important numbers.
Given the availability of hired accountants, computers, and calculators to do our figuring for us, it may be the case that the
domain of number will continue to expand while the power of the
individual to calculate grows rusty with disuse.

This history of numeracy in early America follows the story
from its origins in seventeenth-century England to its flowering in the mid-nineteenth century in America. These were
the years when increasing numbers of people were drawn into a
commercialized economy requiring a competence in the fundamentals of arithmetic. New economic, religious, and political
ideas all stimulated the spread of reckoning skills and contributed
to the prestige of numbers and quantification, a prestige that had
become very great by the antebellum decades. What sorts of
people could reckon and with what degree of sophistication? By
what methods and in what patterns were arithmetical skills diffused? Did a spreading propensity to count and measure indicate
an alteration in the way people thought about what they were
counting and measuring? When could it be said that the era of
mass numeracy had arrived, and what did it bring in its train?
This book explores both the spread of numeracy in the population
and the spread of the domain of number as things once thought
of solely in qualitative terms became subject to quantification.

Since numeracy cannot be exactly measured, evidence for it
must generally be inferred inexactly from the various uses of
numbers in the past. Just as we can infer something about levels
of readership from an examination of published writings and their
circulations, clues to numeracy are reflected in a multitude of
events and documents. The replacement of roman by arabic numerals is one such clue; the exposure to arithmetic in schools and
through textbooks is another. The expansion of occupations that
required mathematical skill, for example in business, surveying,
and engineering, signals an expansion of numeracy. The appear-

ance of numbers and statistics in publications of wide circulation indicates something about the receptivity of the public to such data. Taken together, these and other clues create a clear pattern of the progress of numeracy.

This book is not a comprehensive catalogue of all uses of numbers from the seventeenth to the mid-nineteenth century. Each chapter focuses on a factor or episode that illustrates the scope and limits of numeracy at a particular time: the fad for number, weight, and measure among a small circle of seventeenth-century Englishmen; the controversial inauguration of censuses in Jamestown and the West Indies colonies in the first century of colonization; the debate over the meaning of mortality patterns in the eighteenth-century colonies; the history of arithmetic education; the relation of "statisticks" to statecraft in the young republic; and the furor over the errors in the 1840 census. Each chapter also illuminates a significant enlargement of the domain of number and links quantification with alterations in the way men thought about their social, political, and economic relations. Numeracy profoundly shaped the character of society in the post-Revolutionary years; a knowledge of its history supplies a fresh vantage point from which to view the development of modern America.

1

Numeracy in
Seventeenth-Century
England

No state, no age, no man, nor child, but here may wisdome win
For numbers teach the parts of speech, wher children first begin.
And number beares so great a sway, even from the most to least
That who in numbring hath no skill, is numbred for a beast:
For what more beastly can be thought? nay what more blockish than
Then man to want the onely art, which proper is to man,
For many creatures farre excell mankind in many things,
But never none could number yet, save man, in whom it springs.
If numbring then be (almost) al, betweene a man and beast,
Come learne o men to number then, which arte is here profest.

—THOMAS HILL
The Arte of Vulgar Arithmetick, both in Integers and Fractions
(London, 1600) [Original spellings slightly modified.]

In 1600, Elizabethan England had good reason to sing the praises of the art of arithmetic. The century just brought to a close had been characterized by continual expansion. Marked population growth, monetary inflation, and overseas discoveries stretched the boundaries of thought and custom in ways that called to mind size, number, and measure. Certainly it was an indulgence in hyperbole for the author of the paean to arithmetic, Thomas Hill, to single out counting as the essence of humanity, the skill that distinguished man from the beasts. But the exaggeration served to emphasize the paramount importance of arithmetic in a country rapidly becoming a center of commercial capitalism.

Arithmetic skills had in fact been only rather recently and selectively developed in England when Hill published his book.
Although his poem went on to list nearly a score of occupations
and stations in life for which knowledge of arithmetic was allegedly requisite, including shepherds, philosophers, and soldiers,
Hill was not describing reality so much as he was attempting to
widen the market for his book. In the early seventeenth century,
arithmetic was a commercial subject, studied chiefly by men who
followed the life of commerce. Arabic numerals did not come into
general use until the middle of the sixteenth century, and the
earliest English textbook of the rules of arithmetic appeared in
the 1540s, the first of a trickle that became a flood around 1600.
The expansion of the commercial sector of the population generated a demand for reckoning skills that books like Hill's were
attempting to meet.

As knowledge of arithmetic became slowly diffused in the seventeenth century, the activities of counting and measuring soon
moved somewhat beyond the confines of commerce and found
expression not only in improved methods of navigation and surveying, but in political thought as well. A new word, "pantometry,"
appeared in seventeenth-century dictionaries, indicating that the
measuring of all things could be considered to be one activity
subsumed in one word. Arguments erupted over the true heights
of mountains and the exact number of years since God's creation
of the world. Dozens of men acquired thermometers and barom-
eters and consulted them thrice daily to measure the weather. The
idea of commercial bookkeeping, transposed to the realm of government, led to "political arithmetic," an accounting of the total
resources of the country for the purpose of formulating rational
policy.

To the twentieth-century mind, all these varieties of counting
and measuring may seem to be only remotely related. Today
arithmetic is applied to so many different phenomena that it
scarcely seems instructive to draw connections between sports
statistics and the consumer price index. They have numbers in
common, but, then, number is the new literacy of the twentieth
century; sports and prices are only two of a very large set of items
easily described in quantitative terms. In the seventeenth century,
applications of number were still limited, and many obstacles
stood in the way of an easy diffusion of numeracy. Measuring
things was in fact a kind of sport, relatively few people were

engaged in it, and the set of items thought to be susceptible of quantitative expression was rather small. It is therefore legitimate to ask what bounded that set. What did these instances of quantification have in common, and what limited the further application of numerical reasoning?

A key unifying element is that a mere handful of people produced most of the instances of quantification. An urge to measure had caught the fancy of a number of men, many of whom knew each other through the Royal Society of London or through local mathematics clubs. They became intent on measuring, counting, and weighing as a method of acquiring knowledge, and they moved easily from one sort of measurement to another. Their oddity was that they were trying to affix numerical certainty to what most people were content to leave to supposition, estimate, or qualitative description. A single author would write books on arithmetic, navigation, bookkeeping, gauging (measuring the capacity of containers), and interest rates. The man who coined the term "political arithmetic" had earlier in his career been a navigator and surveyor. A minister fascinated by the demography of his parish readily turned his hand to the problem of the heights of lunar mountains. The mathematical similarity in all these endeavors was precisely what attracted them. Prefaces to gauging and arithmetic books often specified ingenious persons of mathematical bent as part of the intended audience, in addition to bookkeepers or artisans with practical need of specific arithmetic techniques. That was how they saw themselves: as men disposed to delight in numbers.[1]

While the common feature of the new and diverse instances of quantification was their origin amongst a few men, the limiting factor, the constraint that kept quantification confined to certain areas, is less easy to discern. It might appear sufficient to observe that people measure only what they need to measure, and, as the need for precise knowledge expands, the practice of measurement expands with it. Thus it might be argued that the rise of commercial capitalism required that merchants have ways to figure their exact profits and losses on ventures. Trading in distant markets turned the art of gauging into a necessity, for one had to master several intricate systems of weights and measures to be able to compare products from one place with products from another. The mercantilist balance-of-trade theory suggested the utility of an office of import and export statistics. However, to

assume so direct a link between a need for knowledge and an
urge to measure and number is far too simplistic. In fact, most
seventeenth-century capitalists, traders, and mercantilists got
along quite well without using the quantitative techniques—double-entry bookkeeping, geometrical gauging, national account
books—that the quantifiers praised. Something more than plain
need, then, produced the urge to measure among the handful of
quantifying men; clearly, something quite apart from need was at
work in their efforts to measure the heights of mountains or the
heat of the day. Why did they develop curiosity about the dimensions of some things but not others? One clue may lie in their
frequent declarations that numbers brought satisfaction because
they signified certainty, quite apart from any practical application.
What was measured in the seventeenth century, then, was not
only what was thought to be necessary but also what most ur-
gently needed to be made certain.

Arabic numerals filtered into Europe in the tenth century
through North Africa and Spain, but they were hardly
known before the early thirteenth century. Leonardo of
Pisa learned of them in his travels in Egypt and Syria, and on his
return to Italy in 1202 he wrote a treatise describing an amazing
number system that allowed basic computations to be carried out
with the written numbers themselves. Roman numerals, the traditional notation system then in use in Europe, allowed only for
the expression of quantity. There was no way to add, subtract,
multiply, divide, or write fractions by manipulating the written
symbols. Nevertheless, medieval and early modern Italian merchants found this traditional system entirely adequate to their
purposes. In the twelfth and thirteenth centuries Italian city-states
had developed rather complicated systems of trade, exchange,
banking, and credit, and they managed to maintain all records
and transactions with roman numerals. Basic operations were
carried out with an abacus or on a counting board, a table top
with lines representing an abacus and with coins or small stones
used as counting tokens. Business transactions could be concluded right on the counter in this mechanical fashion, without
the use of paper and without the necessity of doing simple sums
in the head.[2]

Leonardo's treatise on arabic numerals had little immediate impact on this traditional system of figuring. Indeed, in 1299 one Italian city, Florence, passed a law against the use of arabic numerals because the numbers were more easily falsified than the roman. It was argued that a zero could be altered into a six or a nine too easily, or a one to a seven. Even more grievous falsification was permitted by the addition of extra digits to the beginning or end of a number; 428 could grow to 4281 with the stroke of a pen. By contrast, roman numerals expressed a number with finality: usually the last letter in a group was given an extra mark to identify it as the last, for example xij instead of xii for 12.[3] These reasons for rejecting arabic numerals show that the basic function of written numbers in medieval and early modern commerce was to record transactions, not to create manipulable bodies of data. Further, the limited availability of paper argued in favor of retaining the old notation, where calculations were carried out on counting boards and only the final results were committed to writing.

In the century between 1450 and 1550 arabic numerals gradually supplanted roman numerals in European commerce. The change-over in England came in the reign of Henry VIII. As that king's title suggests, roman numerals did not entirely fade away. They continued to be used in written documents where specification of quantity or number was essential and where no calculation with the number was intended. Legal documents, wills, and court records retained the roman, as did the days of the month in almanacs, chapter numbers in books, and numerical designations of successive monarchs. But where calculation with numbers was desired, arabic numerals were adopted. Commerce, bookkeeping, navigation, and surveying all were altered under the impact of arabic numerals.

The first English books of arabic arithmetic presented their subject as a systematic set of rules governing the elementary manipulation of the new numbers. Robert Recorde's *Grounde of Arts* appeared in 1543, followed by a second text, *The Whetstone of Witte*, in 1557. The titles squarely placed mathematics on the ground floor of intellectual development by suggesting that arithmetic was the foundation of knowledge as well as an activity that sharpened the mind. Both books were reprinted in many editions over the next century, and they established the model followed by other pure arithmetic texts.[4] They began with numeration and explained the power of arabic place notation, where nine symbols plus zero could express any quantity. The basic operations with numbers were set forth, examples were worked, and a systematic development was sustained from each stage to the next, through the first four "rules" (addition, subtraction, multiplication, division), to fractions and decimals, up to surde (irrational) numbers and the "cossicke practise" (algebra).[5] The reader of such texts learned mathematics as a coherent body of thought about numbers in the abstract.

At the end of the sixteenth century, books of applied arithmetic came on the scene. Most of them presupposed a thorough knowledge of basic arithmetic on the part of the reader. The authors were typically mathematical men whose interests spanned several fields. For example, in the middle years of Elizabeth's reign the mathematician Leonard Digges wrote about navigation, gunnery (the flight of projectiles), architecture, and the all-encompassing "pantometria," the art of measuring all lines, surfaces, and solids. Seventy-five years later one William Leybourn churned out at least twenty books on surveying, navigation, gunnery, "dialing" (constructing sundials), accounting, and "arithmetical recreations." Since they assumed a preexisting mathematical competence, their readership could not have been wide; but the practical applications addressed problems of growing importance in Tudor-Stuart England.

Navigation and surveying, for example, had taken on new importance in this era of overseas expansion, settlement of new lands, and a reorganization of existing land-tenure arrangements at home. To some extent, navigation and surveying have always concerned men of property and of the sea. But there was no premium on mathematical precision when ships clung to coastwise routes or when property lines stayed in their traditional places, coinciding with natural features of the land, such as river bottoms. In the sixteenth and seventeenth centuries, vessels on the high seas required more exact methods of reckoning position. Disruptions of land boundaries, such as those caused by the confiscation of monastery lands by Henry VIII or the parceling-out of confiscated Irish land in the 1650s, sparked large-scale surveying efforts, which required new instruments and mathematical skills, particularly simple geometry and trigonometry.

Navigators in England lagged behind the exploratory Spanish and Portuguese, who in the fifteenth century were already sailing to Africa and the West Indies, guided by the astrolabe and sundial, in use since the twelfth century. The astrolabe, forerunner of the sextant, was not commonly used by English seamen, according to one historian of Tudor navigation. It measured the altitude of the sun or a star above the horizon, and apparently it was too complicated a device for the average English mariner. But then, the problems that English sailors confronted were simpler than the Spaniards'. In the mid-sixteenth century English navigation depended on equipment no more complicated than a lead and line for sounding the depths of the wide continental shelf that extends off the English coast; thus, even when they were far beyond sight of land, mariners could know they were following the coastline.[6] However, the expansion of trade and exploration by the English in Elizabeth's reign created a need for more accurate methods of determining position and direction at sea. Beginning in the 1560s, books on navigation addressed a range of nautical problems, the most pressing of which was how to find the latitude and longitude of a position.

The division of the globe into lines of latitude and longitude was a Ptolemaic idea, rediscovered in the early fifteenth century. Beginning in the mid-sixteenth century, English maps began to use the coordinates as reference points on two-dimensional maps of small areas, in which distortion was negligible. After 1569, when the Flemish geographer Gerhardus Mercator thought of stretching the latitude lines apart near the poles, the guiding lines could be used on large maps.[7] Having such a map, the navigator had only to sail to a desired latitude and then stay on course, east or west, to the destination. The reckoning of latitude was a fairly straightforward matter. Using a quadrant, a navigator measured the angle of the sun at solar noon with the horizon, compared it to a table of the sun's declination for that day (degrees above or below the celestial equator), and entered the numbers in a formula that varied with the time of year.[8] Staying on course, however, was a more difficult matter, so this method of navigation was rather inefficient. In the early seventeenth century, navigation texts introduced the ''sayling triangle'' as an alternate solution to the problem of plotting a ship's course. With a knowledge of a ship's latitude at two different times plus knowledge of the degrees of the angle off North of the ship's course, it was possible to construct a right-angled triangle, since all the angles and one side's length were known; the hypotenuse represented the ship's path.[9] Protractors became essential on-board equipment, along with compasses and quadrants. Not until the invention of the marine chronometer in the eighteenth century would navigation become more exact.

The principles of triangulation were also applied to the measurement of distances on land. Manuals on the art of surveying were in effect practical treatises on geometry. But the audience they addressed was not narrowly vocational. One author claimed that anyone of liberal mind would "take great delight and pleasure to see how by Arte a man may measure the distances and places remote and farre a sunder, approaching nigh none of them," and with greater accuracy than could be achieved by the old method of direct measurement by chains attached to poles.[10] Another author recommended that budding surveyors practice their art by mapping out their home towns, taking sightings from the school, the church, the jail, and the town hall. Quite apart from the obvious practical benefits of surveying, this author justified the study of triangulation as a sort of game for young scholars and gentlemen. Just as the exercise of riding led to health, and merchandising led to wealth, so recreational mathematics was said to lead to happiness, being "amiable company" for "vacant hours."[11]

Measuring the heights of mountains was a kind of competitive sport in the seventeenth century. The measurers used triangulation, and they argued intently over their often conflicting estimates in the pages of successive editions of surveying books. A Captain Samuel Sturmy, in an idle moment in the Canary Islands, decided to test an amazing report that the peak of Teneriffe was sixty miles high; he felt sure that snow could not exist at that altitude. Using his quadrant, he sighted the mountain from several offshore positions and presented two pages of calculation by triangulation in his 1669 text on the mariner's art. He arrived with satisfaction at the altitude 31 and 30/100 miles. In a 1684 edition of the same book, an italicized communication from "John Cotton, Teacher of Mathematics in London," offered a correction of "2100 Geometrical Paces, that is two Miles (of 1000 paces) and 1/100,"

> and this, to all knowing men, will appear to be the truth, rather than this pretended observation of the Authors, for that the Height of Pico, or any other Mountain in the World should be 31 Miles is altogether incredible.[12]

It is in this context of measurement as sport that we should place the "perambulator," a wheel for measuring distances along a road, developed by a Frenchman in 1567.[13] In the seventeenth century, English almanacs began to include lists giving distances along roads and mileage between cities, information derived from either perambulation or triangulation.[14] Mileage seems so eminently useful to know that it is an effort to imagine why earlier almanacs did not include it or what circumstances led to its insertion. Were there more travelers over strange roads? Was the greater movement of goods causing traders to think in terms of cost per mile? Or was there simply a curiosity to measure the distance, aided by new methods and legions of neophyte surveyors? The alternative to mileage is to express distance in travel time, a measure that varies with an individual's speed and with seasonal and geographical impediments. Travel time is a subjective measure, whereas mileage is objective and unchanging. The presence of tables of distances in almanacs is about the only evidence that objective quantitative measurement was of interest to a larger public than that addressed by the specialized mathematical books.

In addition to navigation and surveying texts, a third sort of applied arithmetic book that became very common in England in the mid-seventeenth century covered the problems of measurement and computation in business life. Commercial figuring was far from simple because the systems of money, weights, and measures then in use were very complicated. The problems of adding or multiplying a duodecimal system of money—the base-twelve pound-shilling-pence system of England—using a base-ten number system were compounded by the tremendous variety of meanings given to terms of measurement used in commerce. For example, a gallon of wine differed in volume from a gallon of beer or ale, and in London a barrel of beer contained thirty-two gallons but anywhere else it contained thirty-four; a pound of weight meant sixteen ounces of some materials but twelve of others.[15] In practice the welter of measuring terms probably was not very confusing, for what did it matter if the traditional casks holding beer and wine were of different sizes? (Today's beverage consumers do not require vessels of identical size in order to make a choice between the two.) Up through the eighteenth century most Englishmen found it perfectly reasonable to let the material being measured dictate the unit of measurement. No one suggested a more uniform system of weights and measures, not the least because a new system would have required an improbable administrative fiat to reorder the traditional ways men thought about quantity, by forcing a disassociation between product and measure. But a few men, at least, were disturbed enough by the variety of terms to think that a commercial arithmetic book ought to set forth all the different measures in tables of equivalences and instruct young clerks in the art of measuring all products uniformly.

Some commercial texts assumed that their readers already had a grasp of basic arithmetic and geometry. John Smith, author of *Stereometrie, Or the Art of Practical Gauging* (1673), warned that geometry and decimal fractions were particularly necessary to know before one could learn to measure volumes. Any person "who intends to reap any benefit by reading this Book, should have a proper Genius, not only ready to conceive Mathematical Notions, but apt likewise to take a kind of pleasure in them, for, de quo libet ligno non fit Mercurius." Mercury, signifying quickness of mind, is not made of just any wood.[16]

But this exclusionary attitude was not very practical. If only mercurial minds could learn to measure wine or brandy casks, there would not be nearly enough gaugers around. There was always the traditional but inconvenient method of gauging odd-shaped containers, that is, by pouring the contents into a vessel of known size. But the larger the scale of trade, the more cumbersome that method became. The solution was to teach traders and gaugers a streamlined version of arithmetic that was directly appropriate to their work. From the mid-seventeenth to the late eighteenth century, commerce-oriented texts that assumed no prior knowledge of arithmetic dominated the market.[17] They promised (falsely) to present the subject in such a way that even the meanest capacities could learn enough to function in business and trade. The leading example was Edward Cocker's *Arithmetick*, which was issued in 112 editions in the century after 1677. Also popular were James Hodder's *Arithmetick, or that Necessary Art Made Easy*, first printed in 1661 and reprinted throughout the eighteenth century in England and the American colonies, and Thomas Dilworth's *The Schoolmaster's Assistant*, reissued from 1743 into the nineteenth century.[18] These books became the backbone of arithmetic training, eclipsing books like Robert Recorde's, which had sought to teach mathematics as a coherent system dealing with abstract quantities. Because the commercial books were designed for educating youth "as to Clerkship and Trades," the authors deliberately omitted explanations and demonstrations of why mathematical operations worked, claiming they were too tedious.[19] They not only assumed that their readers were ignorant about basic arithmetic; they also seemed to assume that it was hopeless to try to teach them to understand anything about it. They therefore presented their material in the form of rules to be memorized, followed by examples drawn from business life.

The emphasis on memory rather than reasoning is evident in the catechism of questions and answers that became the standard format for arithmetic texts. The format was justified on the grounds that it kept the book plain and short and therefore made the subject less discouraging to students. Certainly it was easier to memorize than to understand passages such as the following, from Dilworth, which explained how large numbers are written:

Q. How many figures are sufficient to express most ordinary concerns?

A. Nine.

Q. Why does it consist of nine Places, rather than eight or ten?

A. Because they make up three even periods.

Q. What do you mean by a Period?

A. A Period is a Quantity express'd by three Figures, whereof the first to the right Hand signifies so many Units or single Things; the second so many Tens; and the third so many Hundreds.

Q. Why are three Figures called a Period?

A. Because if the Number be increased above three Places, there is still the same periodical Return of the Value of those Places, and every third Figure to the left Hand, will always be Hundreds, if it be never so far extended.[20]

A briefer but no less mystifying explanation of numeration in another text listed the numbers 1 to 9 and warned that "every one, or any, of the abovementioned nine Figures, or Digits, have two values; one certain, and another uncertain"—certain when it stands by itself, uncertain when it stands with other numbers.[21] Thus were students introduced to the concept of place, that unique and powerful feature of arabic notation.

From this elementary but uncertain beginning a student was carried on through addition, subtraction, multiplication, division, and the Rule of Three, an operation for finding the fourth number in a proportion when the other three are known. Next came fractions, and the four basic rules were given again as though they were completely new operations, unrelated to addition or multiplication of whole numbers.[22] The most advanced levels of the commercial texts treated interest, annuities, rebates, brokerage, and the "rule of fellowship," a comradely term for a rule that determined the division of profits in a joint enterprise. Some authors attempted a modicum of explanation, beyond the memorization of operations, as in this definition of zero: "[A cipher is] the beginning of number, or rather the medium between increasing and decreasing numbers, commonly called *absolute* or *whole* numbers, and *negative* or *fractional* numbers."[23] Since whole and fractional numbers had the same meaning then as they have today, perhaps it was a kindness to the students that authors rarely injected such explanations into their texts. For the most part, the authors stuck to rules and examples; they made no attempt to weave the whole into an integrated system of thought, and they omitted reasons because they were "tedious and inconvenient."[24]

The effect of these books on practical arithmetic must certainly have been to discourage and constrain the spread of numerical skills. This they accomplished not only because they made the subject inaccessible to human reason but also because they suffused arithmetic with commercial meanings. Therefore, most young people not destined for a life of commerce did not learn arithmetic at all. Those of high social rank, theoretically above the world of getting and spending, did not deign to study the subject. The most respectable English public schools, like Eton and Harrow, did not offer any instruction in arithmetic until well into the nineteenth century.[25] Nor did Oxford and Cambridge include arithmetic in their curriculum. In 1662 the well-educated Samuel Pepys was forced to take up the subject at the advanced age of thirty, just after his first appointment to public office. He arose at 4:00 A.M. to struggle with the multiplication table, "which is all the trouble I meet withal in my arithmetique."[26] If the well-born could often avoid the subject, the laboring classes never had the opportunity to study it. Adding and subtracting their scarce pennies were their only mathematical needs. Arithmetic became solidly identified with mercantile life, and the young clerks and tradesmen who managed to survive a dose of Cocker's *Arithmetick* probably really learned whatever they needed to know either during their apprenticeship or in lessons from private tutors, who hung out shingles as teachers of arithmetic and bookkeeping. In other words, arithmetic knowledge spread in the seventeenth and eighteenth centuries, but it spread only in the widening groove of bourgeois life and in a manner that did not encourage easy familiarity with mathematics.

The popularity of "ready reckoners" in the seventeenth and eighteenth centuries is a clue to the endemic lack of arithmetic skill among tradesmen. These books offered page after page of tables showing multiples of unit costs for common commodities at a variety of prices. To figure the total cost of a purchase of cloth, for example, one would turn to the page headed by the appropriate cost per yard and then scan down the vertical columns, which specified the price for fractions and multiples of a yard. The earliest of these books appeared in the 1610s and 1620s, and by the 1660s there were dozens of them, bearing such titles as *A Platform for Purchasers, A Mate for Measurers,* and *A Manual of Millions.* In the mid-eighteenth century a new one, titled *The Ready Reckoner,* finally hit the right combination of alliteration and meaning in the title, and, from then on, "ready reckoner" became a generic term. The books could be both substitutes for and checks on the accuracy of paper-and-pen multiplication.[27]

Another clue to both the scope and the limits of mathematical acuity in commerce lies in the history of bookkeeping in Tudor-Stuart England. Well before the sixteenth century, simple merchant or household account books were often maintained to record debts and credits and to monitor expenditures in order to prevent theft by subordinates. In the 1540s a manual on double-entry bookkeeping appeared in English, translated from Italian, and it was followed by several more in the late sixteenth and seventeenth centuries, all of them extolling the virtues of exact record-keeping.[28] Under the new system transactions were entered twice, in both credit and debit accounts; periodic summary balance sheets displayed the financial state of the entire enterprise. In theory the multiple ledgers could lead to calculations of profit and loss on invested capital. But despite the fact that all the features of modern accounting practice were implicit in the system, relatively few commercial establishments ever computed profit-and-loss statements, and only very irregularly did they balance out the books. Thus, though the *form* of the double-entry system was used, the system itself was not generally used in a modern way.[29] Historians of accounting speculate that merchants mentally figured the approximate profits and losses on individual ventures and so did not need accounting to tell them what they already knew.[30] It is also possible that, given the dismal state of commercial arithmetic training, the merchants' clerks did not have the skills requisite to the full use of double-entry books.

Strange as it seems, commercial life both triggered and then limited the development of numeracy in England. The adoption of arabic numerals and arithmetic came as a result of the expansion of commerce in the sixteenth century, but textbook writers then decided that their subject was too difficult for bourgeois lads to learn with any degree of understanding. They tried to strip arithmetic to its essentials, but in fact they cut it into incoherent bits and made it an arcane subject, almost impossible to learn. The relatively small group of men who did take a delight in numbers—the writers of stereometry and pantometry books, the ones who applied calculus to beer barrels and trigonometry to the Pico of Teneriffe—did not emerge from the bourgeois class, learning arithmetic over shop counters.

One result of the disparity between commercial arithmetic and more sophisticated mathematics was that, up until the late seventeenth century, economic writers did not discuss the economy in quantitative terms. The state of the national economy was a matter of great concern in the seventeenth century, chiefly because it was changing so remarkably, in ways that as yet there was no language to describe. Hundreds of writers, mostly from the trading class, groped to conceptualize the new economic order, with its ever-larger markets and its new uses of capital.[31] At the end of the century, some of the men with broad mathematical interests joined the intellectual effort to make sense of the economy, which up to that time had been surprisingly nonquantitative. They proposed an analogy between the bookkeeping practices of merchants and households and an accounting of the resources of the nation. John Arbuthnot, mathematician and member of the Royal Society, explained that

> Arithmetic is not only the great instrument of private commerce, but by it are (or ought to be) kept the public accounts

of a nation; I mean those that regard the whole state of a commonwealth, as to the number, fructification of its people, increase of stock, improvement of lands and manufacturers, balance of trade, public revenues, coinage, military power by sea and land, etc. Those that would judge or reason truly about the state of any nation must go that way to work, subjecting all the forementioned particulars to calculation. This is the true political knowledge.[32]

True political knowledge, perhaps, but it was nearly impossible to "go that way to work," as Arbuthnot recommended, because of the lack of sound data. The analogy between quantifying the assets of a firm and the total resources of the nation had been put forth by several mathematical men as early as the 1660s, but in reality the analogy found practical expression only in the matter of foreign trade. Of all the economic and political endeavors Arbuthnot listed, foreign trade was the only one that could be easily put into numbers. The balance of trade became a substitute for the ultimate balancing of national account books that could not be constructed for lack of data.[33]

The customs service was what made foreign trade so eminently calculable. Since the 1560s customs laws in England required ships to dock and load at specified wharves, in daylight, so that their contents could be assessed by inspectors and the appropriate fees levied. In the 1620s several writers of "discourses on trade" turned their attention to the traffic across borders and argued that the flow of goods and money, conceived of as the balance of trade, bore some relation to the economic health of the nation as a whole. However, almost no attempt was made to aggregate the customs duties, the first step in quantifying the dimensions of the flow. One writer in 1623 ferreted out the customs duties for a year, to demonstrate how the balance of trade could be determined "by science." His effort showed that, in theory, the data were recoverable, since the record-keeping mechanism was firmly in place; but in fact no central office collected data from officers. Other economic writers were content to talk about the balance of trade in nonempirical generalities until the 1650s, when a newly established trade council was charged with keeping an "exact Accompt" of imports and exports "to the end that a perfect Ballance of Trade may be taken." However there is no evidence that the council ever fulfilled this charge.[34] A later incarnation of the council, the Lords of Trade and Plantations, also tried to collect such data, without much success, in the 1670s. Around 1670 a mathematician, John Collins, applied for employment as clerk to the Council of Trade and proposed an interesting scheme for creating an account of trade that balanced not only the value of imports against exports but also, in credit and debit columns, the numerous and conflicting opinions of English writers about trade.[35] (Collins did not reveal how the balance of opinions would be struck.) His proposal illustrates the mathematical approach to policy questions that was just beginning to be articulated in the doctrine of "political arithmetic."

The originator of that doctrine and the foremost spokesman for a numerical approach to economics was Sir William Petty, an unrelenting "numerist" throughout his life.[36] Petty coined the phrase "political arithmetic" to describe what was then considered an unorthodox conjunction between matters of state, a lofty sphere, and the "vulgar art" of arithmetic, with its strong commercial association. He explained his notion in the original version of his *Political Arithmetick,* which was written in the early 1670s but was not published until after his death, in 1690.

> The Method I take to do this is not yet very usual; for instead of using only comparative and superlative Words, and intellectual Arguments, I have taken the course (as a Specimen of the Political Arithmetick I have long aimed at) to express my self in terms of *Number, Weight,* and *Measure;* to use only Arguments of Sense, and to consider only such Causes, as have visible Foundations in Nature; leaving those that depend upon the mutable Minds, Opinions, Appetites and Passions of particular Men, to the Consideration of others.[37]

What is significant about Petty's work is that he forged a link between quantification, economic thought, and the philosophical idea that true knowledge comes only through the senses, from observation of facts. Petty and his circle of friends in the Royal Society revered Sir Francis Bacon, who in the early seventeenth century had formulated the classical statement of scientific method: inductive reasoning practiced on empirical facts. Men of science like Galileo, Hooke, and Boyle sought out quantifiable facts on which to base conclusions about mechanics and physics. Petty combined Bacon's method and the scientists' concern for exact measurement and applied them to the realm of social and economic facts. To Petty, the best empirical facts about society were numerical facts. Number, weight, and measure implied certainty, because once something was measured its dimensions were no longer a matter of subjective opinion. The specificity of numbers conferred objectivity, in Petty's eyes. He therefore thought that true political knowledge would arise out of full, quantitative accounting of social and economic facts.

Petty's quantitative spirit was prefigured in his youth, when he became a mariner at the age of thirteen and learned the art of navigation just when the "sayling triangle" was gaining currency.[38] His days at sea were cut short by a broken leg, and he entered a Jesuit school in the French port of Caen, where his ship had dropped him off. For four years he studied languages, arithmetic, practical geometry, navigation, dialing, and "several mathematical trades" of unspecified sort. He then went off to Holland to take up the study of medicine. Eventually he returned to England, after a stint in Paris, where he made contact with Descartes and other French mathematicians, and by the late 1640s he was a member of a science and medicine group at Oxford, the core of which became the founding membership of the Royal Society of London. In the 1650s he landed the job of surveyor general of Ireland, which put him in charge of the survey of all land forfeited after the Irish Rebellion. His task was monumental, but he accomplished it in thirteen months with a crew of a thousand men, most of whom had to be taught simple surveying techniques.

Petty's mathematical background was, then, both practical, growing out of navigation and surveying, and academic, gleaned from his Jesuit schooling and from his association with French and English mathematicians. Though he prided himself on being very quick in mathematics, he recognized that he was not in the same league as the creative mathematicians of his time.[39] He therefore applied his talents in elementary mathematics to the immediate world and came up with political arithmetic. He probably thought that what he was doing was not different in essence from what a scientist like Robert Boyle did in his meteorological experiments. What he failed to note was that quantitative facts about social and economic matters cannot be measured with the same degree of directness as measurements in the physical sciences. Petty assumed that anything described in numerical terms was objective and accurate, however the number was arrived at.

And he had plenty of numbers. In his *Political Arithmetick* almost every statement susceptible of a numerical rendering received one, even if the figure had to be purely hypothetical. Figures for volume of trade, population, yields per acre, and distance were given with the confidence that numbers made his arguments solid and reliable, even though most of the numbers could have represented only rough estimates or rounded-off guesses. Some historians have suggested that Petty was regrettably careless with numbers, that because he was more enchanted with his method than with the details he became cavalier about accuracy. Careless and enchanted he was, but he was nonetheless convinced that accuracy lay within his grasp. If he could find numbers—say, for population or trade—he characteristically gave no further thought to the problem of shortcomings or errors in the data. Neither did he concern himself with the multiplication of inaccuracy in his long chains of calculations based on specific but sometimes questionable numerical assumptions. For example, this is how he analyzed Holland's financial advantage over England and France in transporting goods to market:

> In Holland and Zealand, there is scarce any place of work or business one Mile distant from a Navigable Water, and the charge of Water carriage is generally but 1/15 or 1/20 part of Land carriage; Wherefore if there be as much Trade there as in France, then the Hollanders can out-sell the French 14/15 of all the expence, of all Travelling Postage and carriage whatsoever, which even in England I take to be 300000 l. p. an. where the very Postage of Letters, costs the People perhaps 50000 l. per annum, though Farmed at much less, and all other Labour of Horses, and Porters, at least six times as much. The value of this conveniency I estimate to be above Three Hundred Thousand pounds per annum.[40]

This sort of hypothetical reasoning shows that Petty was uncritical about numbers even while he claimed to be practicing the science of number, weight, and measure. In his drive to quantify all aspects of the economy, numerical specificity often substituted for accuracy.

Petty had friends and admirers who applauded his efforts to wed arithmetic and scientific method to the study of economics. In the 1690s Charles Davenant, Gregory King, Edmund Halley, and John Arbuthnot began to toy with economic and demographic calculations, which they presented as a branch of political arithmetic.[41] But no one tried to implement Petty's grand scheme, the quantification of all the resources of the country in giant national account books. The data for this undertaking simply did not exist, and Petty's habit of manufacturing hypothetical data eventually undermined the credibility of his plan. Arbuthnot, writing in 1701, acknowledged that Petty often proceeded on the basis of erroneous information but felt that his plan was in theory sound.[42] However, a century later, Adam Smith declared that he had "no great faith in political arithmetic," because the hopelessness of securing accurate data rendered the whole scheme useless, or worse.[43] Smith was sensitive to difficulties in simple counting that Petty and Arbuthnot were unable to imagine because they had never tried to carry out a census or collect trade statistics.

Such efforts were made in the 1690s, and the difficulties inherent in collecting data were then made manifest. In 1696 the Board of Trade was reorganized, and the new members (three of them Fellows of the Royal Society) requested aggregate import and export records from the preceding three years. From these they learned the limitations of customs duties as a measure of trade flow; all grades of linen, for example, were charged the same duty per ell whatever the value, with the result that the total duties paid on linen did not reflect the true value of the trade. In 1696 the board therefore established the new office of Inspector-General of Imports and Exports, whose sole function was to straighten out the anomalies in the customs records and prepare reports on the balance of trade, including both quantities of goods and their total value.[44] For nearly a century raw data piled up in this office. Abstracts were submitted to Parliament annually, but rarely were the data subjected to calculations that could be used as the basis for rational decision-making—for example, figuring yearly averages and projecting trends. In 1701 a member of the Board of Trade produced a table showing comparative data, but this effort was never repeated. In the 1720s the office of Inspector-General became a sinecure held by a succession of uninspired men, and the quality of the accounts was greatly diminished.[45]

In some ways the quantification of the balance of trade echoes the limited use made of the balance of double-entry bookkeeping. Both systems produced descriptions of economic activities that in theory provided a basis for a mathematical approach to decision-making, but neither system exploited that potential in practice. Possibly a quick glance at the annual abstracts of trade sufficed to give the Board an adequate idea of the impact of its policies, just as a merchant might instinctively know the state of his financial affairs without having to set pen to paper to do sums. This might explain why the decline in the quality of the records was of no great moment, because the precise numbers were in fact not playing a paramount role in the establishment of policy. Indeed, there was only a relatively short period when the impulse for empirical accuracy seems to have ranked high in the Board's view, and that was at the inauguration of the office.

The 1690s were a particularly congenial decade for the implementation of grand quantitative schemes, probably because of the influence of Petty and his political arithmetic. In 1694 Parliament enacted a law that in effect required a complete enumeration of the inhabitants of England and Wales as a backdrop to a revenue act taxing vital events and persons of particular stations. The ostensible purpose was to raise revenue by levying a tax on births, deaths, and marriages and annual fines on bachelors over twenty-five and childless widowers. Assessors in each locality were to submit lists of all the inhabitants, specifying their names, so that bachelors and widowers could be tracked from year to year, and also listing their social stations, because the vital-event tax and the individual tax varied according to station. Each year the assessor was to bring his enumeration up to date by adjusting for vital events in the community. The act of 1694 stayed in force for over a decade, lapsing only in 1706.[46] Had it been fully implemented, it would have produced a remarkable and comprehensive annual census of England a full century before decennial censuses became an accepted practice and a half-century before any other European country instituted regular censuses.[47] Very little of the census remains, but the existing fragments indicate that initially the count was extensive and nationwide; the most substantial document is a list of "London Inhabitants within the Walls" for 1695.[48]

The origins of the 1694 act are obscure. Demographic historians sometimes link it to Gregory King, who was keenly interested in questions of population in the early 1690s. King found employment as an enumerator in London and soon after used the material for his 1696 essay *Natural and Political Observations and Conclusions upon the State and Condition of England*. While he clearly benefited from the census and used it to further his demographic speculations, there is no evidence that he participated in any way in the formulation of the act. Nor is there evidence that he did not. In view of the influence of political arithmetic on the Board of Trade in this same period, it is not farfetched to suspect that a similar influence was operating on the government bodies concerned with revenue questions.[49]

In any event, the originators of the act did not sufficiently consider the difficulties involved in instituting an annual census. In addition to the predictable administrative difficulties (still not entirely solved, three centuries later), Parliament guaranteed that the count would be unpopular by tying it to a revenue measure. On top of that, Britons were entirely unfamiliar with the practice of censuses, and there were strong cultural factors, biblical and etymological, preventing an easy adjustment to the practice. The Old Testament told of the "sin of David," who brought a plague on Israel for "numbering" the people. Exactly why that displeased God is not clear from the story, but seventeenth-century Protestants were not likely to ask that question when the punishment so swiftly followed the sin. Throughout the eighteenth century the "sin of David" was occasionally, perhaps selectively, invoked to protest local censuses in both England and America.[50] The etymological factor grew out of the Latin link between *census* and *censor*. Seventeenth-century dictionaries identified the *censor* as the Roman officer who both censed—counted—persons and estates and censured immoral behavior.[51] The two ideas were inextricably joined, and this perhaps explains why English officials usually preferred to avoid the word "census" and instead to talk about "numberings" of the people. Antipathy toward taxes, fear of God's retribution, and alarm about government invasion of privacy were tough obstacles standing in the path of political arithmetic. An Enlightenment idealism might conceivably have inspired one William Wynne as he approached his enumerating task in the town of Newark in 1697, but, if so, he was disabused of this view when "the common people of the town got together in a tumultuous and disorderly manner, and with stone, dirt, and other things forct the said officer from his duty."[52] There was no proud desire in Newark to be counted as a national resource.

Regular, successful census-taking requires a degree of numeracy on the part of the enumerators sponsoring the count. They must perceive that the totality of people can be described quantitatively and that it is worth knowing exactly what that quantity is. Such ideas seem obvious now, but they were not at all prevalent

in the seventeenth century. Most people then thought of the totality of the people as a group; if they differentiated the totality
at all, it was in terms of characteristics—for example, all Englishmen—or in terms of relationships—for example, the body politic,
with its head, arms, and feet. Only a few thought that the *number*
of people might be important to ascertain. Today "population"
means the whole number of people. There is general agreement
in Western countries that the whole number is worth knowing,
and so the subjects of censuses willingly cooperate and allow
themselves to be counted. They have accepted a quantitative
outlook on something that was once thought of as strictly qualitative. That acceptance came gradually, and so a history of censuses illuminates the diffusion of one form of numeracy.

Before the seventeenth century there was no word for population. Administrative and fiscal documents survive from medieval and early modern times and allow historians to reconstruct
past population figures, but no one at the time would have been
interested in such calculations. The famous eleventh-century
Domesday survey was not a census, for it did not pose and then
answer the question How many? Like the Florentine *catastos* of
the early Renaissance and like the medieval "extents" of England, Domesday was essentially a record of financial situations
and responsibilities. It listed certain (but not all) people, hides,
plows, churches, and prices, but it did not count them.[53]

The earliest true censuses came in the mid-sixteenth century,
when ecclesiastical leaders directed the local clergy to count the
"housling" people in each parish, that is, the number of communicants. There were five ecclesiastical censuses in England in
the sixteenth and seventeenth centuries—in 1547, 1563, 1603,
1676, and 1688; these were transitional moments in Reformation
history, so it may be inferred that the Anglican bishops had good
reason to want to know how many communicants there were. On
two occasions they also asked for the number of recusants and
Nonconformists, which strengthens the suspicion that they
wanted to know something about the relative size of church membership.[54] But it is possible that the desire to know how many was
secondary to a desire to exercise authority by counting: inscribing
people's names on an official list of communicants was a way to
remind them of their religious obligations. If so, the early ecclesiastical censuses combined the double meaning of censoring and
censing.

The most explicit statement of the moral use of a census was made by the French Huguenot Jean Bodin in the last part of his *Six Bookes of a Commonweale,* written in 1580 and published in English in 1606.[55] Bodin took up the question "Whether it be expedient to inroll and number the subjects?" and argued that both enrolling and numbering served important purposes. From the number, ages, and quality of persons a government could learn the military and colonizing potential of a country, and it could plan for adequate food in times of siege or famine. But this was not all: as he enrolled the subjects, the censor would also be inspecting and judging them, turning the eye of public inquiry on their lives. The purpose of exposure was

> thereby to expell all drones out of a commonweale, which sucke the honey from the Bees, and to banish vagabonds, idle persons, thieves, cooseners, & ruffians . . . who although they walke in darknesses, yet hereby they should bee seene, noted and known.[56]

There is nothing of numeracy in this second use of the census. Bodin's point was that the very act of identifying crooks and vagabonds would shame them into mending their ways or else disappearing.

A variant on the moral censor's version of a census was the muster list, in which a military officer inscribed the names of all able-bodied men liable for service. In Tudor-Stuart England and in the American colonies as well, the citizen army or local militia began to replace professional troops and private armies. The muster list in effect was a register of names; its purpose was to signal men that they were liable for duty. At the same time, it could be used to give officers an idea of their troop strength. It partook of both the enrolling and numbering features of a census, but usually with emphasis on the former. Sometimes muster lists were never totted up and performed only the function of indicating obligation, but on at least a few occasions the task of compiling the list fell into the hands of a highly numerate individual, who transformed the job far beyond customary expectations. For example, in 1608 the steward of Lord Henry Berkeley's household in Gloucestershire included in his muster list the approximate ages and precise occupations of 19,402 men in the shire. This steward enjoyed a local reputation as a thorough man who habitually took notes on everything. Apparently his thoroughness in this matter was entirely self-inspired; it is not known whether Lord Berkeley was impressed or amused.[57]

Here and there in England a handful of other numerate men of the seventeenth century approached their traditional tasks from the new angle of interest in quantity and produced documents of great value to demographers. Between 1610 and 1628 the rector of Cogenhoe took stock of his communicants nearly annually. At first he listed only Easter communicants; then his interests expanded, and he listed parish households and later added the names of the occupants of each household. Why he compiled these lists is not known; his successor did not continue the practice. Far more valuable are two complete censuses of the village of Clayworth, taken by its rector in 1676 and 1688. The first was taken in response to the archbishop's call for an ecclesiastical census, and the second possibly was also, although the evidence on that point is not clear. The rector of Clayworth was an experienced account-keeper and a man of exact habits. He kept a notebook of weather conditions, crop prices, and the disbursements of parish funds. When called upon to produce a list of communicants in 1676, he went from door to door in the parish and listed all 401 inhabitants, noting callings, familial relationships, and whether each person was a communicant. He repeated his census twelve years later, providing historians with the unparalleled opportunity to glimpse short-run change in the social structure of a preindustrial village.[58]

The Clayworth and Cogenhoe records are the products of nearly unique instances of parish rectors who asked different questions—quantitative questions—in the line of their duties. All English clergy were expected to maintain parish registers recording the baptisms, burials, and marriages at which they officiated; all were expected to teach and encourage communicants in the faith; all were expected to exercise moral influence in their parish by endorsing familial government and discouraging illicit alliances. The successful performance of these duties did not require any arithmetic. But a few men saw their tasks in a new light. They numbered their parishioners, they counted the communicants, and they created a record of their ministration year by year. In doing so they brought a new dimension to their role. Their records enabled them to compare the past with the present and to develop a notion of religious progress.

Comparison of the present with the immediate past had also been the goal behind the political-arithmetic version of the balance of trade and the plan for the general census enumerations enacted in 1694. One reason those plans fell short of the mark was that there was insufficient delight in numbers among the legions of persons whose participation was a necessary feature of both plans. It was a lot to ask of customs officers and revenue collectors that they share a curiosity about numbers and a grasp of the administrative uses to which such numbers could be put. Even Members of Parliament did not agree that determining England's population was a paramount goal of the act of 1694; had they so agreed, they would not have tied the census to a revenue act, which seriously undermined its chances for success. (In contrast, America's Founding Fathers tied their census to a system of fines for noncompliance—certainly a more efficacious combination of counting and money.) Political arithmeticians talked of the importance of knowing the whole number of the people, but the dictionaries of the day still had no word for the idea itself. *Population* finally appeared, but it was defined variously as "a wasting, destroying, robbing, and spoiling of people" or "a wasting or depeopling"; *populosity,* "a fullness of people," came the closest to expressing something about the totality of people, but even then it was still a qualitative, not a quantitative, word.[59] Not until the mid-eighteenth century was there a sufficiently strong interest in population as quantity to ensure that censuses would be seen as useful knowledge and not as sins or as shaming devices. By that time the diffusion of numeracy had begun to eat away at the traditional fears of a censorious census and of a wrathful God.[60]

By the end of the seventeenth century, numeracy had not made rapid progress in England. Probably fewer than four hundred men could be said to be mathematically minded, and that figure includes teachers of navigation as well as Fellows of the Royal Society, with talents varying from the undisciplined mind of William Petty to the genius of Isaac Newton.[61] These men shared a delight in numbers and a keenness to measure, but few other Englishmen participated in their activities. The great mass of the people bumbled along, learning a self-limiting version of commercial arithmetic, or else they avoided the subject altogether. The few highly numerate men accepted this state of affairs and wrote books for each other. If they felt inclined to tinker with the mathematics of population or trade, they generally worked on problems that did not require active cooperation from others fascinated with questions of quantity. For example, John Graunt, a friend of Petty's, turned to the existing London death records to construct his *Natural and Political Observations of the Bills of Mortality*. Graunt found regularities and uniformities where others saw only body counts rising and falling mysteriously, and he paid attention to the limitations of his evidence, since it had been collected for a purpose different from the one he put it to.[62] William Derham, a clergyman and a Fellow of the Royal Society, ransacked parish registers to test out some of Graunt's observations about death rates and sex ratios.[63] Both the parish registers and the bills of mortality were innovations in the early days of arabic-numeral use, around 1530, but neither had ever been intended as anything more than a record of facts.

Highly numerate men were few in number in 1700, but their contribution to Western thought was large. They began to see quantities where, before, men thought of qualities. The body politic could be thought of as a population, death could be comprehended as a mortality rate. Even temperature, which to the average Englishman was a characteristic made up of some mixture of hot and cold with dry and moist, became an ascertainable number of degrees that varied systematically over the day and the year.[64] This new propensity to measure and count meant that certain kinds of experience hitherto considered to be wholly subjective became amenable to objective description through the use of numbers. The warmth or coolness of the day is a matter of opinion, but a numerical reading on a thermometer is precise, repeatable, and value-free. Distances can be traversed quickly or slowly, but, when expressed in miles, distance is no longer variable. Are there too many or too few people?[65] Count them and find out.

What all these forms of quantification had in common was the substitution of objective standards for subjective judgments. The many new and practical uses of numbers in the sixteenth and seventeenth centuries contributed to the belief that whatever was quantifiable was objective, in the sense that it existed apart from any imposition of taste or moral judgment on the part of the viewer. Observer bias in measurement never seems to have troubled anyone.

Nascent quantification—a simple urge to measure and count—appeared in Western culture in a variety of contexts and situations in the sixteenth and seventeenth centuries. On one level, its appearance correlates with important changes in the political, economic, and religious life of those turbulent centuries and to well-known historical processes, such as the growth of centralized government and the expansion of overseas trade. On a deeper level, quantification can be considered as a peculiar mental activity, one that satisfies a need for precision and finitude, and its appearance in a period of numerous crises suggests that more than practical needs for rationality and knowledge were being met.

On the practical level, the distinguishing features of political life in the sixteenth and seventeenth centuries were the rise of powerful monarchies, the geographical consolidation of nations, and the development of new concepts of public administration, which, in the seventeenth century, entailed mercantilism and the government's claimed right to regulate economic activity. In theory this created a justification for evaluating national resources, including the population and the volume of trade, and increasingly such evaluations were quantitative, in varying degrees of accuracy.

In the economic history of the period, three separate strands of development contributed to an elevation of the public consciousness of numbers. The rise of capitalism and of national economies drew greater numbers of people into the world of monetary exchange, where some elementary calculation and bookkeeping were necessary skills. Overseas trading and adventuring stimulated a mathematical approach to navigation and introduced ordinary seamen to the wonders of arithmetic. Finally, the great price rise of the sixteenth century and the concomitant population expansion loosed some men from their roots, setting them adrift in English society, and startled other men, like Bodin, into quantitative inquiries in an effort to create order.

The most fundamental change in society and thought in the sixteenth and seventeenth centuries was the Protestant Reformation, and the historiography of the past fifty years compels us to consider the interrelations between religion and numeracy. The direct, straightforward connections that can be made must be seen as somewhat superficial; for example, the breakup of the monastery lands in England created a need for surveyors. Max

Weber's thesis reaches a deeper level of analysis in stressing the social sanction of economic gain through Protestant asceticism and the doctrine of the calling. The Protestant ethos accounts for the motivation of those who embraced the pecuniary rewards of hard work, but it does not explain why a bookkeeping mentality would become the all-important standard for measuring self-worth. A Protestant could devote himself to his calling on earth and work very hard to establish and advance his business, but none of that devotion and hard work implied the need to be precise or the simple delight in figuring that inspired the bookkeeping manuals and the political arithmeticians. The connection between commerce and a low-level arithmetic skill is certain, but numeracy was probably not enhanced specifically because of a Calvinist cast of mind mediated through business.[66]

If commerce is not the link between religion and numeracy, science is perhaps the next-best candidate. Scientific method called for empirical observations subjected to inductive reasoning; the observations did not have to be quantitative, but in the late seventeenth century they very often were, especially in the work of the Fellows of the Royal Society. English historian Christopher Hill has advanced the argument that Puritanism was especially conducive to the rise of science. To establish this link, he relies on similarity of method: the Puritan insistence on personal experience of God, without intermediaries, parallels the empiricism of Baconian science, which emphasized personal experience (self-reliance) in testing hypotheses. Puritans and scientists relied on their own immediate experiences, rejecting the authority of the Church and the authority of Aristotle. To substantiate his case, Hill demonstrates that a large number of leading scientists in England were of Puritan background.[67]

However, it is hard to maintain the parallel, based on the common ground of personal experience, when the focus narrows to measurement as the specific form of method. A Puritan's religious experience was a unique, direct communion with God; it was emotional, unrepeatable, subjective, and not in any sense measurable. The scientist sought a dispassionate experience in his experiments, and he hoped it would be repeatable and, if at all possible, quantifiable. Both experiences were personal, but they were essentially different. The distinction between them would seem to deny that the roots of quantitative thinking can be traced to a purported common ground between religion and science.

Critics of the Hill thesis have offered an alternative connection between religion and science that can comfortably expand to account for the fact that interest in measurement extended beyond the bounds of science in the seventeenth century. Richard Greaves and T. K. Rabb have each argued that the Puritan revolution of the 1640s and 1650s was the intermediate step linking Puritanism indirectly with the rise of science. The revolutionary fervor of those years, they write, undercut established authority in politics and religion and carried over into the intellectual world of university and urban life. Greaves and Rabb see the revolution as a liberating force, allowing "progress in scientific thought" to move forward.[68] This argument assumes that such progress is natural once the dead weight of past tradition is removed. But it might be fruitful to explore the possibility that it was the chaos and disorder of a revolutionary situation that directly encouraged a quantitative orientation, which then spilled over into a quantitative empiricism in the pursuit of science.

One way to approach this problem is to examine more closely the nature of the quantifying act. Numbers are preeminently descriptive labels. On the most basic level, they enumerate: they tell something definite about the size of a class of counted objects that have something in common, if only the fact that they are part of a countable set. Enumerations create a bond of uniformity around the objects counted; it *is* possible to add apples and oranges if the problem is to know how much fruit there is. On a second level, numbers measure sizes and magnitudes, for example distance, volume, temperature, weight. Here again they create a uniformity among magnitudes that might appear to be of a very different order. Distances over oceans or lands can be compared with the altitudes of mountains or a journey to the moon; the volume of a barrel of ale and that of a tub of lard can be thought of in the same units; the climate of Massachusetts can be precisely contrasted with that of London.

A third aspect of quantification is that numbers can sort out the combined effects of several components. Velocity is a variable of time and distance, population growth is affected by fertility and mortality rates. All rates express a ratio of frequency (an enumeration) over a fixed time period. Numbers of this sort describe something (an object, an event, a series of events) that is in motion or flux. A fourth use of numbers occurs in matters of probability, where a number or series of numbers conveys some notion of risk. All of these attributes or uses of numbers existed in the seventeenth century. Much later, quantification would extend the attributes to more varied types of objects enumerated or magnitudes measured.

Quantification, then, creates a sense of uniformity and finitude; it counts—and accounts in the process; it describes stationary objects and changing relationships; it uncovers patterns, evaluates risks, and predicts outcomes. Quantification can be a powerful method of analysis and a powerful explanatory tool. In the turbulent and disorderly years of the seventeenth century, quantification must have seemed an alluring way to impose order on a world in flux.

Before the seventeenth century in Europe, the order of the cosmos was dictated by classical and, specifically, Aristotelian systems of classification. All aspects of life and nature were comprehensible through the arrangements of categories meant to exhibit significant distinctions and to exhaust the possibilities of reality. The world was composed of four substances, the body had four humours, the life of man was framed by the seven stages of the aging process, and so on. The penchant for classification remained alive in the seventeenth century and found full expression in the Great Chain of Being, an idea that expressed the relations among all creatures on earth and in heaven by making explicit an assumed hierarchy of the natural and supernatural worlds. Linnaeus's classification of the botanical world in the eighteenth century is another example of the use of categorization to make sense of the world.

Classification by categories is a reasonable method for ordering static things that have discrete and distinguishable characteristics. But in the seventeenth century there appeared to be a considerable amount of movement in many areas, both human and material, and the static categories of pure classification could not seem to capture or articulate this movement. Static categories do not admit of exchange among themselves; usually they are defined as mutually exclusive. How could one accept Aristotle's idea that the basic unit of society was the family when family-less people were roving the countryside? What meaning did the seven-ages-of-man concept have for a society where few people actually lived through all the stages, where death occurred in infancy more commonly than in old age, and where men were increasingly sensitive to the wastage of human life?

Quantification emerged in the seventeenth century as an alternative way to make sense of the world, a way that would account for activities newly perceived in the interstices of the classical categories. A vast, undifferentiated sea could not easily be thought about in terms of qualitative units, but a grid of numbered vertical and horizontal divisions, like Mercator's, reduced it to manageable proportions. Overseas trade and human traffic to the colonies were somehow disrupting the economy at home, but no one could quite explain why. Economic quantification made it possible to impose control and order on tobacco, linen, indentured servants; longitudes, latitudes, and navigation methods facilitated control of the ocean. Censuses pinned people down to a time, place, and class; life tables suggested a numerical idea about the stages of life one could expect to live through.

It is not surprising that fear of disorder and charges of disobedience were common in the seventeenth century, for this was an age that experienced social dislocation, the extremes of political authority and revolt, regicide, and the overthrow of long-held beliefs about the nature of God and the physical laws of the universe.[69] Jean Bodin quite explicitly related the problem of out-of-place people to the need for a census: "We see most commonweales swarme with vagabounds, idle persons, and ruffians, who by their deeds and examples corrupt good citisens; and there is no meanes to expell this vermine, but by the Censore." An enumeration of inhabitants by itself would somehow put people back in their rightful place: "A looke, a word, and a dash with a pen, was more bloudie, and touched more to the quick" than traditional legal or religious institutions.[70]

Quantification as a method for ordering reality was born in an era marked by disorder and sometimes by outright chaos. It did not supplant older methods of imposing order, and it appeared first in areas that lent themselves most naturally to the concept of number: in the counting of discrete units and the measuring of space. Within these areas there was, of course, a wide range of objects that could be counted or measured, but it is the *types* of things that seventeenth-century Englishmen chose to count and measure that reveal the most pressing and practical needs to reorder the English universe. No one was yet suggesting quantitative measures of intelligence; that was left for an elite intelligentsia of a later age, who may have felt threatened by a leveling spirit. No one was yet trying to give quantitative expression to the army of

orphans and foundlings begging in London; that awaited an age
of greater sensitivity to the plight of children. In the sixteenth and
seventeenth centuries, numbers appeared to capture the vastness
of the world and the universe, the importance of money, and the
unruliness of people. In presenting these thoughts to Englishmen,
numbers also assumed a reputation for reality and objectivity and
introduced into Western thought the idea that it is possible to
remove values from anything that can be quantified.

2

Colonial Counting

One small corner of the vast universe that some Englishmen were attempting to subdue with numbers was the coast of North America. In the first half of the seventeenth century English joint-stock companies began colonization efforts in the Chesapeake, in New England, and in the West Indies, in imitation of the Spanish colonization of Central and South America. But while Spain's forays into the New World were sponsored and controlled directly by her royal government, England's monarch instead transferred control to private companies, which then developed colonization schemes designed to produce commercial profit. Thus the leaders of the early English colonization efforts were chiefly businessmen with an eye on the balance sheet, not adventurers or political administrators with an eye on the flag. They brought to their task a quantitative outlook that was entirely appropriate for commercial enterprises but that had not yet been extended to the political and social realms. More than half a century before William Petty invented "political arithmetic"— that wedding of vulgar calculation and public policy—the Virginia Company of London was busy collecting censuses and totting up ship lists of emigrants, because in their enterprise people had been reduced to commodities.

Despite auspicious beginnings, numeracy did not proceed very far in seventeenth-century America. The peculiar circumstances of early settlement that fostered the use of numbers did not obtain for long. It is important to bear in mind the rather narrow scope of numeracy in order to understand why the seventeenth-century colonists were not yet "a calculating people." English investors wanted figures, but the settlers themselves had a hard time understanding why. They did not see themselves as units in a business transaction, and business was the only familiar province of arithmetic.

In general, whenever English accounts of the New World featured quantitative information, there was an economic interest lurking not far beneath the surface. Out of a need to attract both investors and emigrants, there quickly sprang up a promotional literature whose authors vied with one another in describing the magnitudes of natural abundance in the several colonies. For much the same reasons, the Virginia Company printed and distributed abstracts of its emigrant ships' lists, to lend an impression that Virginia was a populated and hence popular destination. Later in the seventeenth century the newly formed Lords of Trade and Plantations decided that correct regulation of mercantilism required periodic quantitative reports from the royal governors on the scene. These agencies had a desire to collect quantified data in order to further their own economic ends, but in fact they encountered great difficulty in procuring data. Frequently, authors of promotional tracts simply made up their numbers, as did some royal governors when faced with the perplexing barrage of quantitative questions sent out by the Lords of Trade. The leaders of the Virginia Company did not fabricate data, but they certainly scrambled to hide them when the real tragedy of their traffic in people began to be reflected in population statistics. These examples of numeracy in seventeenth-century America were produced by a small handful of men, who either accepted numbers of dubious authenticity or abandoned efforts to collect precise data at all, once the numbers worked against their economic goals. Their desire to have such data was rarely supported by the general run of new settlers in America, and sometimes it was actively opposed.

The lack of interest in arithmetic among the settlers partly stemmed from the low level of education among them. South of New England, the vast majority of new Americans were untrained, illiterate young people who shipped off to the New World in desperation, because England offered them no future. Once in America they served out (if lucky) numbing years of servitude, doing physical labor, with no more need for calculation skills than their black-skinned coworkers, who also labored in the tobacco, corn, and sugar-cane fields. The fortunate white servant who survived to achieve the status of freeholder found some use for arithmetic if he planned to participate in the commercial market in agricultural products, but, even there, knowledge of numbers could be quite rudimentary, limited to the simple addition and subtraction needed in a barter economy. More sophisticated ideas for using numbers, such as the act calling for a numbering of tobacco plants in Virginia in 1632, in order to control total output, fell dismally into neglect.

The low level of education was not, however, the only cause of innumeracy. In New England, seventeenth-century Puritans were not lacking in education or literacy. The founding generation arrived in Massachusetts in the 1630s with the highest number of university degrees and the highest rates of literacy of any migratory group. Within a decade they instructed towns to establish local grammar schools and had set up Harvard College to provide high-level training for home-grown ministers. But arithmetic was not among the subjects considered basic for Puritan children to learn. If anything, numbers were rather less used in Massachusetts than in Virginia in the early years. A profitable trade ranked high in the scheme of things in Virginia, but the investors and settlers in the Massachusetts Bay Company had something much more important on their mind: religion. No one went to Massachusetts with the expectation of getting rich quick. Their goal was to establish their own biblical commonwealth as a model for corrupt England to follow. The contrast between corruption and purity in religion contained, for the Puritan mind, no quantitative dimension. They could not conceive of any way to measure purity or piety, and numerical thinking did not, in the seventeenth century, develop into a common mode of cognition among them. Religion, however, is not impervious to numbers. Nineteenth- and twentieth-century quantifiers have found ways to hold yardsticks to it, ways that would have been foreign to the Puritans. For example, the religious crisis of declension in the second half of the seventeenth century has been easily and readily comprehended in numerical terms by modern historians, who think of a falling-away from faith in terms of a decline in church membership. For the Puritans, considerations about church membership lay completely outside the realm of things countable. Their worries about declining religiosity did not arise from, or lead to, an attempt to document the decline empirically by reference to church registers of conversions. Their inability to apply numerical

reasoning in this instance tells us much about the limits of the
domain of number in the seventeenth century.

I n the early and middle years of the seventeenth century a
lively production of promotional tracts flooded England, each
pamphlet raving about the wonders of particular American
plantations.[1] These tracts often contained much numerical information, reflecting an English climate newly sensitive to the measurable aspects of reality. The tendency to describe in quantitative
terms was reinforced by the fact that, at first sight, the most
noteworthy characteristics of the new world were marvelous
mainly by virtue of their size or abundance. The early promotional
literature rhapsodized about turkey flocks containing 500 fowl,
bass 19 inches in length, harbors of 30 fathoms, large enough to
hold "500 sayle of ships."[2] Numerical detail of this sort was very
common, but its Bunyanesque character suggests that these tracts
were not at all inspired by the desire for precision and accuracy.
Such numbers were rarely the result of actual measuring; usually
they were simple estimates or wild guesses. And the authors
clearly did not discuss everything they could think of quantifying,
for they usually declined to comment on the number of deaths,
a category of quantification that had well-established meaning for
Englishmen of the seventeenth century, familiar as they were with
the London bills of mortality. These were, after all, promotional
tracts. Thus they give us a selective rather than comprehensive
view of the topics deemed amenable to quantification in that era.
   The true function of quantification in the early promotional
tracts was to augment the credibility of the account by making
even the most extravagant claims appear highly concrete and
objective. It was during these same years in England that numbers
were gaining the reputation for being more objective than qualitative description because something quantified could be resub-
mitted to measurement or count by a different observer, who
would reach the same conclusion. No doubt some of the authors
of promotional tracts thought they were engaging in an objective
description of reality; most, however, were only exploiting a cultural tendency that credited numbers with truth.
   To the former, earnest, class belongs Captain John Smith,
whose outpourings of quantified detail have won him a reputation
as a pathbreaking empiricist in the histories of science in early

America.[3] In his thirty-four-page *Description of New England* (1616), for example, Smith related that on an island at 43.5 degrees of latitude his party caught 40,000 fish and acquired the furs of 1,100 beavers and 100 martens from trade with the natives; the fish sold in England for £5 per hundred and in Spain for "40 royalls the quintall." The coast of America was 2,000 miles long; New England was 75 leagues, containing 40 towns, 25 harbors, and more than 200 islands. Smith assiduously sounded the harbors, the most direct form of measurement he engaged in, and marked the depths on his map for future emigrants. He reported that the New English inhabitants traded 6,000 or 7,000 furs per year, while the French to the north were trading 25,000. If the natives were "untoward," a mere "30 or 40 good men will be sufficient to bring them all in subjection." Smith carefully calculated the costs and profits of commerce in fishing and even estimated the number of fish a tolerably good fisherman could catch in one day. Fish were the gold of North America, and Smith was ready with calculations to show just how much of this "gold" each man could corner. A less quantitatively inclined person might have found it sufficient to remark that there was an abundance of fish. When Smith asked the native Indians how many fish they customarily caught, he learned that "the Saluages compare their store in the sea to the haires of their heads." It is possible they were puzzled by Smith's inquiry.[4]

John Smith was an eager, not to say compulsive, calculator, whose eye automatically gauged everything that came within its purview. His accounts have credibility because he apparently witnessed nearly everything he reported on. Such was not the case with a host of other writers, whose use of numbers had a patently promotional purpose. The author of *A Perfect Description of Virginia* (1649) devoted to his first sentence to declaring that 15,000 English and 300 Negro servants lived in that colony and his following sentences to enumerating the next-most important populations: 20,000 cattle, 200 horses, 50 asses, 3,000 sheep, 5,000 goats, and "six publike Brewhouses." Probably only the last was the product of empirical investigation. Comforting numbers, like the number of ships that docked yearly (30) or the number of pounds of tobacco one man could plant (2,000), were prominently touted. But the accounts of two Indian massacres, which were disasters in the colony's early history, were related in general terms, without the use of numbers. And no mention at all was made of the massive toll taken by "seasoning," the painful and frequently fatal process of acquiring immunities to the diseases that flourished in the Virginia summertime.[5]

Promotional tracts for rival colonies were less hesitant about broaching the subject of Virginia's poor mortality record. Beauchamp Plantagenet, the author of a 1648 pamphlet praising Maryland, emphasized some numbers he claimed Virginians themselves had told him: 100,000 people had died of sickness in the first thirty years, a number allegedly amounting to five out of six emigrants. If true—and there is evidence that the ratio of five out of six was not grossly inaccurate—even London during a plague year was safer than Virginia. The shocking total of 100,000 deaths was nothing but a wild guess, for that many people had not even arrived on Virginia's shores until the early eighteenth century. After deprecating Virginia, Plantagenet developed his theme that "New Albion," just to the north of Virginia, was the land of milk and honey, which he proved with specific numerical reports of weights of turkeys, corn yields per acre, shippings per year, and Indian bowmen for each tribe, complete with a kill ratio of a dozen English marksmen to 300 Indians. Plantagenet noted with satisfaction that an Englishman could shoot thirty pellets from a five-foot caliver over a distance of fifty yards, while a lone Indian could shoot one arrow only thirty yards. Here was a clear instance of how quantitative analysis served to alleviate anxiety; the very certainty of the numbers assured easy military victory over the native population.[6]

America as a land of plenty and abundance was the common theme of all the promotional literature. In particular, comment on the size of turkeys (ranging from twenty to sixty pounds) and on the number of young that deer brought forth each season (said to be three per mother) seem to have been de rigueur.[7] These numbers suggested that rapid growth and easy fertility were assured in the American environment.

The prevalent concern with growth and fertility led the promoters to place special emphasis on the size and growth of the English population in the colonies. In the early seventeenth century, population was not a matter of great interest in England; it was not until late in the century that proponents of mercantilism and political arithmetic introduced the idea that population was a crucial factor in the calculation of a country's wealth. But from the initial settlement, colonial promoters recognized that a reputedly large and growing population signified the vitality of a colony and made it less vulnerable to enemy attack. The reliability of their figures varied greatly, according to the myopia of each author. For example, Thomas Morton in his *New English Canaan* estimated that in 1632 there were 12,000 persons in New England, "as my intelligence gives," but his intelligence was evidently different from that of a ship's captain, who reported to the Privy Council that the Bay Colony's population numbered about 2,000 that year. Morton's myopia had likely been conditioned by his outcast status: he was a maverick, hounded back to England by disapproving Pilgrims for hosting a perpetual riotous party too near to Pilgrim settlements; thus it is not surprising that for every Pilgrim there he saw six.[8] Another pair of conflicting population reports appeared in 1634. In that year Governor John Winthrop estimated the Massachusetts population to be 4,000 (he drew back from counting, because of the sin of David), while an anonymous "Relation Concerning the Estate of New-England" confidently pronounced that Massachusetts had more than 20,000 inhabitants and that New England as a whole had 30,000.[9] Here the discrepancy can perhaps be accounted for by sheer carelessness in the latter document. Its nineteenth-century editor noted that three copies of the "Relation" had been found in England, all in different hands and differing "in particulars, especially in numbers."[10] Evidently, numbers were the least important part of the message: why take care to copy them exactly when they were presumed to be inaccurate in the first place?

A third type of error in estimating population—deliberate fabrication—is evident in some figures for Barbados in the 1660s. One John Scott, an adventurous spy of dubious veracity, produced a string of precise numbers for the population of Barbados in 1645 and 1667. Since his figures are three to five times higher than modern estimates, based on indirect evidence (tax and militia lists), one historian has concluded that Scott simply made up his numbers.[11] That he chose quite specific numbers, such as 82,023 slaves, shows that by the 1660s it was important to be precise in order to be believable, even when one was grossly exaggerating.

The size of the American population had the symbolic value of promoting images of fertility and viability long before it was thought to have a positive economic value as part of the calculable wealth of the state. Strict accuracy in determining the population, therefore, was never of paramount importance, and the general tendency favored exaggeration. An actual census would not have aided these boastful purposes and might in fact have undermined them if the population fell far short of the publicized estimates. There was really no pressure to underestimate population, since England was not exacting taxes based on head counts.

Inflated and contradictory American figures provoked no challenges in the mother country because in the first half of the seventeenth century no one in England seemed to be worrying that the peopling of America would rob England of her vitality and resources. To the contrary, the promotional literature championed massive emigration as a solution for the problem of overpopulation at home. England was said to have a swarming multitude of vagrants and other marginal people. Vivid images in the promotional literature drove the point home; one writer remarked, for example, that

> [it is] most profitable for our State, to rid our multitudes of such as lie at home, pestering the land with vice and villanie, worse than the plague it selfe.[12]

Another said:

> Our multitudes like too much blood in the body do infect our country with plague and poverty . . . ; our land hath brought forth, but it hath not milk sufficient in the breast thereof to nourish all those children which it hath brought forth.[13]

America had the milk to offer (interestingly, many promotional tracts emphasize the abundance of cows and dairy products in the land of milk and honey) and—to continue the mixed metaphor—England apparently needed some bloodletting.

A rapidly growing population was perceived as positive and vital in one area and a cause of disease and infection in another, the difference owing to the actual sizes of the two populations. There is implicit here a nascent theory of optimum population. England had too many people, America too few. No one tried to develop the theory further, with quantitative data to specify an optimum size, because it was entirely possible to talk about too many or too few people without recourse to numbers; one needed only to look at the symptoms, pestilence and penury, to know that there were too many. In fact, had anyone had thought (or been able) to measure the rate of growth in population in the mid-seventeenth century, the results would have been surprising, for

England's population was probably stationary or declining, according to reconstructions made by modern demographers. As one historian has suggested, it is possible that the whole notion of the pressure of overpopulation was part of a calculated plan by colonial promoters, who thereby hoped to encourage emigration to their fledgling outposts.[14] Certainly, England in the reigns of James I and Charles I was suffering from a surfeit of unemployed, marginal people who lacked even a subsistence level of food and who swelled the death registers in time of famine and plague; that seventeenth-century impression of crisis has been confirmed by modern demographic studies.[15] But that overpopulation was the cause—rather than economic dislocation, maldistribution of wealth, high food prices, poor harvests, and black rats—is extremely doubtful.

To have understood those connections, a seventeenth-century person would have had to think of mortality in a distinctly modern way, in terms of death rates specific to ages, classes, and seasons. The pattern of deaths so categorized reveals which groups in a population are unusually vulnerable to death and when and thereby implies something about the cause of death. But until the nineteenth century no one conceptualized death in that way.

Just a simple magnitude of death was as far as any quantifier went in the seventeenth century, and even that was not a usual way to contemplate death in the colonies. For example, when the second shipload of Puritans landed at Massachusetts Bay in 1630, one of the arrivals, Thomas Dudley, noted that eighty people of the first settling had died in the preceding winter, but thereafter he described the subsequent heavy mortality in qualitative terms, using biblical phrases to place death in a sympathetic social context: "There is not an howse where there is not one dead, and in some howses many." Deaths of prominent or virtuous people were noted in particular, while magnitude was merely suggested by the information that "many dyed weekely, yea almost dayley." The rounded number of eighty summarized a mortality that Dudley had not personally witnessed; after his arrival, he experienced the deaths not as abstract numbers but as human events with direct meaning for the survivors. Similarly, William Bradford considered the initial mortality among the Pilgrims worth noting in very rough terms of quantity—more than half of the original one hundred died in the first two or three months—because it was so enormous.[16] But contemporary aggregate accounts of the number of deaths for periods after the first year or two of settlement are extremely rare.[17]

In short, colonists of the seventeenth century tended to maximize estimates of their population and to ignore magnitudes of mortality except when it was unusually heavy, and even then the deaths were likely to be discussed in qualitative rather than quantitative terms. There was little point in keeping records of the totals, since the number of deaths was in any case beyond the control of the living and since reports of high mortality would only drive away future settlers. Growth and fertility made a colony seem attractive; emphasis on mortality was a sign of failure.

Only once in the early seventeenth century was the rule of maximizing growth and minimizing deaths reversed, and the occasion paved the way for an extraordinary series of censuses, the first actual head counts in the British Empire. Virginia in the 1620s suffered from such appalling mortality and mismanagement that the colonists themselves were spurred to gather nominal "lists of the living" in order to demonstrate their need for help, and the British government ordered several more lists to verify the terrible state of affairs. These censuses were truly unusual; they predate any other British colonial census by nearly half a century. Two assumptions inspired their undertaking: the assumption that people could be treated as commodities in an economic system and the assumption that someone was to blame for the heavy mortality. Once the short-run crisis was over in Virginia, the notion of counting a population person by person faded away.

The first assumption, that emigrants could most usefully be regarded as commodities, developed under the shrewd leadership of Sir Edwin Sandys, who in 1619 became treasurer of the Virginia Company of London, the top post in the organization. Sandys did not have a countinghouse background. The son of an archbishop, he attended Oxford and then trained for the law at Middle Temple in London, an education that fitted him for a political career. Beginning in 1586 he was from time to time a member of the House of Commons, where, in the 1610s, he distinguished himself chiefly as a vocal critic of King James I. Nothing in his background pointed to a political-arithmetic approach to colonization, although he was an early investor in several colonial companies. But his deputy was John Ferrar, eldest son of a notable merchant family of London. Ferrar handled all the administrative details of the project, from rounding up emigrants and provisioning ships to keeping account books of expenses and registers of passengers. It was he, more than anyone, who brought a quantitative mentality to the Virginia Company's enterprise, and, ironically it was he, more than anyone, who was to blame for the tragedy that ensued.[18] Through careful calculations he intended to rationalize the company's decisions about the colony, but in fact his miscalculations greatly augmented the colonists' grief.

Since 1607 the Virginia Company had been attempting without great luck to establish a viable colony in the Chesapeake. Intermittently small shiploads of men landed at Jamestown to replace the sick and dying from prior shipments of settlers. Usually the new recruits did not fare much better than their predecessors. Starvation, disease, bad water, ill will, lack of ambition, and poor local leadership kept the colony small and struggling.[19] This situation did not please investors back in London. Rather than cut losses and abandon the project, the company's leaders decided to move colonization into high gear in 1618 by pumping multitudes of people into Virginia quickly and setting them to work on a variety of projects—tobacco culture, silkworm-raising, ironworks, vineyards, and glass-blowing—to see if something could not be made to turn a profit. Sandys and Ferrar took charge of this policy in 1619 and aggressively pursued it to the bitter end.

In contrast to the trickle of emigration before 1619, under Sandys' direction anywhere from 800 to 1,500 began embarking annually for the Chesapeake. Such numbers of passengers represented a very large outlay of money for the company, so Ferrar kept careful records in order to evaluate the success of the strategy. He also wanted to make sure that among the emigrants there was a proper distribution of skills and trades, to carry out the new plans for diversification. Passenger lists showing the name, age, trade, and next of kin of each emigrant were deposited with Ferrar, who digested them into aggregate lists to present as part of the company's periodic reports. In 1619, 1620, and 1621 the aggregate lists were also issued as broadsides, to show to the public the fantastic speed with which Virginia was being settled. On these lists Ferrar noted not only the emigrants sent for the service of the company—the employees one would expect a company to keep records of—but also the numbers sent by private planters and the ones sent to be sold on arrival, such as the ninety young maids sent in 1619 to be bought for brides. The labor expended in this effort to keep track of every emigrant was termed an "incredible trouble" by Sandys; Ferrar allegedly had to neglect his own business and enlist the aid of his brothers to get the records in shape for each quarterly meeting.[20]

Essentially, Sandys and Ferrar thought of the emigrants as raw material; they were treating the population of Virginia as an important part of a business calculation that required precision and accuracy. Barrels of pitch and biscuits, bushels of malt, and numbers of people were all reckoned as part of the inflow of resources; the productive labor of Virginians would determine the profit. In a project of this relatively small scale—where it was clear that the number of people was correlated with fruitful production, where the influx of people was customarily recorded in passenger lists, and where one business, indeed one man, had oversight of the whole operation—it was obvious that population could be a quantitative concept and could enter into calculations.

Sandys and Ferrar not only kept accounts of the flow of human traffic; they also wanted to know the actual size of the resident population, both human and bovine. They had some idea of the size just before they took over, for in 1617 colonist John Rolfe returned to England and reported the population to be 351 people and 144 cattle. The newly codified operating procedures, the company's "Orders and Constitutions" of 1619 and 1620, called for a special book to be kept, along with the account books and letter books, recording the names of all planters residing in Virginia, created from lists supplied by the head of each plantation. In 1621 this plan was reiterated in the set of instructions sent over with Sir Francis Wyatt, the new governor, reminding him to take "a catalogue of the people in every plantation" and to keep a "list of all cattle." These lists have not survived, but it is evident that they were at first kept and sent in, for in 1623 the absence of the yearly list was noted with uneasiness by the faction within the company that opposed Sandys's leadership: "The catalogue of all the peoples names residing in the Colony is appointed by order from hence to be sent ouer euery yeare, that so the Company here may discerne of the strength of the Colony. This is either omitted this yeare or concealed from vs."[21]

As it developed, the anti-Sandys faction had good reason to feel uneasy, but at first there was no demonstrable cause. Dissatisfaction with Sandys surfaced early, in 1620, when some members of the company's council suspected he was concealing news from Virginia; however, his opponents could make no specific

charges against him. They engineered his ouster as official treasurer in 1620 by stirring up the old bitterness between Sandys and
the king, who obliged by declaring Sandys out of the running for
any company office. But there was insufficient voting strength
within the company to unseat Sandys completely from power,
and the new treasurer, the earl of Southampton, was his willing
puppet; the figure-minded Ferrar also continued in his all-important post as deputy. (John Ferrar was deputy until 1623, when his
brother Nicholas took over the post.) The dissatisfaction stemmed
from shady dealings in tobacco contracts as well as worries that
Sandys was perhaps being reckless with both money and lives in
his rapid peopling of Virginia. But, strangely, no one thought to
check the emigrant lists against the resident records until 1623.
Had someone done so, it is possible that the shocking discrep-
ancies would have come to light as early as 1620. In that year a
nasty rumor that Virginia was a sure deathtrap circulated in Plymouth, England, a major port of departure for the Chesapeake, but
the company's only response was to deny it and consider instituting libel proceedings. Dockworkers and waterfront dwellers in
Plymouth knew more by scuttlebutt than Sandys and Ferrar did
with all their careful figures.[22]

Or perhaps they did know but concealed the truth. Pieces of
the story continued to trickle out, however, and suspicions were
transformed into genuine alarm in 1622 and 1623. The Indian
massacre of March, 1622, marked the first concrete news of mass
death in the Chesapeake, but still the company's leaders preferred
to minimize its numerical significance. They expressed shock and
grief over the event, of course, for the Indians had been reckoned
by some as friends, and their bold action of simultaneously at-
tacking all of the white settlements indicated a treachery chilling
in its implications for future Anglo-Indian relations. But the actual
number of settlers murdered was played down as a small fraction
of the population. Edward Waterhouse, secretary of the company,
was assigned the difficult task of putting a good face on the massacre, of making it less frightening so that it would not dampen
enthusiasm for emigration. Waterhouse assured English readers
that 3,570 emigrants had gone to Virginia in the past three years
and that more embarkations were imminent: Indians could not
stem the tide of settlement. The massacre had caused the deaths
of 347, true; but it was far from being the near-total slaughter that
fearful rumor would have it. Perhaps there was even an advantage

to be gained from all the bloodshed, Waterhouse continued, for
the enmity shown by the natives now removed all constraints on
civility, and the English could with clear conscience pursue a
policy of genocide against the native population. Another London
account of the massacre also emphasized the drop-in-the-bucket
version of the deaths: Captain John Smith wrote that "eleuen
parts of twelue" of the Virginians had survived and that the colony
was actually thriving, not dying.[23]

Such, of course, was not the case. John Ferrar, for one, must
have known that the number of survivors was far less than the
published accounts indicated. The spring, 1622, annual enrolling
of the population revealed a total of 1,240 persons alive in the
Chesapeake, not the 3,800 implied by John Smith's account.[24]
Where had the other two and a half thousand disappeared to?
Ferrar preferred not to raise this question. By early 1623 the anti-
Sandys faction was raising the question, finally, and with increasing persistence.

For by spring, 1623, even more settlers had died and Ferrar and
Sandys were no longer able to suppress the news. After the massacre they had rashly continued to send shiploads of settlers,
despite the fact that the Virginians had been forced to abandon
their cultivated lands and retreat to the relative security of Jamestown, making food very scarce. Nearly a thousand newcomers
descended upon them, and the locals were in no position to receive them hospitably. On the rare occasion when the emigrants
arrived with extra provisions to share with the older settlers, the
food caused, rather than alleviated, problems. The ship *Abigail*
sailed up the James River in February, 1623, with a cargo of sickly
people and a supply of "stinking beere," and disease and death
spread rapidly. Virginians blamed the beer and pleaded for re-
venge against one Dupper, the brewer who had made it. Some of
the most pitiful letters of complaint from Virginians date from the
late winter and early spring of 1623; and because they began
addressing their letters to Sandys's opponents, these letters were
saved, as evidence of mismanagement. (The opponents alleged
that Sandys had received such letters earlier but had not shared
them with the company's council.)[25] Edwin Sandys's own younger
brother, George, an official residing in the colony, decided to
lodge his complaint with Samuel Wrote, a company member who
sided with the faction opposed to Sandys's regime:

Who is ignorant how the heavie hand of God hath suppressed us? the lyving being hardlie able to bury the dead through their owne Imbecillitie, insomuch as I am afraid wee have not lost lesse than 500 by sicknes (with a generall weaknes of the rest) which taken out of so small a number (*Farre Short of Yor Conjectures*) I belieue haue not left behind them so mani able men in the Countrye. And by the way I would you Could hang that villaine Dupper who with his Stinking beere hath poisoned most of the Passengers and spred the Infection all over the Collanie which before the Arrivall of the Abigail were recouvered.[26]

George Sandys directed his wrath at Dupper the brewer. But Samuel Wrote began to wonder who really was to blame for the heavy mortality. He drew up a balance sheet, comparing the annual census totals from 1619, 1620, 1621, and 1622 with the records of emigration over those years and discovered that over 3,000 persons were not accounted for and were presumably dead—and this before the massacre. He then added in the thousand dumped on Virginia after the massacre, subtracted the 500 deaths from the foul beer, and concluded that not above 1,700 people could be left alive.[27]

Armed with these alarming data, the opponents of Sandys pressed for a royal investigation of the company. By early summer, 1623, a commission empowered by the Privy Council was sifting through quantitative evidence supplied by both sides. Numbers played a central role in documenting the alleged malfeasance. One side dramatically claimed that, in all the years of colonization, 10,000 people had been sent over and that only 2,000 were now left alive.[28] The figure of 10,000 was overblown, according to Ferrar's careful emigration statistics. Sandys took refuge in the records showing that a total of only 6,000 had been sent since 1607, of whom only 3,500 had been sent since 1619, the year his command began; of these 3,500, 2,500 were now alive, "wherof good proofe is to be made."[29] Sandys's defense was to lay as much of the mortality as possible at the door of the previous regime and to show that the death record had actually improved since 1619 under his management. Though he neglected to add in the roughly 1,000 emigrants sent after the massacre and could in fact offer no proof that 2,500 were still alive, Sandys had to concede, even on the basis of his own moderated figures, that a third of his emigrants had died. His opponents seized on this concession and at the same time tried to produce a more accurate account of the mortality. At issue were the numbers alive in 1618 and the number currently alive; from those figures the crown could assess the charge that Virginia, under Sandys, had become "a slaughterhouse."

The census, which Sandys was sure would exonerate him, did not materialize in 1623. There is good evidence of the colonists' professed intent to take it, for in April, 1623, the resident secretary in Virginia, Christopher Davison, wrote to Ferrar about a head count then in progress:

> I had sent a list, of the names of all the people, that dyed or were slayne, by the Indians, since the massacre, & of all that remayne aliue, but since I could not in tyme procure the bills, from many perticular plantations, I thought it better, to send you a perfect catalogue, by the next ship, then a lame & imperfect one by this.[30]

It is unlikely that this count was completed when promised, for in December, 1623, Davison and other members of the Virginia Council were still prodding local plantation leaders to return the names of the living and all who had died since the massacre.[31] These resident officials in Virginia had good reason to drag their feet, for they knew the census would make the company look bad, and most of them were investors in it. The royal investigators meanwhile decided to launch their own census, and in October, 1623, they appointed commissioners to be sent to Virginia to examine at first hand the complaints of incompetence and mismanagement and to count "the number of plantations, public and private, and the men, women, and children in each."[32]

By the following February the "List of the Living and Dead" was complete, the product of Davison's work, not that of the royal commissioners, since they did not arrive in the colony until early March.[33] Even though the count was done by company men, it was powerful evidence against the company. It showed that only 1,275 souls were alive in Virginia, a number that corroborated the fears of the anti-Sandys faction because it was substantially lower than Samuel Wrote's grim calculations, worked out the previous spring.[34] The large discrepancy between records of the numbers sent and the findings of the census did indeed make Virginia appear to be a slaughterhouse, and the crown began proceedings to dissolve the company.[35]

Just how accurate was this 1624 census? Counting people is not exactly as easy as counting casks of tobacco stacked on wharves, since people can slip around and be counted twice or not at all. And, too, the novelty of the whole operation, for the English counters, might be expected to affect the accuracy of the results. On the other hand, the Virginians were not exactly inexperienced in counting themselves, since they had conducted censuses four times between 1619 and 1622. Moreover, the small size of the population, separated into two dozen distinct locations, made it easier for each geographical division to be fairly accurate in its count. Since a great deal hinged on the accuracy of the census, the investigators took advantage of one of the virtues of measurement—its repeatability—for verification. In early 1625 another census was taken, this time called a muster but in fact much more than a militia list, since it gave the ages, dates of arrival, and amount of provisions on hand as well as names for nearly all Virginians—men, women and children.[36] The Virginia council sent this to the royal officials now in charge and even promised to take another general muster after the fall harvest of 1625 to show by how much they had been "augmented."[37] The instructions to the new governor in April, 1626, directed that he send an account of all the inhabitants as soon as he arrived.[38] (No autumn, 1625, or April, 1626, census has, however, come to light.) Contrast this sort of endeavor, the frequent and repeated measurement of population, with the quality of information obtained from the offhand subjective remark made by one of the royal commissioners, sent over in late 1623: "[We] doe finde the persons heer to be more in number . . . then we expected."[39] It would be hard to dissolve the Virginia Company on the basis of that statement, since it tells more about the commissioners' expectations than anything else.

The muster of 1625 did confirm the picture of few survivors presented by the 1624 List of the Living: some 1,232 Virginians remained out of the 6,000 sent by the company; four out of five had in fact perished.[40] Numbers unambiguously showed that Virginia was not a healthy place to be. But with the Virginia Company disbanded, would there be as much mortality? And would the new royal officials be inclined to monitor the situation? In answering the second question we come up against the constraints that policy often exercises over fact-finding. Emigrants continued to pour into Virginia in the late 1620s and 1630s, in numbers as great or greater than the annual departures under Sandys, and

there continued to be complaints about ill-timed and ill-provi-
sioned (and just plain ill) herds of people arriving to infest the
colony.[41] In theory, the kind of calculations that brought down the
Virginia Company could have been made for the early years of
royal control, at least in the 1630s. The entry of emigrants was
monitored by a registry maintained at the first landfall, Point
Comfort; ships' captains were required to deliver passenger lists,
and each newcomer had to swear allegiance to the king and get
his or her name inscribed in a register.[42] Yearly censuses were
supposed to continue, as stipulated by instructions to governors
and by a law of 1632 passed by the Virginia House of Burgesses,
which set December 1 as the date for the annual census.[43] But
theory was not practice, and the calculations were not made. The
register of emigrants was evaded as much as possible because of
a 6-pence fee levied on each oath-taker, and petitions to the crown
in the 1630s asked that the whole registration system be discontinued. No one was in a mood to follow Ferrar's model and aggregate the register in the cause of good advertising.[44] Nor was
more than one census taken (or, if there were more, they were
not sent back to the royal officials in London). The exception
occurred in 1635, when a general muster of people and cattle was
prepared and the governor, John Harvey, informed the Privy
Council that 4,914 was the exact number of Virginians.[45] This
represented a fourfold increase over the population of a decade
before, in 1625, which sounds like rapid growth until one recalls
the relatively small numbers that are involved. If an average of
a thousand emigrants had gone to Virginia each year in that decade—not an unreasonable supposition—these, combined with
the population alive in 1625, would yield a total of 11,200 if there
were no natural increase and no mortality. But Harvey reported
only 4,914. Clearly, death was still a problem in the Chesapeake.[46]
How much of a problem it was did not interest the new authorities,
and no further censuses were taken in Virginia until 1699.

No census of people, that is. In 1632 a plan was advanced to
count all tobacco plants growing in the colony. Here was the
pure form of a censorious census. Tobacco prices had fallen pre-
cipitously in the late 1620s, prompting planters to plant more in
an effort to maintain income. The crown wanted to reverse that—
to curtail tobacco production—in the hope that Virginians would
plant food crops, since food shortages continued to be a problem.
Governor Harvey was just the sort to turn to a census to enforce

the crown's policy. He had first come to Virginia in 1624 as a commissioner sent to count the inhabitants, and when he returned as governor in 1630 he sent in frequent estimates of the population, culminating in the exact-appearing muster of 1635. In the first assembly called by Harvey, in 1630, the burgesses were persuaded to pass a law limiting cultivation to 2,000 tobacco plants per capita. Two years later a new version of the law instituted a novel method of enforcement:

> to prevent any greater quantities, every planter or mayster of a famylie plantinge a cropp of tobacco more or lesse, shall be tyed to procure one of his neighbours, or some sufficient man to come and nomber his or theire plants of tobacco, who will uppon his oath declare and testifie unto the commander of that place, before the tenth day of July that he hath counted and nombred the sayd plants, and shall say in his conscience the iust and true number of them.[47]

Planters caught with excessive numbers of plants were doomed to suffer the loss of their entire crops as penalty. Commanders, who might understandably be reluctant to mow down a neighbor's field, faced imprisonment if they neglected their duty. Apparently the law had some effect, for Harvey reported that the production of staples had risen dramatically in 1633 and 1634.[48] However, when the law was renewed in 1638, the burgesses spent a month debating it, and Harvey wrote home that the colonists had "no inclination to embrace" a guaranteed market and price offered by the crown in exchange for reduced production.[49] By the early 1640s tobacco was planted freely again, its price at an all-time low, and watchful eyes no longer tallied the neighbor's crop. Gone, too, was Harvey, dismissed from office in 1639 through the machinations of his own council, whom he had alienated from the beginning by his meddling policies.[50] His successors were not at all inclined to control by counting.

After the 1635 census in Virginia, no census of people was taken in any British colony for nearly three decades. The English Civil War and interregnum of the 1640s and 1650s seriously disrupted the government's interest and ability to assert control over overseas colonies. With the Restoration in 1660 Britain put her internal disputes behind her and turned to the task of ordering the colonies for the maximum benefit of the mother country. From 1660 to the mid-1690s there was a gradual proliferation of acts, councils, and bureaucratic functionaries, the chief purpose of which was to bring some order into the growing trans-Atlantic trade and to build English profits at the expense of the Dutch. Periodic censuses and surveys of a few colonies were only rather inconsequential by-products of the administrative apparatus, which may seem surprising to twentieth-century historians. To our minds, an effort to control trade or redirect it seems almost impossible in the absence of accurate knowledge of its dimensions, but the architects of the nascent colonial system were for the most part content with very general guesses and approximations of the volume of trade and the numbers of people. Only in a few isolated instances did anything like an accurate inventory occur. In the 1690s, however, the flourishing interest in political arithmetic among the new Board of Trade members gave rise to a systematic, quantitative approach to imperial administration.

The first half-dozen censuses of the Restoration period were all taken in Jamaica between 1661 and 1680.[51] Such a flurry of enumerations, followed by a long hiatus, should signal that, as in the case of early Virginia, these censuses were not part of a larger, more general effort to know the number of people under colonial rule but rather arose out of a situation peculiar to Jamaica, one that did not obtain even in the other island colonies. In 1661 Jamaica had been inhabited by the English for only five years. The toehold its small population had gained was continually threatened by Spanish invasion. In 1660 the last of the Spaniards were finally driven off, an informal survey of the state of affairs was submitted to the Privy Council, and Jamaica became a royal colony.[52] At almost the same time, in December, 1660, a newly reorganized Council for Foreign Plantations was appointed by the crown and was given instructions to investigate the affairs and governments of all the colonies. The only instruction specifying numerical information directed the council to inquire into the "number of men, fortifications, &c." in each colony—information of evident military value.[53] Jamaica's informal survey of 1660 had included the number of soldiers and most of the other information the council wanted, and yet, just one year later, the council received a far more detailed numerical account of the population of Jamaica. In 1661 and again in 1662, 1665, 1670, 1671, 1673, and 1680, officials in Jamaica completed reports about the numbers of people, sometimes with age, race, and sex included as well, and sometimes giving acreage granted, annual production of sugar and cocoa, and the like.[54] The agricultural information was meant to answer direct requests of the council; the details on population, however, far exceeded the council's requests. Why were these censuses taken, if not to satisfy superiors in the hierarchy of colonial administration?

The initial census in 1661 is something of a mystery.[55] The first royal governor, Thomas Windsor, was appointed only in late 1661 and did not embark for the island until March, 1662. He carried instructions to draw up a "register of the plantations to be sent home as soon as possible."[56] Such a register would presumably record who owned land and, perhaps, how much; it was not a request for a population count. No such register appears in the *Calendar of State Papers* during Windsor's term, and it seems likely that the only population information that he submitted to England was an exact count of the militia, amounting to 2,030 men, in December 1662.[57] The number of military men was supplied in answer to an explicit request of the Council for Foreign Plantations, which apparently saw no need for further information on population. Yet, in 1662, another enumeration was carried out, one that counted and distinguished white men, women, and children and black slaves.[58] There are also indications that in 1665 and in 1668 further head counts took place, which either were not sent to, or have not survived in, the Colonial Office in London.[59] In 1670 Windsor's successor, Governor Thomas Modyford, submitted a nominal list of property owners by parish, each with his acreage noted.[60] Perhaps this was the plantation register that the royal instructions had initially requested. But Modyford supplied information beyond landholding; for each parish, the number of family heads was totaled (not always correctly), and a figure for "people by estimation" was set down beside it. In two cases the estimation appears to be a simple multiple (by 10) of the number of families; in other cases it is an exact number arrived at by unknown methods. The tallies are tabulated and summed in a table at the end, which shows total number of acres, total number of families, and total number of persons. A concern for comprehensive accuracy in the number of persons was not preeminent, however, since an area of four parishes on the north of the island was not surveyed, "as not worth it, by reason of its distance and new settlements"; to account for those, the compiler of the survey tossed in 1,500 more people, plus 2,500 "lusty, able" buccaneers and sailors and another 3,300 for the populations of the two towns.[61] In other words, the final population figure, although it appears to be the result of an exact count (because of its specificity, 15,198), is actually only slightly better than the general estimates of population that other royal governors were content to report.

The real significance of the survey of 1670 is that it suggests the reason why all the enumerations in the 1660s were made and why between 1662 and 1670 they were not reported to London. The chief purpose of the 1670 survey was to demonstrate how many acres of land had been granted to settlers; the total was just over 200,000 acres. At the time the survey was being completed, another Modyford, Charles, was presenting a proposal to the Privy Council to revise Jamaica's system of collecting revenues. Instead of basing the tax on cultivated acres, Charles Modyford suggested that when the acreage granted exceeded 200,000 a flat tax be imposed per acre, regardless of cultivation, because it was "a great trouble for His Majesty's officers always to be running out [measuring] the manured land to find how many pennies are due."[62] The old system of taxation had required repeated surveys in the 1660s, since the base of the assessment, cultivated acres, changed rapidly from year to year. Under the proposed system, taxes could be easily calculated from a one-time-only record of landholdings. The 1670 survey created that record and also demonstrated that the threshold number of 200,000 acres had already been passed.

Thus it appears that the population enumerations of the 1660s were by-products of tax surveys, frequently repeated. Earlier surveys were not reported to the London council because, as the governor put it, they showed the island to be "so thinly inhabited till the end of the Dutch war" that he was "both afraid and ashamed to send it, lest it might fall into the enemy's hands." But now that the population had grown so large—Jamaica had quadrupled her population in the preceding eight years, with by far the largest component of increase due to the arrival of thousands of slaves—he would not mind having the survey results printed and publicized.[63]

There is yet another reason why the 1670 Jamaica survey was undertaken and sent on to London. A recent change in the London bureaucracy led Modyford to believe that a new era of planned development was under way and that the planners would begin to require more information as a basis for decisionmaking. The

original Council for Foreign Plantations, which was established
in 1660 as an adjunct to the Privy Council, had been composed
of two separate and quite large committees, with a total membership of 110. Its unwieldy size contributed to its lack of rigor
in dealing with the colonies, and, after 1665, local events (the
London plague, war, and fire) caused it to disband altogether. A
second council, commissioned in 1668, was similarly inactive,
and in July, 1670, the king set up yet another new select Committee
on Foreign Plantations.[64] Thomas Modyford was informed in
June, 1670, of the new council's imminent creation and was given
to understand that it would have the special interests of Jamaican
development close to its heart; Modyford was therefore requested
to "furnish said Council with all lights sufficient for their perfect
information in relation to the government which his Majesty looks
upon as the most valuable he has, or at least, capable of being
made so."[65] Modyford, overjoyed at the prospect of some new
favor from London, replied that he could not "too much celebrate
his Majesty's care in erecting a particular Council for these West
India Plantations," and he pledged to send a survey of his island.[66]
A month later, he made good on his promise with the 1670 survey,
completed at great speed by the "extraordinary diligence" of an
aide. He admitted that it was not perfect, but he hoped to refine
it by the following March.[67] He was not given that chance: in
January, 1671, his commission as governor was revoked because
he was known to have encouraged privateers to operate out of
Jamaica.[68] That he included the privateers in his survey and estimated their numbers at about one in six of the entire population
(slaves included) might have sealed his fate. His zealous effort
to respond to favorable overtures from the royal government supplied the government with the exact information that justified his
removal from office.

Modyford had been quick to send off his survey before he
actually received a formal request from the newly reconstituted
council, and so, with all his data, he did not manage to supply
the information most sought by the royal commissioners. The
king's instructions had directed them to collect "minute information," particularly as to the number of planters and servants
in each colony, "and if any be overstocked with servants or slaves
to consider the best means of conveying them."[69] Here were new
notions: that a proper balance should obtain between the free and
the unfree; that a quantitative assessment of the population could

reveal whether the proper balance existed; and, further, that steps could be taken to redress the balance by redistributing the unfree. At its very inception the council had embarked in a new direction in the use of numbers. The commissioners did not want to know the mere numbers of people in each colony; they had a vaguely formulated idea that they could manipulate the numbers and redistribute people according to some rational plan with respect to the supply of labor. This was truly a radical departure from previous attitudes toward population in England in the seventeenth century. The new council made a second and equally radical move: it not only requested information about population, but it asked that the information be sent annually. The numbers would facilitate comparisons of the past and present situations of the colonies and, by enabling the commissioners to search out trends, would allow them to make reasonable assessments for the future.

> You shall send to us and to our Commissioners for Trade and Plantations By the First Conveyance an Account of the present number of planters and inhabitants, MEN, women, and children, as well masters as servants, free and unfree, and of the slaves in our said province, as also a yearly Account of the increase or decrease of them, and how many of them are fit to bear arms in the Militia of our said province.[70]

One of the last official acts of Governor Modyford was to answer this inquiry, along with many other questions that the council asked. In reply to question 16, "What number of planters, servants, slaves, and parishes?" he directed the council to a mass of documents appended to his report. However, among the lists of ships, tonnages, guns, and so forth, there was no account of the population.[71]

It is indeed possible that he did not enclose one at all, because an exact determination of the legal status of all Jamaicans would have necessitated a more thorough survey than the one taken the preceding September. Two years later Modyford's successor, Thomas Lynch, claimed that Modyford's 1670 census had been "made by guess" and that his own new census was "a true account of all the families . . . very exactly done." In remitting this census of 1673 Lynch revealed something about the method employed for conducting the enumeration: his account was short one parish from being complete, "occasioned by Col. Vassall's absence [at about the time of] the survey of the island." Col.

Vassall was identified as the militia leader for his parish, so it appears that the governor entrusted the enumeration to local militia leaders. They were already presumably familiar with the arms-bearing men in their parish and so were a logical choice for this new responsibility.[72] The 1673 census distinguished white men, women, and children and black slaves.[73]

In 1675 there was a third important revision in the structure and membership of the Council for Foreign Plantations. The resulting and more powerful body, the Lords of Trade, demanded information from the royal governors ever more frequently and with emphasis on greater detail.[74] The earlier request for annual information had not met with much success in any colony, but the Lords of Trade were determined to get it. On one day in January, 1680, they fired off identical instructions to Jamaica, Barbados, the Leeward Islands, and Virginia, requesting quarterly accounts of "all matters of importance," particularly proposals and debates in the colony's government, anything concerning trade, and abstracts of all important papers of any nature whatsoever.[75] Jamaica responded to this blanket request by sending back a multitude of quantified data, including an abstract of all land surveyed, .nuster rolls, and a partial census of black and white inhabitants, noting births and deaths in the past two years.[76] The census was partial, the report said, because as yet only two of the seven men identified as the "Custos Rotulorum"—the justice of the peace—had been able to do it.[77] The two precincts completed corresponded to the two "surviving fragments" of what has hitherto been presumed to have been a more complete census in that year.[78] No further parts of this census appear to have been sent. It is very likely that the immediate deluge of facts and figures—whatever the governor of Jamaica could get his hands on in a very short time—was intended to flood the Lords of Trade with data and so make them regret or forget their request. The population data, although incomplete for the island, gave surprisingly full details about the households in the two enumerated precincts: the name of the head of household and the number of white women and children, servants, and adult and child slaves.[79] Jamaica would not conduct a detailed census again until 1730.

The governor of Barbados gave a similarly abundant response to the 1680 request for information from the Lords of Trade, and the reason postulated for the Jamaican flood of data is demonstrably present here. Sir Jonathan Atkins, who had been governor of Barbados since 1673, had from the beginning of his term seemed reluctant or unable to comply with requests for quantitative information. Historians identify two censuses earlier than the 1680 mass of data, one taken in or before 1673 and another in 1676, but only the earlier one has any resemblance to a census.[80] The later one was simply an Atkins fabrication.

The census of 1673 was forwarded to the council by Atkins's predecessor, an interim governor who took charge following the death of the old governor, Lord Willoughby. It was an "account of the inhabitants and public stores" formulated as part of a request for more powder, ammunition and small arms; the clear intention was to demonstrate that Barbados had too few arms in relation to its population. The number of inhabitants was said to have been taken from "lists taken during Lord Willoughby's life," and there were explicit numbers of men over the age of sixteen; boys; all females; and slaves, divided into men and boys, women and girls.[81] Evidently, some sort of census had been taken prior to Willoughby's death—but not necessarily in 1673. This source suggests the purpose of the census: "forasmuch as there ran a report that these lists were taking [sic] in order to a tax on negroes [sic], [the interim governor] is of opinion that one third of the negroes is not given."[82]

In February, 1676, Governor Atkins submitted "An Account of His Majesty's Island of Barbados" to fulfill the general request by circular letter of the council. But Atkins did not bother to conduct any census; evidently he took at least some of the numbers from the previous list, juggled them a bit, and supplied the Lords with concrete data that were inaccurate and out of date.[83] It appears that his figures for the slave population were taken wholesale from the earlier list, despite the acknowledged underenumeration of blacks. It is possible that the white population was recounted in some way. But the similarity in numbers suggests a readdition of old lists for the white females and a rounding-off of the number of adult males.

	1673 Report from Undetermined Earlier List (Taken for tax purposes)	Atkins's 1676 report
White:		
Men	9,274	10,000
Boys	3,600	3,030
Women, girls	8,435	8,695
Black:		
Men	10,236	10,525
Boys	5,827	5,827
Women	11,914 ⎫ = [17,121]	16,121
Girls	5,207 ⎭	

Atkins consistently showed a reluctance to comply with the Lords' requests for information. Throughout the late 1670s they continually reprimanded him for sending in laws after they had expired and for ignoring requests for information. Atkins, on his part, claimed that he had no records in Barbados from which he could get reliable information. In July, 1676, he explained that no records of baptisms and burials had been kept until very recently, and then only in the Church of England; the Anabaptists, Jews, and Quakers "bury where they please" and "the negroes bury one another in the ground of the plantations where they die." People were married by license, but no records were kept; no bills of mortality were kept; and there was no way to assess the total wealth of the island, for "no merchant will tell [me] or anybody what he is worth, for his chief guard is his credit."[84]

The Lords were not satisfied with these excuses, and they directed Atkins to remedy the lack of vital records. "Planters, masters, servants, and slaves" were the numbers they wanted, and accounts of christenings, burials, and marriages.[85] Finally, in January, 1680, along with the general "heads of inquiries" letter sent to all the island colonies, a special note to Atkins from the Lords again detailed his failings in reporting laws and information and finally threatened that, without a "punctual compliance with our desires," they would recommend that the king replace him.[86] Atkins immediately filled a trunk with a wide variety of records and sent them with a covering letter, explaining how each piece of information had been collected and who could attest to its accuracy. He sent: lists of the inhabitants of each town or parish (broken down by parents, children, hired servants, bought servants, and slaves) and the acreage owned by each; baptisms and burials for the previous two years for each parish, listed by name; an account of the number of Negroes received in the previous two years; a forty-page list of all persons who had bought tickets to leave Barbados in the preceding year, alphabetized, plus a box of duplicates of all of the tickets themselves; lengthy lists of the members of eight regiments, totaling 5,588 men; and the names of all judges, council members, and assemblymen.[87] The burials and baptisms were countersigned by the ministers and church-wardens, as were the general lists of inhabitants, "since I find that I have so little credit with your Lordships." To verify the departure list, "that you may be the better informed, I have sent you all the tickets"—in all, 583 tickets. Atkins was indeed bitter.

At the same time that he transmitted all these data, he expressed doubts that they were truly accurate in some instances. Apparently each planter had been asked to declare his acreage and slaveholdings, and "your Lordships have no conception of the difficulty with which they have been obtained. The inquiries as to their land and the number of their negroes raised a hundred apprehensions of heavy taxation." The burials were taken from parish registers, but many people still buried the dead in their own gardens and never reported them. The militia lists were witnessed by the colonels of each regiment, but there was no regular muster-master in charge of keeping lists, "nor will they allow any, so the rolls may seem a little confused."[88] Barbadians seemed singularly resistant to being registered or counted by anyone.

The Lords of Trade were still not pleased with Atkins's mass of quantitative facts. They wrote him a stiff rebuke, questioning the accuracy of his data on several points.

> If the taking the number of the negroes excites such apprehensions, it is because it happens so seldom, whereas we expect it to be frequently done by your order, whereby all suspicions will be removed. . . . We are much surprised to find the Militia, horse and foot, reduced to 5,588, the more so, since your letter of 3rd February 1675[76] told us that the foot alone were 8,000 men. . . . The number of inhabitants according to your lists is but 5,504, which we attribute to the omission of the women and children. This is vastly different from your first computation of 21,722 [contained in the alleged census of 1676].[89]

The Lords had asked for an account of imports and exports, which Atkins said he could not furnish, there being no customhouse in Barbados, only a naval officer. So the Lords ordered him to send an account kept by the officer. Less than a month after the rebuke, with no time for Atkins to redeem himself, the king recalled him as governor.[90]

It is ironic that, although Atkins's 1680 account of Barbados seemed faulty and deficient in the eyes of the Lords of Trade, and although Atkins probably meant to discourage the Lords by sending them an incoherent mass of data and figures, the report has turned out to be one of the richest sources for seventeenth-century social history. It helps answer modern questions about the distribution of the island's wealth, the social origins of the richest elite, the correlation between wealth and officeholding, family size and structure, and—the hardest of all demographic variables to quantify—emigration patterns, based on those 583 tickets, complete with destination.[91] None of those questions would have occurred to anyone in the seventeenth century, of course, and the Lords of Trade simply filed the papers away in the Colonial Office, holding them as evidence of Atkins's failure to respond adequately to their new quest for quantitative data on which to base decisions.

The new governor, in his first response to the Lords' "heads of inquiry," in June, 1681, did not improve on Atkins's record for population or vital statistics, and he noted many of the same obstacles to the collection of that information. But he sent quarterly accounts of trade and of the acts of the island's council, and apparently this regularity satisfied the Lords of Trade.[92] In 1684 a census was taken, the last until 1712. Only an abstract of it survives, but historian Richard Dunn supposes that it was originally as detailed as the 1680 census because there is evidence that one parish paid three men for "drawing up several lists of the people of this Town and Parish."[93] It appears that, in Barbados, census-taking most appropriately devolved on the local minister or someone hired by him, in contrast to Jamaica, where the "custos rotulorum" and/or militia leader was thought to be the logical enumerator.

Two other British colonies, the Leeward Islands and Newfoundland, were able to satisfy the requests of the Lords of Trade in the 1670s with reports of population composition. The governor of the Leeward Islands was directed to submit a "distinct account" of all the inhabitants, organized by sex, race, and ethnic background, plus a record of baptisms and burials. About ten months later the report was complete, a massive 97-page document "taken 28th January 1678," which contained the numbers and, for some areas, the names of the householders, along with numbers of women, children, and slaves for each. The next census of the Leeward Islands came three decades later, in 1707.[94]

Newfoundland also came under close scrutiny in the 1670s. Before 1675 the northern colony had a very small and constantly fluctuating English population, which increased and decreased with the seasonal fishing trade. In 1675 the Lords agreed that stability would be gained and the danger of a French takeover lessened if the king would appoint a royal governor and would attempt to increase colonization. The first governor to arrive in Newfoundland, in the summer of 1675, had men scout the creeks and bays in order to take the "exact account as directed"; two months later he sent back details on the number of fishermen, planters, families, and boats, cattle, quantities of fish, and "train-fats" (whale oil). In 1676 another census was taken, similar to the first. A third head count was taken in 1677, which gave only numbers, no names; none was taken in 1678, and only an estimate was provided in 1679. There was still a consistent annual concern about the population of Newfoundland, but the degree of specificity declined rapidly after the first two years. At first the Lords had no clear idea of who was living there and what they were producing; once they had a clear idea, however, estimates and rounded numbers were quite sufficient to keep them informed. In all these years the English population varied between 1,500 and 1,700, so the difficulty of an initial enumeration was not nearly so great as in the West Indies colonies, whose population was in the range of 20,000 to 50,000 persons. The last census in Newfoundland, in this series, was a nominal census in 1680, taken in response to the general request the Lords sent to several governors that year.[95]

Unlike the West Indies governors, the governor of Newfoundland evidenced no irritation in responding to the inquiries. Information flowed smoothly compared to the other colonies, probably because Newfoundland had a rather small population and because the governor came and went annually, along with the fishing fleet. By collecting population statistics he was informing himself as well as the Lords about the most salient features of Newfoundland life. Since he was not an all-year-round resident, he did not in-

timately know the inhabitants and their desires, needs, and griev-
ances. In the absence of more personal knowledge, numbers
became a kind of shorthand information regarding the well-being
of the colony. Resident governors in the West Indies, on the other
hand, were familiar with the qualitative condition of the colonies
they controlled. They did not need to keep quantitative records
to know the general condition of trade or population, and so they
had to make strenuous efforts to comply with the Lords' requests
for succinct and accurate data.

From about 1680 on, the importance attached to numbers as-
cended sharply in colonial administrative circles, for several reasons. Influential men on the Privy Council and the Lords of Trade
regarded quantitative information as a superior substitute for personal or impressionistic reports, because for the first time, in the
late seventeenth century, they expected that numerical reports of
population and trade would be based on actual enumerations or
tallies of customs registers. As numbers became more accurate
representations of reality, they were given greater weight in government reports. They provided an empirical underpinning for
mercantilism, an elaborate theory of politics and economics,
which postulated that the number of people in a country was a
component of a country's wealth and that the balance of trade,
as measured by import and export statistics, was the crucial sign
of economic well-being. Increasingly, what the colonial administrators measured was what they thought they should *control*.
The purpose of having periodic reports on numbers of masters
and slaves, or barrels of sugar, or militia and arms, was that these
quantities could be adjusted if they were found to deviate from
some ideal conception of how things ought to be. Navigation Acts
and emigration laws could shape the flow of people and commodities, and quantitative records of the flow could in turn shape
policy.

All these strands of thought were related, of course, and they
reinforced each other in the late seventeenth century. Mercantilism spawned the Navigation Acts, which in turn led to naval
officers' being stationed in every port in 1673 to collect and record
the duties paid on enumerated items.[96] In 1680 the naval officers
were for the first time required to submit regular summaries of
the trade that flowed past them.[97] By this move the Lords of Trade
hoped to use established registers to derive aggregate information
on the volume of trade for certain commodities. Their desires fell

short of fulfillment, however, because the naval officers, for the most part, did not share their interest in compiling figures or in calculating quantities. "These accounts are very imperfect and made up in such shape and fashion that no exact computation can be made from them," complained one of the Lords about the Naval Office lists, thereby revealing both the intent of the Lords of Trade and the failings of the officers.[98]

Finally, in 1696, a more systematic application of empiricism to the theory of the balance of trade was attempted. In that year the financial and foreign trade departments of the government underwent a massive reorganization following a crisis over the balance of payments and internal inflation.[99] A new council, the Board of Trade, replaced the old Lords of Trade, and the turnover in personnel was substantial and significant: three of the ten new members were Fellows of the Royal Society, experts in economics and exponents of empiricism in the sciences.[100] The new board established the office of Inspector-General of Imports and Exports, whose job it was to maintain annual trade statistics. These statistics could be used to monitor and control foreign trade; they could also be used by individual merchants, who had begun to recognize their predictive value for making business decisions. In fact, starting in the early 1690s, a private group in London was already publishing trade statistics based on the Naval Office lists and was selling them to private subscribers.[101]

The new Board of Trade moved swiftly to collect census information from nearly all the colonies, not just the ones with important trade or having a potential servant-slave problem. In the next few years there was a huge burst of census-taking, led by Newfoundland, which made counts in 1698, 1688, 1700, and 1701. Bermuda responded in 1698; Maryland in 1701 and 1704; Virginia in 1699 and 1701; New York and possibly New Jersey in 1698 and 1703; and Rhode Island in 1708.[102] Massachusetts, Connecticut, New Hampshire, and Pennsylvania did not conduct colony-wide censuses and remained beyond the purview of the Board. Their absence, undoubtedly intentional, from the record of populations in America suggests that a census was an avenue of English control—an avenue that these relatively autonomous colonies did not intend to open up.[103]

I n realms of life considered to fall outside the bounds of human agency altogether, quantification made no headway in the seventeenth century. Religion was such a realm for the Puritans, and a contrast between them and the Anglicans on the matter of counting souls saved and members converted illustrates the connection between quantification and the desire for rational control that is so evident in the Board of Trade's censuses.

The declension of Puritanism has long been a classic chapter in the history of New England. Sermons of the 1650s and 1660s bewailed the irreligion and worldliness eclipsing the piety of the founding generation. Ministers complained of the decline in religious fervor among the young, and the Half Way Covenant of 1662 was designed to recapture the attention of children of partial members and to reverse the decreasing religiosity of the population. To the twentieth-century scholar, the declension of Puritanism has a distinctly quantitative meaning. For a long time, modern historians assumed that church membership *did* decline in some potentially measurable way; but recently a historian has performed the obvious measurements of church membership and has discovered that in fact church admissions were rising throughout the second half of the seventeenth century.[104] How could the Puritans have been so mistaken?

The simple answer is they did not keep track of membership and conversion by numbers; they did not compile statistics of religion. Their records consisted of official notations of the changed status of individuals, not of a census of souls. It is quite possible that they did not perceive a quantitative meaning in declension at all but rather viewed it as a *qualitative* shift in the centrality of religion to people's lives. Further, it could have made no sense to keep an account book with God because there was no way by which one could study the books and use them to devise schemes to increase the "profit" figured in the number of souls saved. Predestination would proscribe that concept: since one cannot work to increase the number of the elect beyond what is already established by God, there is not much point in maintaining aggregate records.

In contrast, the Anglicans during the seventeenth century were retreating from the doctrine of predestination in its Calvinist sense, and Anglican ministers in America were being directed to keep careful accounts of their progress in converting nonbelievers:

Each of them [must] keep a register of his Parishioners' Names, Profession of Religion, Baptism, &c. according to the Scheme annexed, No. I for his own Satisfaction, and the Benefit of the People. That they send every six Months an Account of the State of their respective Parishes, according to the Scheme annexed, No. II.[105]

There followed two charts, with spaces for number of inhabitants, number of baptized, number of Dissenters, and so on. The Society for the Propagation of the Gospel explained the purpose of these detailed tally sheets: it is "so that the Corporation may, from Time to Time, see the Progress they make in the Good Work; and if any Difficulties should arise, consider how they may apply proper Remedies."[106] For the Anglicans, human agency had made inroads on God's providential powers and had thereby fostered the extension of numeracy.

3

Patterns and
Providence

n 1735 the *Pennsylvania Gazette* extolled the virtues of mathematics to a Philadelphia audience, the most urban and mercantile population center in the American colonies. "On the Usefulness of the Mathematicks" ran the headline, to flag the attention of those who valued utility. The lead paragraph defined the word, in case anyone should be uncertain of its meaning:

> *Mathematicks*, originally signifies any kind of Discipline or Learning, but now it is taken for that Science, which teaches or contemplates whatever is capable of being numbered or measured: That part of the *Mathematicks* which relates to *Numbers* only, is called Arithmetick; and that which is concerned about *Measure* in general, whether *Length*, *Breadth*, *Motion*, *Force*, &c. is called *Geometry*.

The main burden of the article was the claim that the benefits of the science of number extended well beyond the trading classes. "All sorts and Degrees of men, from the highest to the lowest" could apply numbers to their mundane affairs, the author promised, although his explicit examples of calculating occupations were drawn from a predictable and limited sphere of callings: merchant, astronomer, mariner, geographer, architect, engineer, surveyor, gauger. The manual laborer had to be content with the vague assertion that he would somehow do better with arithmetic and would not regret learning it; the author did not or could not pinpoint its actual utility to the laboring class of workers. Even if practical mathematics could not be made to seem indispensable to all mankind, the author argued that mathematics was a form of logic, which stretched the mind and improved the faculty for exact reasoning. Nonmathematical subjects could be thought about more clearly by a person with mathematical training; the best rulers in mankind's history had been men of mathematical skill, he alleged. Even dull minds could be sharpened a bit, and a sharp mind was highly esteemed by this author, the young Ben Franklin.[1]

Now Franklin was certainly no sluggard when it came to exercises for mental improvement. But as a child he had failed, not once but twice, in his initial encounters with the science of numbers in a Boston school, and it was not until he experienced shame arising from his ignorance of arithmetic, at the age of sixteen, that he took up the subject in earnest and taught himself from Edward Cocker's *Arithmetick,* the workhorse of English commercial texts. He also dipped into geometry, using books on navigation, but "never proceeded far in that science." It would seem that arithmetic and geometry were not the foundations of his own extraordinary mental acuity.[2]

Franklin's plea for the usefulness of mathematics suggests rather the contrary of what he intended. Far from being a utilitarian skill, useful and familiar to all, mathematics in the eighteenth-century American colonies remained an arcane and difficult subject. Bright lads like Franklin had to struggle to learn it. It had to be defined before it could be discussed in newspapers of the day. Little wonder, then, that the generality of the population did not exhibit a reverence for numbers or a mania for measurement. Despite the stepped-up pace of commerce, the call of the sea, the growth of population, the building of fair-sized cities, and, in general, the louder hum of the economy, numeracy did not burst forth as the preeminent skill of the day. If many farmers now sold their surplus off their farms and engaged by day in market transactions, they did not necessarily spend their nights gloating over profit figures or calculating anticipated crop yields.[3] Merchants in Salem, Boston, Philadelphia, and Charleston might well have derived satisfaction from the mathematics of bookkeeping, but accountancy in ledger books might also be a headache or a danger, the former where barter dominated over cash and the latter when a merchant's profits came from smuggling (a not altogether uncommon situation).[4]

Strangely, what progress there was in numeracy in pre-Revolutionary America came not as a tangent to commercial growth but as the result of a slow but fundamental shift in the way men thought about human affairs and divine intervention. The progress did not come through wider applications of advanced mathematics but rather through the extension of a simple form of quantitative reasoning to an aspect of life previously thought of only in qualitative terms. The Puritans of the seventeenth century did not keep running totals of souls saved because of their fatalistic view that the number of the elect was already determined. They did not expect to be able to improve on God's plan, so it made no sense to quantify it. They also did not expect to be able to second-guess God's plan, so there was no point in looking for empirical patterns by which to predict who would saved. Even more basic, it was vain to suppose that the saved could be be identified by mere mortals with anything approaching certainty, and that meant that the critical characteristic under observation, the state of grace, was not really amenable to counting in the first place. In other words, fatalism, unpredictability, and uncertainty were obstacles to the application of a mathematical sense to religion. The decline of fatalism and uncertainty and the discovery of peculiar regularities in events once thought to be under inscrutable divine control encouraged the evolution of a mathematical sense in the eighteenth century.

Nowhere was this more evident than in discussions about death and mortality among eighteenth-century clerics and physicians. Demographic speculations in America were first stimulated by the ideas of the English political arithmeticians. Works by William Petty, Edmund Halley, and William Derham circulated among the educated colonial elites and even filtered down to the literate masses when almanacs and newspapers printed snippets of their writings. It was actually newsworthy to print a table showing the regularity of deaths by age.[5] From the start, American ministers were warm to the idea that vital events taken in the aggregate exhibited patterns with mysterious constancy, for it bolstered the fatalistic concept that God controlled these events entirely. The wondrous appearance of a pattern implied a Divine Order, which the Divine Hand must guide and preserve.[6] As always, God and not man controlled the entrance to and exit from life, but now it was discovered that his control displayed a kind of numerical elegance as well. The faithful were exhorted in church to study the numerical patterns of death and to use demographic facts to reflect on their own mortality, ever a fit subject for a Christian to contemplate.

All of this was fine until a few eager empiricists in America began to amass their own local data. It then became apparent that those patterns were not so immutably ordered after all. They were not only different in different places—a clue to environmental relativity—but on occasion they were also manipulable by man. The gradual realization that man could, in theory, control mortality accelerated the decline of the notion of an omnipotent God and hastened the arrival of autonomous man, directing his own destiny. Fatalism and uncertainty began to give way to control and predictability, exercised through the medium of numbers.

The emergent history of a quantitative approach to death forms the main body of this chapter. But it must be noted that demography was not the only domain of number that was new in the eighteenth century. It claims prime attention because it was, after commerce, the commonest point of contact between ordinary people and numbers. Discussions of population growth and decline and reports of numbers of births and deaths were featured in newspapers, sermons, and pamphlets, and through popularized demography the reading public was introduced to a form of quantitative reasoning about human behavior. In a few moments of extreme crisis, when smallpox and inoculation competed for victims during epidemics, ordinary folk even began to place trust in quantitative reasoning (after initial hesitation). But there were other areas where numbers, arithmetic, and measurement were employed, some in traditional fields like navigation and surveying, and some in other ways that foreshadow the nineteenth-century fascination with numerical facts and statistics.

The traditional area where quantitative thought flourished in the eighteenth century was among the mathematical practitioners, a small number of craftsmen or teachers who either made specialized measuring instruments or taught their use in evening schools in the coastal cities. There had been such men in England in the seventeenth century, and they took root in America in the early eighteenth century as cities grew and the need for competent surveyors, cartographers, and navigators mushroomed. When Franklin wrote about the "Usefulness of the Mathematicks," it was chiefly these men he had in mind. They were identified as mathematicians by trade, and colonial governments would hire them to do the measurements and calculations on large boundary questions, which involved problems beyond the scope of local surveyors, who ran property lines with rods and chains. A recent historian of these practitioners has documented the existence of 134 instrument-makers and just under three dozen teachers of the mathematics of navigation and surveying in evening schools in the colonies in the hundred years preceding the Revolution.[7]

The impact these men had on the population at large is rather hard to assess. As teachers of mathematics they obviously elevated the numerical skills of their students into the realms of algebra, geometry, and trigonometry. How many students they had and how well they taught cannot be known. One teacher in Philadelphia in the 1730s claimed that his course on "Arithmetick in all its Parts, *Geometry, Mensuration, Surveying, Gauging, Trigonometry, Navigation, Dialling* and *Astronomy,* the use of the *Globes* and other *Mathematical Instruments . . . Algebra,* and the *Analytical Art,* with the *Laws* and *Properties* of *Motion"* could be mastered in three months, "provided the Person have a tolerable Genius and observes a constant application." A Boston teacher in 1767 advertised that he could teach surveying and navigation in as little as forty-eight hours.[8] Perhaps other teachers were more thorough in their instruction. In any event, the existence of these few specialized centers for mathematical learning perpetuated the segregation of the mathematical arts from general education and in that way presented an obstacle to the diffusion of numeracy. While it might be argued that the mathematicians' complex almanac calculations brought numbers into nearly every American household, even a quick perusal of eighteenth-century almanacs reveals that they made no arithmetic demands on the user. Almanacs functioned as calendars and timepieces, providing information on sunrise and sunset, lunar phases, tides, eclipses, and the positions of planets and constellations throughout the year. An occasional "Philomath" (a favorite pseudonym for almanac authors) dressed up his almanac with brief essays on the history of calendars or on the Copernican system, but there was no effort to instruct the readership on any of the mysteries of mathematics or astronomical calculations. Almanacs did not become compendia of quantitative facts and statistics until the early nineteenth century.[9]

The other new usage of numbers in the eighteenth century was limited to an even smaller collection of men than the practitioners and philomaths, but it is significant because of its portent for the future. A compulsive habit to quantify afflicted a handful of unusual individuals. John Lining, a Charleston physician; Ezra

Stiles, president of Yale College; and Thomas Jefferson, scientist and philosopher *par excellence,* became confirmed calculators well ahead of the age of calculative enthusiasm. The historian of science will recognize these men as part of a much larger catalogue of colonial contributors to science.[10] But science before the Revolution was not especially or pointedly quantitative in method, even though empiricism and experiment were the accepted modes of advancing knowledge. Observation, description, and classification of the qualitative properties of things and phenomena took precedence over experiments that generated numerical data. Were earthquakes waves or electrical jolts? Was electricity a fluid? Such hypotheses could be tested by experiments that did not require counting or mathematics. What was distinct about Lining, Stiles, and Jefferson was their predilection for quantitative data, and their fascination with counting often spilled over into realms of life not usually thought of as scientific. In that they stood at a distance from their scientific compatriots as well as from the general American population.

Because they were rather unusual, prefiguring a mentality that became pervasive only in the nineteenth century, they deserve a closer look. In their esoteric proclivity for numbers, maintained in a climate not yet readily supportive of that style of thought, they help to illuminate the psychological attraction of quantification. Later generations of calculating Americans imbibed a style of thought in childhood that everywhere surrounded them; the historian must therefore be cautious in pointing out a resonance between personality quirks and a desire to quantify when that desire has become one of the "givens" of a culture. With these eighteenth-century men, the link between the impulse to quantify and individual psychology is more direct. We will return to them at the end of this chapter, after an extended discussion of the quantification of death.

The earliest and most extensive collection of bills of mortality in America began in Boston in the opening years of the eighteenth century. Massachusetts had had vital registration laws on the books since the 1640s, but those laws provided only for the recording of each individual event, not for periodic summaries of events in the aggregate.[11] The idea of aggregating the deaths into a yearly summary occurred contemporaneously with the appearance of the first regularly published newspaper in Boston, the *Boston News-Letter,* and it is likely that there was a connection between the two events. Newspapers look for news to publish; in the early eighteenth century they rarely printed local news, on the assumption that what was local was already known to their readers. But bills of mortality were a type of local news that was not common knowledge, and that made them publishable material. And so, in 1704, the *Boston News-Letter* embarked on a project of collecting and printing annual bills of mortality for Boston, dipping back in the records to 1701 to start the series.

"Because it may carry some useful Information in it, we have thought it not amiss, to give the Publick, the BILL OF MORTALITY for the Three years last past," announced the editor.[12] But he did not elaborate on exactly how such information might be "useful," and the modern historian is left to puzzle about the thoughts that occurred to the Bostonians of 1704 as they perused the dry table of the deaths that had occurred in each month from 1701 to 1703.

Their use was not the same as the London bills of mortality. The London bills had been collected throughout the seventeenth century, so the notion of a quantitative assessment of death was by no means unfamiliar to Bostonians. But the English bills were published as weekly fliers, enumerating the causes as well as the numbers of deaths, and so they served as warnings to the inhabitants of the approach of epidemic diseases. The bills' descriptions of the waxing and waning of various maladies were thus both newsworthy and practical.[13] But the Boston bills did not include information on the cause of death; all that Bostonians could ponder was the seasonal rise and fall of deaths, and that only some months after those deaths had occurred. How did the editor construe this information to be "useful"?

One way to answer that question is to study the editorial comments that occasionally accompanied the bills, directing the reader's attention to particular features. Such comments appeared with the early sets of data in the *News-Letter* and can also be found when the entire series of yearly death totals was republished in another periodical. The bills were maintained up until 1774, when the will for such recording evidently lost out to the revolutionary turmoil enveloping Boston. Moreover, they were unusual enough to engender public interest beyond the confines of Boston. For example, in 1753 the series to that date was presented

in the *Gentleman's Magazine* of London, in a communication
from the Reverend Thomas Prince of Boston. Benjamin Franklin
published thirty years of the series in 1731, in an early issue of
his *Pennsylvania Gazette*. And at the end of the century, the
Massachusetts Historical Society printed the entire series to grat-
ify "a certain class of readers, whose studies are thought by some
to be *more curious* than useful."[14]

From editorial comments and from the contexts of the several
publications of the series, it is possible to reconstruct something
of the meaning that eighteenth-century men attached to annual
death totals. The editor of the *News-Letter* suggested one practical application: that the numbers could be used to judge the
salubrity of Boston as compared to other places. "It has been
observed by some, that in Times of Health, (such as we now
Enjoy) Mortality ordinarily carries off, somewhat about a Fiftieth
Part of the People Every year. Queere, How far will that Observation Hold for this Town?" However, the editor made no attempt
to supply the calculation for his readers, either because he did
not have any figure at hand for Boston's population or because
there was an acknowledged imperfection in the number of deaths
reported: "Many Inhabitants of Boston, have their Employments
at Sea; and many of these Dying abroad (in proportion, much
more than at home) they are not reckoned in our Catalogue."[15]

Over the next several years the *News-Letter* supplied annual
bills each March, maintaining the month-by-month format and
adding a separate category of Negro deaths. The editor usually
limited himself to vague allusions about the newsworthy quality
of the figures, making unsubstantiated claims that the deaths were
not many, in comparison to the population. "It is much for so
populous a Town, to bury no more of its Inhabitants," he asserted
in early 1707; "the Survivors of any Consideration will understand
how to make their profitable *Reflections* both *Political* and *Religious* upon a Bill of this Importance laid before them."[16]

Political reflections could take any of several forms, as the
editor himself had demonstrated over the several years he had
been printing the data. On the simplest level, one could reflect
with pride, along with the editor, on how healthful a place Boston
was. However, this was a nonquantitative reflection, since there
were no comparative figures on which to base that pride. A rather
more unusual type of political reflection had appeared in an early
issue of the *News-Letter,* after the categorization of deaths by

race had begun. The editor translated the forty-four Negro dead
in 1705 into cash terms: those forty-four represented a loss of
£1,320, calculated at £30 per head, a sum that led him to conclude
that it was cheaper to buy white indentured servants. "And here
you see that in one year the Town of Boston has lost 1320 l. by
44 Negroes, which is also a Loss to the Country in General, and
for a less Loss, (if it may improperly be so called) for a 1000 l.
the Country may have 500 Men in 5 years time for the 44 Negroes
dead in one year."[17]

Religious reflections on the bills of mortality were not so certainly grounded in the data and yet were more immediately appealing and apparent than political reflections. There was indeed
agreement that the bills had important religious implications.
When the *Boston Gazette,* in its infancy, published a synopsis of
the account of burials from 1701 to 1720, it said the account was
"offered unto the Publick, that the Survivers [*sic*], (especially in
Boston) may Form their Pious and proper Sentiments upon it."[18]
At the conclusion of the table, the *Gazette* reported the total
number of deaths over the twenty-year period to be 6,429. There
was no suggestion of a political or social meaning revealed by the
figure 6,429, which might have been manifest had the *Gazette*
rearranged that figure into average deaths per year or compared
it to the total population or to births. Any of these calculations
would have been leaped to by William Petty in England. (Indeed,
Petty would probably have compared the death toll to the number
of doctors in the town, because "the number of people dying
where the faculty of Medicine is numerous & where the same is
otherwise, shewes the value and effect of that art. The same may
bee sayd of professors of the Law.")[19] Instead, the large and exact
number of 6,429 stood alone and simply denoted the number of
souls that had met their end in Boston.

At this most basic level, an account of the number of deaths
simply called to mind the fact of death itself. Death had always
been a central event on the Christian's road to heaven or hell,
and so anything that served to augment an awareness of the tem-
poral nature of life could easily be construed as having an important and self-evident religious significance. A periodical reminder
of the presence of death encouraged a proper Christian's pious
contemplation of mortality.[20] That some early eighteenth-century
Englishmen understood the bills on this level can be seen in the
comments of essayist Joseph Addison in *The Spectator* for 1712.

He reported that he regularly inspected the weekly London bills in his local coffeeshop, which led him to "consider the several Ways through which we pass from Life to Eternity. I am very well pleased with these weekly Admonitions, that bring into my Mind such Thoughts as ought to be the daily Entertainment of Every reasonable Creature."[21]

But seventeenth-century Puritans had not needed a numerical formulation of death to bring to mind religious reflections about the meaning of life. Especially in times of heavy mortality, an exact or even inexact count of the dead was not essential to pious thought. For example, Edward Johnson, in his *Wonder-Working Providence,* described 1650 as "the first noted year wherein any store of people died"—in this case, from a disease that carried off an unknown but grievous number of people, most of them children. Johnson reflected that this "correction of the Lord" spurred the survivors to redouble their preparations for "the great work of the Lord Jesus." The surviving children in particular were instructed to reflect "for what end the Lord hath spared their lives, when he cut off others by death, namely to prosecute the work that he hath given them to do in the power of his might, with the greater zeal and courage." God's meaning was clear even without a body count.[22]

However, three-quarters of a century later an epidemic that also affected ages differentially was viewed in quite another way. When diphtheria broke out in several Massachusetts towns in 1735, one hardly needed to count to realize that the victims were almost all children, yet that is exactly what some ministers did when they prepared sermons and "addresses to the bereaved." John Brown, minister of Haverhill, published a book of case histories of the death-bed scenes of the children under his care and prefaced the whole with a remarkable table of deaths separated by age: under 10, under 15, 20, 30, 40, and above. The death toll stood at 256, and the table showed that all but 46 of the victims were under age 10. Brown presented some further figures to maximize the impact of the toll: 140 families were bereaved and 23 were left completely childless; 72 families had lost one member, 36 had lost two, 21 had lost three, 6 had lost four, and a sorrowful 5 families had lost five members apiece.[23] At this point the publisher inserted a note to request other ministers to submit "accounts of the Number and Ages of Persons" who were victims of this distemper of the throat, because he planned a general publication on the epidemic containing "suitable Reflections on this awful Providence."[24]

What reflections might arise from an exact accounting of deaths by age? Jabez Fitch, a minister of Portsmouth, New Hampshire, also collected and printed death tolls in a pamphlet on the throat distemper. He categorized deaths by age for more than a dozen New Hampshire towns, giving the rationale that "Providence having made such a remarkable Distinction [in striking chiefly children], I thought it Proper to take Notice of it in the following Account." Why make the account at all? It was so that the "extraordinary Mortality . . . should ever be remembered to our Humiliation."[25] This affliction was so extraordinary and so distinct in its pattern of visitation that these ministers felt compelled to quantify it to show just how truly terrible it was. The Reverend Joseph Emerson of Malden, Massachusetts, preached effusively to his congregation about the horrors of this epidemic that had struck so many: "What Terror and Amazement, what Distress and Anguish, what Wailing and Lamentation, has this Judgment occasion'd! How many Scores, Hundreds, Thousands, have been swept away by this Besom of Destruction?" Emerson did not mean this question to be a rhetorical flourish, for he immediately provided the answer for his town: "Forty in this Place have died of the Distemper since the beginning of last July; Two Families buried 3, two more 4 apiece, and one Family buried 5 children."[26] It was not sufficient to assert that *many* had died, as it had been in the seventeenth century; now ministers wanted to record precise numbers and add them up from town to town, to prove that the epidemic was a calamity on the order of an earthquake—that it affected everyone, not just the sinful and wicked. "However it may fare with some particular Persons, yet as the generality of a People are, so they may expect to fare in respect of the Dispensations of God's Providence towards them."[27] A calamity that afflicted the generality of people throughout the colony suggested an ungodliness among the generality.

Furthermore, the systematic totaling of the victims by age showed not only the generality of the affliction but also pointed to a specific meaning in this act of God. The fact that the victims were nearly all children forcefully reminded Puritans that death could strike at any age, including the young and hearty.

The Grave is a Land of Darkness without any Order, which has of late been remarkably seen, in respect of the Age of those that have been brought to it, when so many Younger ones have gone to their Home long before the Elder; Yet every one may be said to die in his own Order, in respect to God's appointment, who has determin'd the Time of every one's Death.[28]

Here the Reverend Fitch reminded his readers that one's lifespan was predestined by God and that children were just as likely to die as adults—more likely, in this case. Parents were therefore advised to prepare their remaining offspring, as well as themselves, for the end that could come at any time.[29] Moreover, parents were not only directed to awaken their children to religion; they were also reminded to feel chastened themselves for putting too much store in their children. "The great Mortality that has been among Children, should make Parents very sensible, that their Children are *uncertain* Comforts," said Fitch. Parents who had lost one or two children should be thankful they had not lost more (the data showed it could happen) and should waste no time training the living ones for their eventual encounter with Christ; for, if they were prepared, then, whether the children lived or died, a parent could take comfort in them.[30] Taking comfort from a dead but virtuous child was the message that Fitch, Emerson, and Brown preached—Brown especially, with his stirring deathbed scenes—but one suspects that the parents did not accept the misfortune with much equanimity. After a century of greatly improved mortality rates for both children and adults in New England, and just at a time when the Western world in general was increasingly coming to see children as comforting objects of affection, eighteenth-century Puritans were probably not so stoical about childhood death as their predestinarian doctrines would suggest.[31]

The idea that God had ordained the time of everyone's death and that one's life-span, whether short or long, was fixed in advance seemed to be borne out by the diphtheria-epidemic death tolls. Puritans also believed that in times of ordinary mortality people had to be prepared for death at any age, and so it was probably gratifying to discover the mortality tables constructed by English political arithmeticians like Halley, which did indeed show that no age was spared the risk of death.

In using these mortality tables, Puritans were translating a traditional religious concern for death into a quantitative frame of reference familiar to educated Englishmen in the late seventeenth and early eighteenth centuries. Cotton Mather, for example, demonstrated a blend of the two mentalities in a 1712 sermon, "Seasonable Thoughts Upon Mortality," which was prompted by the "raging of a Mortal Sickness" in Connecticut. "The King of Terrors [is] walking his dismal Rounds," Mather said, and "for us to be deaf unto the Cry, would be a *Stupidity* uncapable of an *Apology."* Death could happen to anyone, not only to the old and infirm, and to prove it Mather referred not to the immediate experience of his listeners but to the political arithmeticians:

> They that have made Nice Remarks, on Bills of Mortality, will tell you: That one half of those that are Born, don't Live Seventeen years: That but about Forty of an hundred, are found Alive, at Sixteen years; That but Ten out of an hundred, at Forty Six; but Six, at Fifty Six; but Three at Sixty-six; but One at Seventy-five.[32]

The lesson of this grim recital was that only the exceptional few would live to be over forty, and so the young, even the strong and hearty among them, must be on good terms with God so as to be prepared at every moment for death.

Mather's blend of the old and the new, so truly seasonable for 1712, had difficult implications, which were not, however, immediately apparent to those who tried to combine divine will with empirical observation. Puritans were supposed to accept the idea that anyone might die at any time, regardless of age or prior health, because God had ordained the time of death for each person; they did not share our notion that a young person's death is untimely or premature.[33] The aggregate analysis of mortality confirmed that people died at all ages, and even preponderantly in the young ages, and so it was immensely attractive to ministers who wanted to remind everyone of God's omnipotence. Such analysis also seemed to show that there was a pattern to the mortality, that regular numbers of people died off at every age, and this was interpreted as further proof of the orderly nature of the universe—for surely there would be no pattern without the hand of God behind it. But what if the pattern were not constant? What if it were susceptible to change by the actions of man?

In 1712 Mather did not yet perceive such difficulties in constructing quantitative proofs of God's ordered universe. Indeed, in his "Seasonable Thoughts" sermon he was content to cite mortality patterns for a European city as though they were completely applicable to Boston. In the next twenty-five years in America, other popularizers of the political arithmeticians would also rest content with the idea that fixed mortality patterns prevailed everywhere and were evidence of a divine order. In 1731 both the *New York Gazette* and the *Pennsylvania Gazette* reprinted lengthy extracts from a British journal on political arithmetic, containing the observation that, since more than half of those who die in London die before age ten, "Mothers ought not to grieve so much for the loss of some of their Children, for every Mother that has a fifth Part of the Children she has born arrived at the Age of ten or above, ought to be thankful, and consider that her Lot must be better than the Lot of most other Mothers."[34] (Actually, it would seem that any mother with only a *fifth part* of her children surviving beyond age ten would be entitled to feel that an unfair share of grief had come her way, since in London only half died before age ten.) A Boston almanac for 1736 used as filler several paragraphs of Halley's life table and concluded: "How unjustly we repine at the shortness of our Lives, and think our selves wrong'd, if we attain not to Old Age; whereas it appears that the *One Half* of those that are Born, die in *Seventeen* Years Time."[35] The study of political arithmetic led to such admonitions as: count it a "great Blessing" to live to be over seventeen; or be thankful every morning and night that you are not among the one-sixth that die of accidents.[36] No importance was attached to the European provenance of the data. Demographers now know that life-expectancy in America was considerably higher than in European cities, so in a way the unintentional misuse of the data struck hard at egotistical presumption. Survivors who defied the odds were supposed to feel grateful, even lucky; no one should presume to be entitled to long years of life.

The 1721 smallpox epidemic in Boston occasioned the first suspicions that man could alter God's plan. The inoculation controversy that gripped Boston almost as tightly as the disease itself has received much historical attention because it represents an early instance of scientific experimentation in battle with religion. One standard interpretation has been that daring innovators, chief among them Cotton Mather, encouraged the artificial transmission of smallpox through inoculation of virulent matter in the hope that the patient would get only a mild case that would confer immunity. Mather has won praise as "the first significant figure in American medicine,'' and the entire controversy usually takes on the aspect of an ancients-versus-the-moderns debate, in which science triumphs over superstition.[37] The innovators have seemed especially modern because of their empirical approach to the problem. Public outrage over inoculation led them to assemble medical statistics to prove that inoculation worked, and so they have been hailed as the founders of the statistics of epidemiology.[38]

However, the motives of the anti- and proinoculation forces need to be examined more closely. The rhetoric of the controversy reveals that extreme resistance to inoculation developed not over the question of whether or not the procedure worked—although there was, to be sure, some debate on that point—but over the question of how inoculation affected God's power to ordain deaths and send punishing providences in the form of epidemics. The prevention of disease was perceived to be essentially different from ministering aid and medicine to people who were already sick, for in the latter case the illness itself was a providence and God still retained the power to let the medicine work or not, as he saw fit. Inoculation presented an entirely new problem: preventing a disease altogether seemed to place the choice of life or death in the hands of man, and it seemed to remove smallpox from God's arsenal of warnings. It was a problem that engaged the best minds of Boston in 1721.[39]

The inoculation controversy illuminates how old and new mentalities intersected. On one side was a small group of empirically minded people who believed that the argument for inoculation could be presented most convincingly with the help of comparative mortality statistics. On the other side was a large mass of people who failed to be impressed by numerical presentations. A third group, which objected to inoculation on medical grounds, also gathered some figures of their own to prove the terrible dangers. Thus the two groups who could be called quantifiers worked against each other. The middle group, probably the majority of people, objected to inoculation on religious grounds, and they viewed numerical proofs as irrelevant. For the duration of the controversy, the value of epidemic statistics as a measure of the validity of inoculation became obscured as the two groups of quantifiers resorted to religious arguments to persuade Bostonians of the benefits or dangers of inoculation. A review of the familiar events of 1721 and 1722 and a closer look at the three groups involved reveal much about the uses and the limits of quantitative thinking in the early eighteenth century.

The chief proponents of inoculation, Cotton Mather and Dr. Zabdiel Boylston, were supported by a very small coterie of ministers and doctors.[40] The opponents on medical grounds, led by Dr. William Douglass, the only trained medical doctor in town,, included most of the other physicians, the town selectmen, and editor James Franklin of the *New England Courant,* a paper founded in the midst of the controversy to give the opponents a forum. The articulate abilities of both groups and their access to printing presses have ensured that their arguments have been preserved in abundance. The nonquantitative populace at large was characterized as a fearful, Satanic mob in Cotton Mather's diary; it was most forcefully represented by the anonymous persons who hurled a grenade into Mather's house in November and a few more-literate men, like Samuel Grainger, who joined the pamphlet war to urge that citations of numbers and demonstrated success were far from sufficient proof that inoculation was lawful.[41] Even though this group had fewer articulate spokesmen, the power of their argument, that inoculation was inconsistent with providence and predestination, can be inferred from the amount of space the proponents of inoculation devoted to answering it.

When smallpox broke out in Boston in the spring of 1721, the town government monitored the progress of the disease on three successive Saturdays and issued reports on the number of sick, which were printed in the *Boston News-Letter.*[42] The third townwide search uncovered only one case, a man said to be on the mend, and the prematurely optimistic report pronounced the disease nearly gone. Cotton Mather, a man familiar with the progress of smallpox cases and not inclined to be optimistic, sent around to the doctors of the town a letter proposing that they consider inoculation. Mather's authority for the practice was the *Philosophical Transactions* of the Royal Society, which several years earlier had printed two accounts of inoculation in Turkey with explicit instructions on how to perform the operation. Neither article presented a statistical proof of the benefit of inoculation, for the simple reason that both had claimed complete success for the method.[43] Mather did not at first manage to convince any doctors that they should proceed with inoculation, probably because there seemed to be no immediate need to resort to drastic measures; but by the end of June the number of cases was rising rapidly (this we know from the lamentations in Mather's diary, for there were no official inquiries until July), and Mather pressed the medical community again to consider this reputedly perfect preventative. This time he found a willing practitioner, Zabdiel Boylston, who perhaps matched Mather in his terror for the safety of his children, because he chose his own six-year-old son to be among his first three patients.[44]

Within four days a "horrid Clamour" had arisen over inoculation, and by mid-July the battle lines were drawn. Boylston, convinced by the success of his first three cases, proceeded to inoculate a few people every day (until the selectmen ordered him to stop, an order he obeyed for only two weeks), and he publicized his actions in the *Boston Gazette*.[45] "W. Philanthropos" led the counteroffense in a scathing article in the *News-Letter* of July 23, calling Boylston illiterate and the whole procedure rash and ill-thought-out. It was "Philanthropos" who first raised the difficult question of how inoculation could be consistent with man's subjection to God. He asked "how the trusting more the extra groundless *Machinations of Men* than to our Preserver in the ordinary course of Nature, may be consistent with that Devotion and Subjection we owe to the all-wise Providence of GOD Almighty."[46] Historians have assumed this was not an entirely serious question, since Philanthropos is assumed to have been Dr. William Douglass himself, who in writings under his own name did not much trouble himself with questions of providence. Whatever Douglass personally felt about the religious implications of inoculation, he certainly touched a responsive chord in the populace of Boston. The fury of the town in mid-July was such that Cotton Mather concluded that Satan himself had taken possession of the people, turning them into "Ideots" and "Franticks," because only Satan could be against something that so obviously and certainly saved lives.[47]

But it was just that certainty of the inoculators about the results of inoculation that particularly raised the ire of religious objectors. Mather's private diary actually reveals great anguish about the possible deadly results of self-inflicted smallpox, especially when he decided to have his children undergo the operation, but publicly he and Boylston maintained their claim that inoculation guaranteed a milder and nonfatal case.[48] This very certainty was attacked by Samuel Grainger in an essay excoriating proof by empirical evidence. Grainger was no innumerate yokel; he was in fact a mathematical practitioner in Boston and ran a school for writing, arithmetic, and advanced mathematics, so it is interesting to see that even he considered argument by number to be irrelevant compared to the religious implications of inoculation. Whoever claims that no man ever died from inoculation must be a "great Traveller," Grainger sarcastically commented, and he who promises that no one will ever die from it is very presumptuous; if inoculation promises absolute safety to the weak and strong, to the holy and profane, all alike, it must be wicked.[49] In Grainger's traditional view, an epidemic represented a visitation from God for a national sinfulness; to prevent it, to overrule it, was thus clearly blasphemous. Grainger was not opposed to other forms of medicine to ameliorate disease, but complete prevention suggested an erroneous belief that God's power could be usurped by man. He warned those inclined toward inoculation not to be "Seduced by its suppos'd success," for "to urge the Lawfulness of this practice from its success, is a very weak argument to prove it so. For should Success become a sufficient plea for the Lawfulness of any action, Every wicked action successfully acted, would become Lawful at that rate." And just to make sure that no one would be seduced by the large numbers of successful inoculations, he specified that

> Arguments of Example, Number, and Success, are very insufficient, though supported with the Testimony of the News Paper. . . . To bring Armies of Africans and Troops of Mahometans [as Mather had done], to prove it lawful by their Success with it, is like their proving the Religion of Mahomet as true Religion, because successfully propagated . . . by vast numbers.[50]

The obvious answer to Grainger's objection was that although smallpox was a providence, a sign from God, surely inoculation was likewise a providence, and perhaps it was even sinful to shun the remedy that God had so graciously provided. All of the proinoculation people used some form of this answer, but the issue remained troublesome.[51] Even William Cooper, one of the "inoculating ministers" (the six who publicly supported Boylston) later admitted he had had difficulty with the problem of assured safety. Cooper seemed almost relieved when it became evident that inoculation did not absolutely protect a patient from death, that it was not completely successful. In a pamphlet published in

early November, at the height of the epidemic, Cooper systematically subdivided the religious objection into nearly a dozen
separate questions, such as: Is it lawful to make yourself sick?
Are we not taking God's work out of his hands? Has not God
already predetermined the time of everyone's death? After making it past all those thorny points, Cooper addressed the penul-
timate question: Can we be assured of safety with inoculation?
and he jubilantly replied, No, one's life is still in God's hands.
Just as minor ills, for example a tooth extraction, could on rare
occasions lead to death, so inoculation also had produced a few
fatal cases, and that proved that God was sovereign and that he
retained the power of death. The fact that so few had died of
inoculation, Cooper said, was a powerful argument in its favor—
a striking point precisely because it had to be argued.

> Nay, if one in an hundred should die in this way, while there
> is Demonstration (as then there would be) that it is ten times
> as safe as the common way of infection, This I humbly con-
> ceive, would be sufficient to justify my going into it: tho' I
> must confess, in this particular, I was once of another mind.[52]

And if death should result from inoculation, Cooper wondered,
was the deceased person responsible for bringing on his own
death? Clearly he was not, because he had died trying to take
advantage of God's remedy and God had ordained him to die
anyway.

The idea that death from inoculation could help ease one's
conscience about the practice did not sit well at all with the medical and official opponents of inoculation. The town selectmen
had prohibited further inoculations in July after hearing sworn
testimony from a French doctor about thirteen cases of inoculation tried out in the French army a quarter of a century earlier.
Of the thirteen, four were alleged to have died of smallpox; six
recovered, but with bizarre and permanent side effects; and the
remaining three showed no effect of the inoculation at all. These
were medical statistics enough for the selectmen, and they were
not willing to let Boylston continue his experiments to see whether
the French results would be repeated in Boston.[53]

Neither were they interested in computing, for comparative
purposes, the chances of death from smallpox contracted in the
"natural" way, even though they collected the figures that alone
made that comparison possible. Just as they had at the very start

of the epidemic, the selectmen authorized door-to-door searches
of the town on four later Saturdays at critical points in the course
of the disease; these searches were conducted by the clerks
of the Train-Bands (militia units), who counted the cumulative
totals of the sick and the dead. The first took place on July 29,
just after Boylston had been ordered to cease inoculating and
when fear ran high in the town; the tally was 168 sick and 18
dead. On September 23 the clerks reported that 110 had died and
more than 1,500 had been or were still sick. Two weeks later, on
October 6, the toll had leaped to 203 buried and 2,757 sick or
recovered.[54] Early October was evidently the acceleration period
for the epidemic, and that probably motivated the selectmen to
take those last two surveys so close together. There were no more
door-to-door counts until February 24, 1722, when the epidemic
was at an end. Thus we see that the desire for a count was not
a regular feature of a public-health program of Boston but was
rather a sporadic effort stimulated by perceptions of being at the
beginning, end, or critical turning point in the progress of the
disease.

It is most interesting that the selectmen inquired about the
number who had been sick, not the number currently sick. A
current figure would have revealed something about the immediate stage of the epidemic, whether it was increasing or dimin-
ishing in intensity. The cumulative figures, however, could yield
that information only if presented in series to show whether the
increase in cases was accelerating or decelerating. When the reports were published, they were never presented in that manner,
so the monitoring of a trend was not the intent in collecting the
figures in the first place. Happily for those who did want to compare relative mortality rates for smallpox in the natural and inoculated forms, the cumulative format of cases easily allowed
such a contrast, since the number reported dead was also a cumulative number. But the selectmen's reports did not supply the
calculation, and the *Boston News-Letter,* in printing the reports,
did not point out this feature of the numbers. We can only surmise
that the selectmen's clerks collected the information in this format
out of a sense of fatalism: it was probably assumed that everyone
in the town, sooner or later, would get smallpox, if they had not
already had it, and so the cumulative totals of the sick indicated
how far along the disease was on its progress toward natural
extinction, which it would reach when it ran out of victims.

William Douglass's attack on inoculation initially stemmed from his fears that patients risked death by submitting to the incision, but he found he could not maintain that argument in the face of the empirical evidence that unfolded during the epidemic. By January, 1722, he was willing to admit that inoculation worked but that it had to be sharply regulated to avoid the danger of enhancing the spread of the disease. From the beginning Douglass had charged that inoculated patients could infect other healthy people with a normal case of smallpox, as indeed they could; it does appear that the inoculators took insufficient precautions to isolate their patients. Douglass compared the progress of the mortality with its progress in the 1702 epidemic in order to show that the current one had spread much more quickly. In 1702, the greatest month of mortality was December, when 80 people died; this time, in the greatest month, October, more than 400 had died. Douglass was convinced that inoculation was the cause of the magnified mortality.[55]

It was also obvious to Douglass that a mathematical sense was essential to understanding a medical experiment of this kind, and he charged that such a sense was quite lacking in Mather. "Tho' unacquainted with the first Principles of the Mathematics," Douglass said, Mather had had the vanity to submit answers to two abstruse problems in the Royal Society's *Philosophical Transactions,* one on squaring the circle and the other on finding longitude at sea, "the Discovery of which for many Years has been endeavoured by the best Mathematicians." Obviously, "a Man guilty of such *Absurdities* is no good Voucher for an Experiment of Consequences," Douglass stated, and he proceeded to validate his own credentials by discussing longitude and latitude knowledgeably.[56]

A mathematical sense was indeed what was necessary to evaluate the success of inoculation. Dr. Zabdiel Boylston kept careful records of his activities, which he made public only once during the course of the epidemic, in the *Boston Gazette* in the last week of October, 1721. "A Faithful Account of what has occurr'd under the late Experiments of the Small-Pox managed and governed in the way of Inoculation" was the promise of the headline, and the print below informed Bostonians that, of the more than threescore persons who had undergone inoculation, "five or Six" came to a less than satisfactory (and unspecified) conclusion because they had probably already caught the disease the common way;

of the rest, not one case miscarried.[57] This glowing account appeared just at the height of the epidemic; October was the most
mortal month by far, and the more than 1,000 newly ill persons
counted in the October 6 survey were still in the throes of the
disease. Nevertheless, Boylston's account did not swing the
weight of public opinion in favor of inoculation. He found only
a few patients each day who were willing to risk infection by
choice. Not until the end of November did his work pick up; from
the 22nd on, he was rushing about from Cambridge to Roxbury
doing as many as ten or fifteen operations a day, mostly on people
from the neighboring area, who were worried that the pox would
spread to their towns.[58] From this evidence it appears that hard
empirical data of the type that Boylston privately collected and
published only once in late October did not play a significant role
in convincing anyone that smallpox inoculation was lawful, successful, or desirable.

Even at the end of the epidemic, no one besides Boylston
seemed to have had a precise idea of how many people had been
inoculated and how many had died as a result. Commentators
charged that "several" had died, and rumors that many had died
after voluntarily contracting the disease were rife. Boylston had
kept records on each case under his care, but he did not publish
the complete figures until 1726, in a pamphlet printed in London
and reprinted in Boston in 1730, at the start of another bout of
smallpox.[59]

In this pamphlet Boylston showed his mettle as a competent
researcher who was sure that numbers were the only convincing
proof he needed to establish the worth of his undertaking. He
recounted the progress of each case chronologically, with names,
ages, and general physical condition of each of his patients, the
days to the onset of symptoms, and in some cases the approximate
number of pustules as a measure of the severity of the case. He
then summarized the data in several tables designed to highlight
important features of his experiment. In one table he listed his
cases (247 of them, which he personally attended) by age group-
ings; then, within each group, he showed how many had been
"perfect" cases of smallpox, how many "imperfect," how many
showed no effect, and how many were suspected to have died of
it. (Interestingly, his totals for "perfect," "imperfect," and "no
effect" do not add up to 247, as they should; even the quantitatively minded, it seems, can be careless in arithmetic.) Boylston

also regrouped his inoculations by month to show that most of
the unfortunate deaths occurred in winter weather, which was
presumed to be more health-threatening. Finally, he considered
the sex breakdown of the group and tossed out that "it may be
worthy of Note" that, of the 80 adult men inoculated, only 1 had
died, whereas 5 of the women and children had died.[60]

Boylston calculated that 1 in 46 of the inoculated cases had
died compared to one in "six or seven" who had caught the
disease the natural way, a calculation he made from the selectmen's final reckoning. (The ratio is actually 1 in 47, not 1 in 46.)[61]
The comparison led to a firm conclusion:

> Now if there be any one that can give a faithful Account or
> History of any Other Method of Practice that has carried such
> a Number, of all Ages, Sexes, Constitutions, and Colours, and
> in the worst Seasons of the Year, thro' the Small Pox . . . with
> better Success, then I will alter my Opinion.

Cotton Mather also recognized the value of quantitative records
as a test of inoculation, and shortly after the epidemic, in March,
1722, he sent his figures to the Royal Society of London. Mather
did not trouble himself with precision, reporting that some 300
had been inoculated (286 according to Boylston) and "5 or 6"
had died, for a death rate expressed as 1 in 60. It is possible that
Mather did not know the precise numbers, which is perhaps further indication that medical statistics were not in the forefront of
the argument in favor of inoculation.[62]

The ingenious William Douglass was not deterred from con-
cocting his own calculation, which he based on the bare numbers
of dead per year that he could get for Boston from the annual bills
of mortality. In 1730, on the eve of another outbreak of the disease
in several American cities, Douglass published *A Dissertation
Concerning Inoculation of the Small-Pox*, in which he purported
to relate the straight story of what had transpired in 1721, "laying
aside all prejudices." Although Douglass was now of the opinion
that inoculation was beneficial, he still could give no credit to his
enemies of 1721. He reported Boylston's figure for suspected
deaths among the inoculated but cast doubt on it by asserting that
the relatives of an inoculated person who died would have been
very unlikely to admit that they had facilitated his death by allowing the incision. "The precise number of those who dy'd by
Inoculation in Boston, I am afraid will never be known, because

of the croud of the Sick and Dead while Inoculation prevailed most." He was more certain of figures for inoculation at Roxbury, where he claimed that 5 out of 72 or 73 had died, or 1 in 14, a death rate far higher than Boylston's 1 in 46 or Mather's 1 in 60.[63]

On the other side of the problem—the risk of dying from smallpox the natural way—Douglass produced positively cheerful numbers, providing one could suffer through his string of calculations:

> As Chearfulness of mind is the best preparative for, and re-storative in the Small Pox; for the comfort of those who have not had the Small Pox, I shall make an estimate of the *net Small Pox deaths* in *Boston,* A. 1721. There died that year of all distempers 1102, whereof 844 were Small-Pox, is only 258 of other diseases [*sic*]; but at a *medium* of 6 preceeding, A. 1721, there dyed *per. an.* 359, and at a *medium* of 6 years following, A. 1722 (I do not include A. 1722 because the *premature deaths* of 1721 had much lessened the burials for that year) there dyed 411: the mean is 385, from which deduct the above 258, remains 127 deaths of *valetudinarians* who . . . must have dyed that year of other ails: or if we compute thus A. 1722 dyed only 273, therefore the former year had *anticipated* this 118 of its due Burials; the *medium* of both computations is 122, which deducted from 5989 and from 844 leaves 722 deaths in 5867 is something more than 1 in 8 [*sic*].[64]

One in eight was a slightly more cheerful view of smallpox deaths when compared to Boylston's one in six; it served to narrow the gap between deaths from the two forms of the disease. Douglass committed two errors in his welter of calculations, however. He subtracted wrongly when he figured the number of deaths expected in 1722 that were anticipated by the smallpox: 385 minus 273 is 112, not 118. He then for some reason *averaged* the two adjustments to the death toll, the 127 who died of smallpox but might have been expected to die of something else in 1721, and the 118 deaths that were anticipated from the 1722 total; whereas the only thing that makes sense is to add those two numbers together, the sum being the number of people who would have died in any case in 1721 and 1722, with no epidemic. That would further reduce the extra deaths by smallpox to 599 out of 5,744 sick, for a death rate of 1 in 9.5. Douglass's disdainful attitude toward Mather's mathematical skills seems a bit unkind, since his own wrestling with figures led to less than perfect results.

The appearance in print of inventive but unrigorous calculations indicates something of the state of the quantitative arts in America in 1730. Numbers impressed, and so William Douglass whipped out a few quick calculations that could convince only inattentive readers. Evidently he did not expect that his numerical logic would be subject to close scrutiny, and he was right.

Smallpox returned to the American colonies several more times in the eighteenth century, and with each passing epidemic the success of inoculation persuaded more and more people to try it. In the 1730 outbreak in Boston the safety of inoculation was no longer much disputed, and the religious argument remained alive only through the reprinting of old pamphlets, not through new statements of the problem. This time the selectmen did not prohibit the operation but required the doctors to adopt Boylston's empiricism and report weekly on the number of patients inoculated and the result of each case. This allowed the town government to monitor the course of the disease and to prohibit inoculation if it appeared to contribute to its spread. The statistics themselves were not publicly announced or otherwise preserved (except for accounts by two doctors), so it would be stretching things to say that the town had embraced a quantitative approach to public policy analysis.[65]

For the time of the next epidemic in Boston, in 1752, it may not be an exaggeration to advance that claim. The tide had turned completely in favor of a quantitative proof of the lawfulness of inoculation, and the religious objection, if mentioned at all, was dismissed summarily and with great carelessness compared to the intense analysis of the problem in 1721–22. Once it was clear that an epidemic was under way, people flocked to be inoculated. After the disease had run its course, the selectmen canvassed the entire town and counted those who had got the natural disease, those who had been inoculated, those who had had the disease before, those who had moved out of town, and then a small final category, those in town who miraculously did not get the disease. Every person was supposedly accounted for in this survey, not just the sick and the dead, who had been the only ones counted in 1722. The numbers showed that in a population of 15,684 only 174 persons who remained in Boston managed to escape the disease altogether. The rest had either had the disease before, by inoculation or naturally, or else had got it this time—clear evidence,

if any was still needed, that one could hardly presume to escape
the pox altogether once it struck.[66]

The Reverend Thomas Prince submitted the 1752 figures to the
Gentleman's Magazine of London the following year to see
"whether the mother may not be instructed by the daughter,"
since inoculation was still being hotly disputed in parts of England.
The figures proved to Prince that God "so distinguishingly pros-
pered inoculation above the other way" that of course he meant
man to use it.

> All these things are under the superintendency of the highest
> intelligent cause; who uses all kinds of natural causes, both of
> the ignorance and skill, the folly and wisdom, the inadvertency
> and care of moral agents, to accomplish his wise designs and
> complete his plan of providence. But they are extremely ig-
> norant of true divinity, who imagine this precludes our liberty
> and duty to make a careful enquiry into the operations of cre-
> ated causes, to find out the more dangerous and safer methods,
> and to use all our wisdom, skill and care, and therein resign
> to the supreme disposal.[67]

In this explanation Prince overlooked the point of the earlier
providence problem, which had hinged on a distinction between
ordinary caution and accepted medical practices on the one hand
and an arrogant assumption of absolute control over a visitation
from God on the other. According to Prince, people had not only
a liberty but a duty to seek out safety from smallpox because in
doing so they were simply using their God-given wisdom, which
was part of the scheme of the universe. What had changed was
that smallpox was no longer a visitation for sins that had to be
borne humbly but was rather an unfortunate event that threatened
the public health and the economy of the town and, as such, was
something to be prevented in any way possible.

Several years later, in 1756, another pamphlet on inoculation
showed how far the providence argument had disintegrated.
Lauchlin Macleane of Philadelphia published *An Essay on the
Expediency of Inoculation;* the title alone indicates that prudence
had unseated providence. There were several proinoculation arguments, Macleane said, but the strongest argument "is drawn
from Facts, an Argument which admits of no Reply, and against
which all Reasoning would be vain and absurd." He then proceeded to summarize "the Facts," which proved to be inoculation

statistics juggled around by the Royal Society in a 1723 essay based in part on Cotton Mather's imprecise data. In an effort to be fair and full to the opponents of inoculation, Macleane listed six objections most frequently brought up against the practice, some medical and some religious, and answered each one. To the statement that "it is a presumption to inflict this, or any other Distemper" on anyone without God's permission, Macleane's reply was that the great success of inoculation, proved numerically, showed that the people had God's permission. To the objection that "our Fate is already decreed, and therefore Inoculation, if not sinfull, must at least be unprofitable," Macleane equivocated, saying that this was a "metaphysical question" not likely ever to be decided. His only reply was a bit of twisted logic cast in conditionals: perhaps, if one fell sick, God had decreed that he would recover if he used inoculation and that he would die if he did not use it. This solution completely overlooked the fact that one is not sick when one chooses to be inoculated and that one chooses it to avoid becoming sick in a natural way. Macleane sensed that his argument was flimsy and so quickly moved on to an excuse that he hoped would persuade those who still wavered on this objection. The people of Boston are firm believers in predestination, he said, and yet they also inoculate; the horrors of the disease first drove them to it, and the success of the method kept them at it. Desire to live was decisive, once inoculation statistics proved that a patient would live.[68]

On this last point he was quite correct, for when the smallpox again threatened Boston in 1764, 699 people caught regular cases of it but 4,977 chose to be inoculated, according to the selectmen's survey.[69] Apparently inoculation no longer posed a threat either to concepts of predestination or to the idea of a punishing providence. By the late eighteenth century, when the Massachusetts Historical Society offered its readers a set of vital statistics for Boston since 1702, they prefaced the statistics on smallpox with the hazy recollection that once there had been opposition to inoculation but that the success of the method had overcome all objections.[70]

It is clear that, by the late eighteenth century, Americans had become convinced that inoculation was relatively safe and that statistical medical evidence, which in 1721 had seemed irrelevant to the key issue of God's control of human life, was now an acceptable means of verifying its safety and effectiveness. The success of inoculation suggested to many people that God intended man to use it, but, more significantly, people became less disposed to submit to God's punishing power and more disposed to view man as somewhat autonomous.

If quantitative reasoning alone did not effect this change in attitude, it may be argued that demographic reality, in the form of improved mortality, or, more precisely, a general sense of demographic reality, conflicted with established religious ideas, and it may further be argued that the growing awareness of this conflict may have induced people to perceive numerical argument as realistic. Recent colonial demographic studies have shown that northern colonists who lived to age twenty, past the hazards of childhood disease, had a remarkable chance to survive into old age.[71] Mortality in New England, and particularly adult mortality, was much improved over England's experience. It certainly was not true that half of those born never lived to see age seventeen, and there must have been a general shared knowledge that people were living longer than ever before.

Yet religion remained preoccupied with death. It has been suggested that this morbid preoccupation was consistent with the continuing high visibility of death when it did occur.[72] But the colonists must certainly have perceived, however dimly, that people in their middle years died far less frequently than the very young or the very old and that the middle years had stretched to encompass many decades. In short, expectations of long life must have been on the rise, just as surely as life-expectancy itself was on the rise.

Thus, the new attitude toward numbers and the respective powers of God and man consisted of these key, novel notions: that man could alter the course of nature; that quantification was essential both as a tool for altering nature and as a means of assessing the extent of the alteration; and that one was entitled to live out his "full" life. These notions probably reinforced one another. The consciousness of a general demographic change may very well have made people receptive to numerical demonstration. For quantification could make concrete what must have seemed barely tangible, and so numbers could assume a greater reality, while old religious ideas began to lose their bearing on daily life.

Three men who evinced unusual delight in numbers in the eighteenth century were Dr. John Lining, the Reverend Ezra Stiles, and Thomas Jefferson. Each of them utilized numerate abilities in striking ways that foreshadow the nineteenth-century enthusiasm for calculation. Undoubtedly there were a few more like them, scattered here and there among college faculties, merchants' countinghouses, and the shops of the mathematical practitioners. But there were not many. Ben Franklin at first would seem to be a likely candidate for inclusion, but in fact he does not quite fit the role. He even had a few harsh words for quantifiers.

John Lining was born in Scotland in 1708 and came to America around 1730, with a solid Edinburgh medical education behind him. The climate of Charleston, South Carolina, his new home, was rather different from the one of his youth. He acquired meteorological instruments and began making daily weather observations, noting the temperature, precipitation, humidity, and wind for more than two decades. In doing so he was participating in one of the most quantitative of endeavors in vogue among the scientific elite in the colonies. In the North and the South there were dozens of little individual weather stations, whose owners checked their instruments two or three times a day and logged the readings into tables. One purpose was to look for patterns in the weather, as an aid to prediction. Averages by month of temperature, rainfall, and snowfall were sometimes calculated from the readings, although just as commonly the raw data were published, in charts thick with numbers, without any guide for the reader. Another purpose was to study the causes of disease. Many of the observers were physicians, like Lining, who were hoping to explain the apparent connection between weather and disease, so evident in epidemics of malaria and yellow fever. The general practice was to compare detailed weather records with bills of mortality, when they could be obtained, in the hope that some pattern would emerge.[73]

John Lining took the theory of a weather-disease connection into new territory. While others contemplated aggregate deaths, by season, in relation to weather, Lining investigated his own body as a possible barometer for meteorological change. For a year, in 1741 and 1742, he measured and weighed his intake of solids and fluids as well as all his bodily excretions—urine, stools, and somehow, perspiration; he also weighed himself day and night, took his pulse twice daily, and unflaggingly continued with his meteorological observations. At the end of a year, he sent all the data to the Royal Society of London, along with his favorite recipe for rum punch, which according to his charts he consumed in impressive quantities (as much as eighty-five ounces daily). This feat of "statical" ingenuity was published in the Society's *Philosophical Transactions* and achieved notoriety for Dr. Lining.[74]

Lining's enormous effort commands less attention now than in his own time, partly because it conflicts with our current understanding of the relationship of weather to disease, but also because it seems a rather improbable experiment to continue for a year. For example, Lining carefully detailed the type of instrument he used for each measurement, except for perspiration (nowhere does he hint how he calculated that, in ounces and drams, diurnally and nocturnally). Actually, Lining was proceeding on a solid hunch. Diseases in South Carolina did come and go with changes in the weather, he observed, and so he assumed a direct connection between the weather and the human body that disposed persons to become ill during certain weather conditions. "And are not the Increments and Decrements of the sensible and insensible Excretions, Regard at the same time being had to the Quantity and Quality of the *Ingesta,* and to the Exercise, &c. the only *Index* of the Changes produced in the human constitution, by the Vicissitudes of the Weather?"[75] He was seeking to establish a correlation between weather and changes in the body, and so he based his experiments on the most logical—because measurable— short-term change that he could observe in the body as an index to disease-disposing changes that might be less visible and less measurable. He was wrong, but the concept was striking and the execution admirable.

It is not known whether Ezra Stiles ever weighed his intake of food or his excretions, but he certainly expressed himself in number, weight, and measure whenever he could. Stiles was a Connecticut Congregationalist, born in 1727, a generation younger than Lining. He studied law and theology at Yale in the 1740s, a time when the college's new president, Thomas Clap, was moving the college swiftly into a more advanced program of mathematics. Whether the new curriculum sparked Stiles's interest in numbers or merely enhanced it is hard to determine, but as a young adult he adopted the habit of counting and measuring, noting his quantitative observations on scraps of paper carefully preserved, on blank pages in almanacs, and, later, in a regular journal. He recorded the number of rings on a tree stump he passed, the height of church steeples, the number of sheep in New Haven. One autumn in Newport, Rhode Island, he counted 888 dwelling houses, 439 warehouses, 16 stills, 16 windmills, 177,791 square feet of wharf surface, 3780¼ tons of vessels in the harbor, 77 oxen, 353 cows, and 1,601 sheep. A few months later he counted the Indians on Cape Cod, merely to satisfy his curiosity. Each of his six children was measured and weighed at birth and at regular intervals thereafter, the information stowed away in his diary. One day in 1766 he weighed them all before breakfast and again after dinner to see what each had gained; then he added up all their prebreakfast weights for a grand total of 223 pounds. If the children represented some sort of immortal extension of Stiles into the future, Stiles knew exactly how much that extension amounted to.[76]

Here is a not untypical entry from Stiles's diary, dated 26 April 1769. In it he describes a spinning contest held in Newport to encourage home production of cloth during the Townshend Duties crisis. The event was a political act in support of the nonimportation and nonconsumption agreements; the industrious contest and gala dinner following made for fine communal celebration of a patriotic cause. Consider how differently John Adams (or Peter Oliver) would have described such an event.

> Spinning Match at my House, thirty-seven Wheels; the Women br't their flax—& spun ninety-four fifteen-knotted skeins: about five skeins & a half to the pound of 16 ounces. They made us a present of the whole. The Spinners were two Quakers, six Baptists, twenty-nine of my own Society. There were beside fourteen Reelers, &c. In the evening & next day, Eighteen 14-knotted skeins more were sent in to us by several that spun at home the same day. Upon sorting & reducing of it, the whole amounts to One hundred & eleven fifteen-knotted Skeins. We dined sixty persons. My p'ple sent in 4 lb. Tea, 9 lb. Coffee, Loaf Sugar, above 3 qrs. veal, 1½ doz. Wine, Gammons, Flour, Bread, Rice, &c., &c., &c., to Amount of £150. Old Tenor, or about twenty Dollars: of which we spent about one-half. In the course of the day, the Spinners were visited by I judge six hundred Spectators.[77]

Stiles also focused his compulsive measuring on a few long-range projects. Like Lining, he kept meteorological records, taking the temperature twice a day and noting the wind direction and the general weather condition. Two friends in Newport, both physicians, also took daily temperature readings and regularly compared notes with Stiles. Stiles kept up his observations for more than thirty years, from 1763 to 1795, and published them for a time in the local newspaper. Population questions also intrigued him. He read widely in the literature on political arithmetic, as other colonists did, but he was also inspired to collect whatever quantitative information he could about the American population; tax lists, birth and marriage registers, bills of mortality, data from tombstones and accounts of midwives, no tidbit was too small to gain admission to his notebooks. He featured careful demographic calculations in a speech he delivered in 1760 to a convention of ministers, *Discourse on the Christian Union,* in which he used past and projected figures of the New England population to show how God favored the Puritans. A few years later he set to work to calculate the number of souls who had existed from the time of Adam and Eve to the present (some 120 billion, he reckoned), and he concluded that the universe must be "perpetually enlarging" to accommodate the ever-increasing numbers.[78]

Thomas Jefferson was another keen observer of details who was drawn to measurement and counting. Throughout his life he kept meticulous records of his daily expenses and classified and aggregated them in ways that would probably withstand an Internal Revenue Service tax audit today. Like Lining and Stiles, he kept meteorological records over various periods of time and analyzed the data for patterns; in one seven-year period he figured he had taken 3,905 observations. On his travels he jotted down sizes of gardens and waterfalls, and when at home he measured out rooms and paced the distances between trees. (The colonial governor's palace in Williamsburg burned in 1781, but because Jefferson lived there in the 1770s and measured the rooms, the wall thicknesses, the chimneys, and the windows of the first floor, the building has been accurately reconstructed.) His calculating interests ranged from habitual notes on the length of the growing season of many crops to lofty plans to create a decimal system of money, weights, and measures for the new republic.[79]

Jefferson's fondness for numerical detail cannot be explained as the product of parsimony; it was no cheap streak in his personality that drove him to calculate. His mind was drawn to quantification for intellectual, not economic, reasons. He had long had an interest in mathematics, and his favorite teacher at the College of William and Mary was a professor of mathematics, a Scotsman named William Small, whom Jefferson regarded as a second father. Jefferson learned mathematics from him as an orderly, rational system of thought, and thereafter he turned to it as a way of imposing order and rationality on his life. His plans to decimalize money, weights, and measures discarded centuries of tradition in favor of an elegant, rational, and presumably natural form of measuring. The plans were also a way of simplifying arithmetic so that men of ordinary capacities could become as facile as he in the calculations of daily life. Jefferson even proposed to increase the mile so that one square mile would equal a thousand acres, out of the sheer beauty of the idea. His plan to impose a rectangular-grid survey system over the western domain subdued a wilderness into geometrical regularity and also was meant to eliminate ambiguous property boundaries, since all the major lines would be fixed mathematically by the stars and all the lines would be at perfect right angles. Things that were counted and measured perfectly were fixed for certain; precision defied ambiguity. That was the attraction of mathematics. (In practice, the grid pattern posed some problems. Meridian lines have to converge, since the earth is a sphere, so legions of perfect little squares will not quite do. And unobliging hills and valleys also make for a lumpy quilt of townships.)[80]

Jefferson preferred certainty and was not very tolerant of ambiguity. Of course there were many ambiguous and ambivalent aspects within his personality; there is hardly another Founding Father who can rival him for genuine ambiguity, which is why new Jefferson biographies will continue to appear. Jefferson himself did not dwell on his ambiguous personal feelings; he did not use a diary to explore inconsistencies of the heart or mind. He often avoided discussing feelings altogether, as in this entry about the funeral of the best friend of his youth:

> 2. hands grubbed the Grave yard 80.f.sq = $\frac{1}{7}$ of an acre in $3\frac{1}{2}$ hours so that one would have done it in 7. hours, and would grub an acre in 49. hours = 4. days.[81]

Jefferson loved his friend deeply and said so in the inscription he wrote for his tombstone. Yet he reined in his emotions through cool and detached quantitative observation. Exclusive focus on the quantitative relegated feelings to the shadowy background.[82]

Ben Franklin is yet another eighteenth-century American who might be included in this list of quantifiers. As the author of "The Way to Wealth" and *Poor Richard's Almanack* Franklin coined many an aphorism about vigilant frugality. "Time is money" and "A penny saved is a penny earned" suggest a compulsive attention to account books, but Franklin was no pure personification of the Protestant work ethic, nor was he obsessed with quantitative details. His own arithmetic training was sketchy and elementary, and he did not hold the discipline in reverence. In fact, he even joked about it. He once advised a much younger and attractive woman that she ought to study arithmetic: "You must practise *addition* to your husband's Estate, by Industry and Frugality; *subtraction* of all unnecessary Expenses; *Multiplication* (I would gladly have taught you that myself, but you thought it was time enough, & wou'dn't learn) he will soon make you a Mistress of it." He recommended that she become an expert in the Rule of Three so that she would have babies all around her skirts the next time he saw her.[83]

Franklin was interested in political arithmetic and published short essays on population questions in his *Poor Richard* in 1750, but he had no patience for ferreting out empirical evidence. His own well-known contribution to demography, *Observations Concerning the Increase of Mankind, Peopling of Countries, &c.* (Boston, 1755) was entirely speculative. He asserted that the American population doubled every twenty years (characteristically, he said twenty-five years in a second place in the essay) on the basis of several improbable and undocumented assumptions: that all colonists married at age twenty, had eight children, and had only half survive to marry.[84] That he was close to correct about the doubling period obscures the fact that it was a shrewd guess and not a mathematical calculation. Precision in details was just not his style, nor did he find such precision congenial in others. An early member of Franklin's club for mutual improvement, the Junto, was Thomas Godfrey, a Philadelphia glazier, smitten with mathematics, who calculated almanacs and invented a superior quadrant. Godfrey did not stay a Junto member for long. He was "not a pleasing companion," said Franklin, "as like most mathematicians I have met with, he expected unusual precision in everything said, or was forever denying or distinguishing upon trifles to the disturbance of all conversation."[85]

"Unusual precision . . . distinguishing upon trifles": to Franklin these were signs of a mind constricted by mathematics. An eye for precision and detail is what was shared by Lining, Stiles, Jefferson, and some others, and they did not see it as constricting. There were benefits to be gained by approaching the world with calipers in hand. Numbers conferred certainty; to know the number of children dead in an epidemic or the exact rapid rise of population was to know the measure of God's pleasure or displeasure with his people. Numbers contributed to knowledge; the survival rates for inoculation proved it was a preferable method and finally a legitimate choice. Numbers revealed regularities; deaths by month suggested a connection between weather and disease. Numbers also could create regularity where none existed before; a record of daily expenses kept one mindful of one's budget, and a numerical overlay on the map contained and controlled western settlement. Numbers fostered detachment; if only the measurable is attended to, feelings, passions, and tumults go unremarked.

Not everyone welcomed these benefits of numbers. The author of an essay called "A Mathematical Question" rebuked the certainty of numbers as a form of false pride. The essay, originally printed in England, was published in six New England editions in the eighteenth century. As a youth, the author said, "I found a peculiar taste to *mathematical studies*." But then he met a real mathematician, who demolished all his interest in the subject. There followed an extended allegory about his travels to an island ruled by a Grand Geometrician but invaded by an evil foreigner, who commits adultery with the princess and creates a monster. The Mathematical Question thrust at him is to describe the monster quantitatively: his weight, height, and thickness, the number of his limbs, the loudness of his voice, his age, and an estimate of the mischief he will do. "In this distress, I began to reflect on my former vanity, in imagining myself able to number the sand, to weigh the mountains, to sound the depth of the seas, and to measure the heavens." After sixty more pages of hopelessness and despair come redemption and salvation; the Grand Geometrician alone can answer the question, and the answer is not numerical. The monster is sin, and its weight is insupportable.[86] Moral: there are some things that cannot be known with precision and exactitude.

4

Republican
Arithmetic

I n 1801 the editor of a fledgling Philadelphia journal of literary
miscellany wrote a brief article in which he described, in a
light and humorous style, his aversion to arithmetic. "Oliver
Oldschool"—the pen name is significant—confessed to readers
of *The Portfolio* that he had never studied much arithmetic because he considered it a shopkeeper's business: "It always appeared to me that a scholar could attain the object of his mission
to the university, without any assistance from the first four rules
[of arithmetic]." His college friends had ridiculed him, but in
rebuttal he cited such diverse authorities as Shakespeare, Dr.
Johnson, and the Calvinist John Knox to show in what low esteem
past worthies had held arithmetic. He readily dismissed a current
theory of the value of arithmetic: "We are magisterially told that
this study, of all others, most closely fixes the attention. An argument shallow, untrue, and easily vanquished. Any object, that
engrosses the mind, will induce a habit of attention."[1]

The significance of Oldschool's objection to arithmetic lies in
the fact that an antiarithmetic argument with a long and serious
tradition had by 1801 come to be presented as an amusing filler
piece. It was undoubtedly Oldschool's personal view that too
close an attention to numbers was demeaning, that "the influence
that arithmetical minutiae has gradually obtained over the heart"
was deplorable; yet he titled his essay "Farrago No. V" (farrago
means "hodgepodge"), and he led off with a bit of entertaining
doggerel that detracted from the potential seriousness of his message:

Our youth, proficients in a noble art,
Divide a farthing to the hundredth part.

116

Well done, my boy, the joyful father cries,
Addition and Subtraction make us wise.

Oldschool was treading this thin line between serious cultural commentary and trivial amusement because at the beginning of the nineteenth century arithmetic itself was undergoing an important transformation. Since the seventeenth century, arithmetic had been thought of as a body of numerical rules and definitions that applied primarily to commercial life; arithmetic had no other uses, in the popular view, and only certain groups of people needed to know it. But at the end of the eighteenth century arithmetic began to lose its commercial taint because more applications were evident and because commerce itself was no longer restricted to a small segment of the American population. At the same time it was beginning to be argued that arithmetic had the power to improve the logical and rational faculties of the mind and was therefore particularly worthy of attention in a republican education. Oldschool was giving voice to rather old-fashioned arguments against the study of mathematics, and he must have recognized that his view was increasingly untenable. He ended his article abruptly, alluding to further criticisms he refrained from making because "the world, quoth Prudence, will not bear it," for "tis a penny-getting, pound-hoarding world."

Oldschool's antimodernism probably evoked agreement in some readers, a blush of guilt in others, but derisive scorn in the majority. In the first two decades of the nineteenth century, the American public's sensitivity to quantified material was considerably heightened by economic, political, and social changes that were making numbers an integral part of life. The commercial revolution stimulated reckoning skills as it pulled more people into a market economy. The political revolution that mandated the pursuit of happiness as an important end of government found its proof of the public's happiness in statistics of growth and progress. The proliferation of public schools, designed to ensure an educated electorate, provided a vehicle for transmitting numerical skills to many more people. These were the years when arithmetic became democratized—and also sex-typed. The history of the ways of teaching arithmetic, from the private tutors of colonial cities to the "mental arithmetic" theory of the 1820s, illuminates deep shifts in American attitudes toward commerce, democracy, and gender relations.[2]

I n seventeenth-century America there were few formal institutions of learning, and what few there were generally ignored
arithmetic. The Puritans' remarkable provision for both primary and advanced education, extending from town schoolhouses
to Harvard College, did not embrace the subject. But then, the
men who designed Puritan schooling were themselves products
of the English system, which considered arithmetic a vulgar study
not properly part of a high-quality education. The ultimate end
of a Puritan education was theological, not mercantile or scientific. Puritan children were to know how to read the Bible, and
Puritan ministers endeavored to learn how to interpret and translate theological imponderables. There was no need to waste time
learning much mathematics. Indeed, the 1648 inaugural rules for
a grammar school in New Haven specifically directed that the
pupils be taught to read, spell, write and ''cypher for numeracion,
& addicion, noe further.''[3] Perhaps the English mathematician
John Arbuthnot was entirely correct when he charged that the
typical American living in barbarous circumstances could not
reckon over twenty.[4] Most of them were farmers in a subsistence
economy; they would, indeed, have had little use for arithmetic
beyond the simple addition of small numbers.

In the eighteenth century, basic arithmetic training in the
schools barely improved. In New England, which boasted the
most advanced system of public education in all the colonies,
local primary schools still did not teach arithmetic as part of their
regular course of instruction. But the grounds for excluding it had
now shifted. Whereas arithmetic was earlier ignored because it
was not thought valuable, in the mid-eighteenth century it was
regarded as too difficult for children younger than ten or twelve
to study.[5] However, since children older than twelve rarely continued to attend school, the result, a low level of numeracy, was
still the same.

On occasion a group of older boys might prevail upon a schoolmaster to offer special arithmetic instruction. The custom was to
hold the class in the evening, probably because, during the day,
the youths were engaged in work and the schoolmaster was tied
up teaching younger pupils to read and write. The popular English
texts by Cocker and Hodder generally provided the structure for
these evening classes, thus ensuring that in America, as in England, arithmetic would be identified with commerce.[6] To what
extent the youthful scholars were serious about their study of

arithmetic was a question a schoolmaster had to resolve before he agreed to take on the extra work of evening lessons. One Connecticut teacher recalled that in the late eighteenth century he held evening arithmetic classes "by particular request of the pupils: but I always avoided them when I could . . . because I had reason to doubt both the motives of those pupils who were the loudest petitioners on the subject, and their practical utility whenever they were permitted."[7] It is a revealing commentary on the attractions of home and hearth in this period that boys would ask to have an evening school, where they would pursue a subject of dubious utility in their lives, from texts that certainly were not entertaining and were probably frustrating, and from a schoolmaster suspicious of their motives. Another district school-teacher in early nineteenth-century New England recalled that that there had been "a most determined opposition" to the idea of transferring arithmetic to the day school; unfortunately, he did not elaborate on who opposed it and why.[8] Was it the parents, who felt, perhaps, that arithmetic should remain an elective subject? Or was it the adolescent boys, who would lose their chance for an evening out?

Boys who went beyond the district school, into Latin grammar schools or, in the late eighteenth century, into the academies, encountered basic arithmetic in their required programs. But the traditional English gentlemanly disdain for the subject survived in muted form in America. Isaac Greenwood, first Hollis Professor of Mathematics at Harvard, published an elementary arithmetic text in 1729 for "Persons of some Education and Curiosity," yet he felt obliged to apologize to his elite readers: "It cannot be thought an unprofitable task for a Gentleman, especially of Curiosity and Learning, once in his Life to pass through the Rules in this Art."[9] Apparently the teachers in the Latin schools agreed that it was not prohibitively vulgar and set their older pupils to work at elementary arithmetic.[10] Benjamin Franklin's proposed curriculum for a Philadelphia academy in 1749 was more boldly utilitarian and included "Arithmetick, Accounts, and some of the first Principles of Geometry and Astronomy" near the top of his list of useful subjects.[11] Daniel Webster was first introduced to arithmetic when he entered the Phillips Academy at Exeter in the 1790s, having learned only reading and writing in his district school in New Hampshire.[12]

The inclusion of arithmetic in a Latin school or academy curriculum did not necessarily mean that the students actually
learned much arithmetic. Caleb Bingham, an education reformer
of the mid-nineteenth century, charged that an academy teacher
of the 1790s, one of the most respected in Boston, had no idea
how to do simple calculations. He took problems out of the copybook he had used as a boy and set them in the books of his
beginning students, who were eleven years old: "Any boy could
copy the work from the manuscript of any other further advanced
than himself, and the writer never heard any explanation of any
principle of arithmetic while he was at school. Indeed, the pupils
believed that the master could not do the sums he set for them."
Bingham added a predictable story about a boy who contradicted
a sum in the master's book and incurred great displeasure, until
the teacher reasserted his authority by altering the terms of the
problem.[13]

Copybooks were widely used in the eighteenth century as substitutes for textbooks, ever in short supply. The teacher dictated
rules and problems to be copied into blank books, and the students
worked out the answers with varying degrees of individual effort.
A collection of sixty surviving arithmetic copybooks dating from
the period 1739 to 1820 affords a glimpse of student interaction
with the fundamentals of mathematics.[14] Most of the books are
neat and orderly, showing that penmanship as well as accuracy
in problem-solving mattered a great deal. A few schoolboys succumbed to the temptation to doodle in the margins or to write
names endlessly over the flyleaf, but most look like what they in
fact became: books written to be saved a long time, for later
reference. (Some contain other information, of the character of
a permanent record: dates of children's births, commercial accounts, names of debtors and creditors; one writer even listed the
dates on which various cows of his "went to bull" in the summer
of 1775.) Those that contain dates reveal that the student completed his course of study in the subject in one or two years, and,
if steadiness of hand is any guide to a child's age, it appears that
all these scholars were older than ten when they began their study.
(One recorded his age—thirteen.) The books trace a standard
progression from addition, subtraction, multiplication, and division to the Rule of Three, single and double, inverse and direct.
A few repeat these rules with fractions and decimals, and a very
few go beyond, to simple measurement of angles. The most ad-

vanced copybook covers practical trigonometry and geometry as applied to problems in surveying and navigation.

Merely to list the subjects contained in the copybooks does not reveal the sufferings endured by these students. Types of problems that would be relatively easy for a high-school student of today take on nightmarish qualities when translated into the measurements and currencies of the eighteenth century and tackled with eighteenth-century methods. Arithmetic was a commercial subject through and through and was therefore burdened with the denominations of commerce. Addition was not merely simple addition with abstract numbers, it was the art of summing up compound numbers in many denominations—pounds, shillings, pence; gallons, quarts, and pints (differing in volume depending on the substance being measured); acres and rods, pounds and ounces (both troy and avoirdupois), firkins and barrels, and so on. Eighteenth-century copybooks show that students had to memorize all these tables of equivalences before embarking on the basic rules and operations. A large chunk of time was spent on a subject called "reduction": learning to reduce a compound number to its smallest unit to facilitate calculations. Students would practice on questions like How many seconds since the creation of the world? How many inches in 3 furlongs and 58 yards? This would prepare them for more advanced problems, such as What will ten pairs of shoes cost at 25 s. 6 d. a pair?

Eighteenth-century methods of problem-solving further confounded all but the best students because they deliberately relied on memory, not on understanding. The English assumption that arithmetic was too difficult to explain persisted in America; printed texts and students' copybooks contained a plethora of rules (sometimes in verse to aid memorization) to cover every conceivable sort of problem. The student's task was to match the problem to the correct rule and grind out the solution mechanically. Independent thought was not encouraged by this system. There were rules of simple addition, addition of compound numbers, and addition of fractions, often in widely separated chapters of a text, with no clue to the fact that they are all variations of the same operation. There were the Rule of Three Direct, the Rule of Three Inverse, the Rule of Fellowship, the Rule of Interest, and dozens more.

Here is a problem in "discount": "What is the present worth of $5,150 due in 4½ months at 8% per annum and 1% for prompt payment?'' The modern student would be likely to set up an equation that expressed the relation of all numbers to the unknown, the present value. The hapless copybook writer had no algebra or experience with equations to help him think logically about the problem. Instead, a rote rule in discount was applied and the answer ground out, with no sense that this type of problem might in any way be related to lots of other problems not involving interest and present values.

The famous Rule of Three illustrates nicely the potential for confusion in eighteenth-century arithmetic. After the rules of addition, subtraction, multiplication, and division of whole numbers, the Rule of Three was the next step and the most basic operation of business—so basic that it was often called the Golden Rule. Many students' entire arithmetic education ended with the Rule of Three. "Given three parts, to find the fourth," is the way the rule was often stated. If 7 yards of cloth cost 21 shillings, how much do 19 yards cost? The Rule of Three instructed the student to set down 7:21::19 on paper and then multiply the middle times the last number and divide the product by the first. Writing the numbers in the wrong order was a major source of grief to students. But the real problem with this rule was that the first step of the solution leads to a meaningless number: 21 shillings by 19 yards equals 399 units of what? It is only with the second step, dividing 399 by 7 yards, that the calculation makes any sense. A more logical way to do the problem is to figure out what one yard costs and go on from there.

This pitfall in the Rule of Three made it hard for students to realize when they had gone awry in a problem. Here is a typical word problem, typical in its complexity and in its use of current events to suggest the utility of arithmetic:

> Suppose General Washington had 800 men and was supplied with provision for but two months, how many of his men must leave him, that his provision may serve the remaining five months?

In this particular case the student mechanically applied the Rule of Three, writing 2:800::5 and then dividing 5 into 2 × 800 to get a final answer of 320. Now, 320 is the number of men who can be fed for five months, not the number who must leave; so Washington's troops would have gone hungry had this schoolboy or his master been in charge of provisioning. One suspects that a real military man would have put the question in a different way: How much food must I commandeer to feed my 800 troops for three more months? But then, problems were not always totally practical: "How many minutes [were there] from the commencement of the war between America and England, April 19, 1775, to the settlement of a general peace, which took place January 20, 1783?"[15]

If these copybooks accurately reflect the substance of arithmetic instruction in academies and grammar schools, then it is easy to see why colonial colleges in general regarded arithmetic as a vulgar subject that could safely be ignored by men heading for a clerical or legal calling. But, gradually, colonial colleges in the eighteenth century became more rigorous in their mathematics curricula and requirements for admission. Although Harvard had established a mathematics professorship in 1726, it still relegated arithmetic, geometry, and astronomy to a mere two hours a week in the senior year. Sometime before the 1780s arithmetic became a first-year subject, leaving room for algebra, geometry, and higher branches in the following years. Yale offered arithmetic as a senior course as early as 1716, and in the 1740s, under the presidency of the mathematically-minded Thomas Clap, it made arithmetic a first-year subject and added algebra and geometry to the curriculum. A few advanced students even studied conic sections and fluxions—calculus—in their senior year. In 1745 Yale daringly began to require a mastery of basic arithmetic before admission to the college, as did Princeton in 1760; but Harvard waited until 1802 to institute a similar rule. The mathematics programs at William and Mary, the University of Pennsylvania, and Dartmouth were strong by the end of the eighteenth century, but, like Harvard, they all began with a quick course in the first four rules. The general assumption was that entering students had a fairly low or even nonexistent acquaintance with basic arithmetic.[16]

Although public schools and academies were less than thorough in their arithmetic instruction, there was a second and much more common way to gain mathematical knowledge in the cities of colonial America: from mathematical practitioners and other private masters in day and evening schools. Throughout the eighteenth century, newspapers carried advertisements for special courses in writing and arithmetic, in the tradition of the English petty school. Sometimes the notices promised great scope and advanced mathematical learning, as in this item from the *Boston Gazette:*

> At the House formerly Sir Charles Hobby's are taught, Grammar, Writing after a free and easy manner, in all the hands usually practiced, Arithmetick Vulgar and Decimal in a concise and practical Method, Merchants Accompts, Geometry, Algebra, Mensuration, Geography, Trigonometry, Astronomy, Navigation, and other parts of the Mathematicks, with the use of the Globes and other Mathematical Instruments, by Samuel Grainger.[17]

Another advanced teacher was Isaac Greenwood, who set himself up as a private master after he was removed from his position at Harvard for intemperance in 1738, as did Nathan Prince, another mathematician of repute, who lost the competition for Greenwood's chair to John Winthrop.[18] But more often the advertisements for lessons offered less impressive programs and were placed by men who had no connection to the scientific elite in the colonies. In South Carolina Stephen Hartley offered reading, writing in several hands, and "Arithmetick, in all its Parts, Merchant's Accompts, or the Italian Method of Bookkeeping" to Charleston residents in June of 1744; three months later George Brownell and John Pratt placed a notice offering the same subjects plus dancing; and the competition was joined by a husband-and-wife team, who included needlework and drawing for young ladies in their program.[19]

It is evident that these evening schools filled a need for basic education that was being met in no other way. The teachers were ordinarily men who had probably learned the material from a private master themselves. Teaching was something they could always fall back on when other types of employment did not work out, as is evident in this plea by a seemingly multitalented Thomas Smith of Virginia:

> To the PUBLIC. A CLERGYMAN of character, of the church of England, addresses himself to the churches of all his Majesty's plantations, that if they want a sober young man for their Minister, on trial, on reasonable terms: Or, he proposes to teach young Gentlemen and Ladies French, Latin, Greek, and English, book keeping by double entry, algebra, geometry, measuring, surveying, mechanics, fortification, gunnery, navigation, and the use of the globes and maps.[20]

So, although arithmetic was not taught in the district schools and was given only cursory attention in higher schools, there were other avenues for acquiring mathematical skills. Indeed, it would be very surprising if this society, whose elite class derived its status from commercial activity, had not created some institutional or formal method for maintaining the requisite numerical skills.

The advertisements for evening schools and writing schools are only the most visible evidence of the ways by which arithmetic knowledge was conveyed. Less formal (and therefore less visible to historians) was the education conveyed from master to apprentice and from parent to child. Apprenticeship laws in the seventeenth century specified that masters be directed to teach their charges to read and write; in the eighteenth century in several colonies the law was enlarged to include "ciphering as far as the rule of three."[21] Probably not a few masters in urban areas sent their apprentices to the evening schools to fulfill this part of their obligation. As for the instruction that passed from parent to child, little trace remains. Common sense suggests that whenever a parent knew some arithmetic and also found it useful in his vocation, he would teach it to his child if no institution did.[22] Or, lacking time but not money, a parent could hire a tutor: "Wanted soon: A TUTOR for a private family, who among other things, thoroughly understands the mathematics."[23] Finally, we should not overlook the possibility that unusually able men could learn arithmetic on their own. Several of the most famous colonial scientists were entirely self-taught: David Rittenhouse, Nathaniel Bowditch, and Benjamin Banneker.[24] Benjamin Franklin had failed to prosper under a teacher, but at the age of sixteen he "took Cocker's book of arithmetic, and went through the whole by myself with the greatest ease"—a truly commendable feat, considering the obfuscating nature of Cocker's text.[25] Clearly, it was possible in eighteenth-century America to learn the rudiments of arithmetic if one needed it in life.

That there were, then, a number of different avenues for learning arithmetic should not obscure the overriding fact that arithmetic instruction remained inflexible and barren of innovation throughout the eighteenth century. It was recognized to be a troublesome subject, but no one made an effort to simplify it. The response instead was to postpone teaching it until a child was ten or twelve (or older). Only those with a future in commerce made a thorough study of it, and, even then, there were shortcuts to reduce reliance on calculations and ways to make up for poor training.

For those who found that they lacked quickness and skill, there were ready reckoners to provide a handy method of computation. Just like English reckoners, these were books consisting of hundreds of tables listing multiples of various unit prices, so that one could look up the price of any amount of a commodity.

> Although this book be chiefly calculated for the use of people unacquainted with figures, yet there is no doubt of its being of advantage, to those who may be perfect in arithmetic; as mistakes will frequently escape the readiest Penmen, when in the hury [sic] of business.[26]

In addition to the unit-price tables, ready reckoners provided other sorts of tables that reflected the changing needs of the public. A 1774 edition compared the value of Pennsylvania and New York currency in terms of gold and silver, an appropriate nod to the increasing interdependency of the colonies; a 1789 edition presented "A Scale of Depreciation, for the Settlement of old debts" for Pennsylvania and Maryland; and a 1794 edition provided a table converting cents to pounds, shillings, and pence, "very useful to all Persons who may be concerned in the Duties established by the Revenue Laws of Congress."[27]

An early and ambitious American version of the reckoner was a reference work written in 1731 by Thomas Prince, a Boston clergyman; he called it *Vade Mecum for America: or a Companion for Traders and Travellers*. Prince grandly claimed that his book was the first of its kind and of such "great advantage, that we need not speak a word in its Commendation."[28] He combined the price tables of the ready reckoner with the sort of miscellany more often included in almanacs. After more than 150 pages of tables showing the value of any quantity of a commodity, there followed a table of interest at 6 percent for a variety of principals; a list of counties and towns in New England and the court dates of colonies as far south as Virginia; the dates of Quaker meetings and fairs; an account of the principal stages along the roads from Boston and the distance between each tavern, down to the nearest half-mile; and a table of weights and measures in all their eighteenth-century complexity. This much was undoubtedly of use to readers, but, from there on, Prince got carried away with his compilation of quantitative information. He provided a chronology of the kings and queens of England, noting dates of birth and death, the date of the beginning of each reign, and then the length of each reign, figured in years, months, and days. The curious reader next encountered an alphabetical list of all the streets in Boston, followed by a neat summary: 60 streets, 41 lanes, and 12 alleys.[29] It is hard to imagine what practical use Prince thought this information might have. Here we encounter an extreme of the quantitative mentality in the eighteenth century: a pure love of counting and computation. Prince, in his position as Congregationalist minister, followed with interest the patterns of vital events among his parishioners and on occasion brought demography and political arithmetic into his sermons. Evidently the same spirit of data collection carried over into his *Vade Mecum*.[30] American ready reckoners after Prince's were limited to tables of prices and interest; the courts and roads, fairs and meetings, were left to the almanac trade, the weights and measures to arithmetic books. No one else bothered to disseminate information about the duration of monarchs or the number of streets, lanes, and alleys in a town—eloquent testimony to the low level of interest such quantitative trivia commanded in the eighteenth century.[31]

The appeal of basic ready reckoners persisted in the eighteenth century because the tables facilitated commercial transactions in a society where few were adept at juggling pounds and shillings along with ells and firkins. But by the second decade of the nineteenth century the use of reckoners had died out, for two reasons. The gradual shift to a decimal monetary system, begun in 1792, greatly simplified price calculations; proponents of the new federal money claimed that they were democratizing commerce by putting computation within the reach of nearly all. At the same time, the self-consciously utilitarian spirit of the new nation invaded education and elevated arithmetic to the status of a basic skill along with reading and writing. Decimal money and arithmetic education were justified as fruits of republican ideology; numeracy was hailed as a cornerstone of free markets and a free society.

Thomas Jefferson proposed that the United States adopt decimal money in 1784, when the Continental Congress was struggling to create order amidst the financial chaos of the Confederation period. As obvious as the virtue of a decimal money system may

seem today, it was not so obvious in the 1780s. In fact, Jefferson's
plan to decimalize the currency was not the first standardization
plan that came before the Continental Congress. In 1782 Gou-
verneur Morris, assistant to financier Robert Morris, drew up a
proposal to base the currency on the unit of silver that was the
lowest common denominator of all the various states' pennies.
This he determined to be one quarter-grain of silver, and from
that base a standardized dollar would contain 1,440 units, a crown,
1,600 units. The virtue of this system was its compatibility with
the state coins; its drawback was that it created terrifying prices.
As Jefferson pointed out, a loaf of bread costing one-twentieth
of a dollar would instead cost 72 units; a pound of butter, 288
units; a horse, 115,200 units; and the public debt—in 1782 a matter
of mounting concern—would be too shocking to contemplate.[32]

Congress tabled Morris's report for two years, then referred
it to a committee, of which Jefferson was a member. The committee then proposed a new system of dollars, divided into dimes
and cents, and established a fixed ratio of gold and silver values
to standardize it. The new plan was accepted by Congress, and
in 1792 the Mint, established at Philadelphia, began to make pennies and half-pennies. By 1796, with the issue of dimes and half-
dimes, Jefferson's prediction about the superior ease of reckoning
in decimals could be tested:

> The facility which this would introduce into the vulgar arith-
> metic would, unquestionably, be soon and sensibly felt by the
> whole mass of people, who would thereby be enabled to com-
> pute for themselves whatever they should have occasion to
> buy, to sell, or measure, which the present complicated and
> difficult ratios place beyond their computation for the most
> part.[33]

Before the facility could be sensibly felt, however, people would
have to be instructed in the use of the new money, and several
books and pamphlets appeared in 1795 and 1796 to that end. Some
were mere broadsides—tables of exchange rates between old and
new currency, suitable for nailing to the wall in stores.[34] Others
were complete arithmetic texts that recast the first four rules with
examples in federal money, specifically for the benefit of all who
wanted to join the "rapid strides towards commercial grandeur"
then under way but who had felt excluded and confused by the
intricacies of the old system of money.[35] *The Assistant, or A*

Treatise on the Currency of the United States (1796), addressed itself to "Traders, Mechanics and young persons" and gave rules and examples "sufficient to teach the smallest capacity, without the assistance of an instructor."[36] In *An Introduction to Arithmetic for the Use of Common Schools* (1796), author Erastus Root specified his audience as future farmers and mechanics and made explicit the patriotic interconnections between common arithmetic, decimal money, and republican government:

> . . . it is expected that before many years, nay, many months, shall elapse, this mode of reckoning will become general throughout the United States. . . . Then let us, I beg of you, Fellow-Citizens, no longer meanly follow the British intricate mode of reckoning.—Let them have their own way—and us, ours.—Their mode is suited to the genius of their government, for it seems to be the policy of tyrants, to keep their accounts in as intricate, and perplexing a method as possible; that the smaller number of their subjects may be able to estimate their enormous impositions and exactions. But Republican money ought to be simple, and adapted to the meanest capacity.[37]

Decimals had been studied by mathematicians for two hundred years, but America was the first country to put them to practical use, Root boasted, drawing a parallel to the ancient Tree of Liberty, existing eternally but blossoming only in the hospitable American environment. This line of thinking unavoidably required a comment on France, which had followed America in both liberty and decimals. By 1796 France had adopted decimal coins, metric weights and measures, and a revamped calendar of ten-day weeks, which afforded Root an opportunity to make a pun: just as they had gone too far in republicanism, "so have they stretched decimal simplicity beyond its proper limits, even into decadary infidelity."[38]

The introduction of decimal money removed a significant obstacle to the study of arithmetic, inasmuch as arithmetic was still taught and thought of primarily in a commercial context. Dollars, dimes, and cents were certainly easier to figure with than pounds, shillings, and pence; they alleviated a lot of the pain associated with denominate arithmetic. The new system of money also required the publication of new arithmetic texts, ones appropriate to American life. Cultural chauvinism, already set in motion by the Revolution, led to a decline in the pirating of English texts and to their replacement by American texts written by Americans. With the introduction of federal money, the American authors had reason to begin to alter the substance of arithmetic texts; no longer did strict adherence to tradition prevail.

A second development in the late eighteenth century further eroded the traditional memory-based version of arithmetic. The arrival of republican government provoked intense speculation about the form and content of education appropriate to a republic. The consensus was that education should be widespread and that it should teach future citizens to think. Several leading figures in the 1780s and 1790s wrote essays describing the sort of education best suited to the rising generations in the new United States, and there was universal agreement that arithmetic was essential and should be elevated to the level of a basic skill. In its new role as a required subject, arithmetic would promote the spread of the commercial frame of mind and at the same time foster a citizenry able to reason clearly. In *Notes on Virginia* (1782) Thomas Jefferson proposed a system of local schools, open to all, that taught reading, writing, and "common arithmetic"; the best of the pupils would have the opportunity to study "the higher branches of numerical arithmetic" at the next step up, the grammar school.[39] Benjamin Rush, the Philadelphia physician, advocated that free district schools teach reading, writing, and the "use of figures."[40] Noah Webster agreed that the yeomanry in district schools should learn about commerce and money, but he kept to the traditional view that boys at age ten were still too immature to reason about abstract mathematics.[41] Two other men, a journalist and an educator, who shared a prize from the American Philosophical Society in 1797 for their essays on education, both matter-of-factly included arithmetic in their proposed primary-school curricula.[42]

While a new consensus was emerging on the value of arithmetic, none of these early advocates of republican education considered whether the method of teaching it ought to be altered. In the 1790s the subject was frozen in the structured texts of Cocker, Hodder, Dilworth, and their imitators, though their complexity had been ameliorated somewhat by the substitution of decimal money in the examples. Arithmetic was still a laborious study, dependent on rules, catechisms, and memory work. Thus it had been since the seventeenth century, and no one had stopped to wonder whether there might be a better pedagogic approach. In the process of making arithmetic a required subject for all young pupils, educators finally had to conclude that the traditional method of instruction simply did not work very well. A self-selected group of fifteen-year-old boys could wrestle with Cocker and finally make sense of it, but the average eight- or ten-year-old needed explanation and help that schoolmasters of the young republic were not well trained to give.

The problem is illustrated by what happened in Boston, which in 1789 passed its own Education Act, a part of which specified that boys aged eleven to fourteen were to learn a standardized course of arithmetic through fractions. Prior to this act, arithmetic had not been required in the Boston schools at all. Within a few years a group of Boston businessmen protested to the School Committee that the pupils taught by the method of arithmetic instruction then in use were totally unprepared for business. Unfortunately, the educators in this case insisted that they were doing an adequate job and refused to make changes in their program.[43]

In general it appears that, although the value of arithmetic knowledge was finally recognized, most communities lacked the skilled teachers and comprehensible texts needed for transmitting it. In the district schools in New England arithmetic was repeatedly judged to be in "a very low state."[44] Benjamin Latrobe, a prominent architect and engineer, pinpointed an obstacle that had yet to be overcome:

> Arithmetic is generally a heavy study to boys, because it is rendered entirely a business of memory, no reasons being assigned for the rules. A schoolbook of arithmetic accompanied with demonstrations is much wanted. We do boys from seven to fifteen years old a great injustice in supposing they cannot reason.[45]

Here Latrobe touched on a claim that had long been accepted for more advanced mathematics: that the ability to reason carefully and logically was associated with mathematical skill.[46] However, elementary arithmetic had been so closely allied to commercial exchange since the seventeenth century that it had been overlooked as a purely intellectual exercise for the mind. With the changing attitudes toward public education and the desire for a

populace well attuned to reason and logic as a solid foundation
for republican government, there emerged the idea that even very
basic arithmetic could help train men to think well. In the summer
of 1788 George Washington expressed this idea in a letter to
Nicolas Pike, the author of the first purely American elementary
arithmetic text to be published in the new republic: "The science
of figures, to a certain degree, is not only indispensably requisite
in every walk of civilised life, but the investigation of mathematical truths accustoms the mind to method and correctness in
reasoning, and is an employm. peculiarly worthy of rational
beings."[47] Next, Washington rather cloudily affirmed the psychological satisfaction inherent in arithmetical precision: "In a cloudy
state of existence, where so many things appear precarious to the
bewildered research, it is here that the rational faculties find a
firm foundation to rest upon."[48]

Washington's youthful experiences as a surveyor supported his
belief that mathematics could be the cornerstone of rationality.
Jefferson, who had also been a surveyor, praised the numerical
art as delightful in itself and as a good preparation for other intellectual endeavors: "The faculties of the mind, like the members
of the body, are strengthened and improved by exercise. Mathematical reasoning and deductions are, therefore, a fine preparation for investigating the abstruse speculations of the law."[49]
Many journal articles of the early nineteenth century repeated the
notion that arithmetic had a double function: it was useful for
practical life and it was an exercise for the mind. Not everyone
agreed with this view, but opponents did not flock to the literary
and education journals to express antimathematical sentiments.
An 1821 article in the *North American Review* elaborated on
objections to the study of mathematics in order to refute them,
and perhaps this paragraph can be taken as a fair representation
of the antimathematics view:

> It is sometimes objected to the study of mathematics, that it
> contracts the mind, and, by circumscribing its view, opposes
> the exercise of invention; that it tends to form a mechanical
> and skeptical character, rendering the mind incapable of com-
> prehending an extensive subject, and insensible to those nice
> shades of evidence, and unsusceptible of that accurate per-
> ception of beauty and truth, so requisite to quick and fair judg-
> ment in matters of taste and morals. This charge, if well
> founded, would be sufficient to prove this study to be danger-

ous; and we have no doubt that a belief more or less confident, of its justice, still operates on many persons in prejudice of mathematical pursuits.[50]

Perhaps so, but the "many persons" who adhered to this prejudice did not find the courage to voice their objections to the growing acceptance of mathematics education. Oliver Oldschool's "Farrago No. V" stands out as an unusual editorial comment swimming against the tide.

With all the new emphasis on arithmetic as a foundation for rational thinking, it became especially clear that eighteenth-century texts, based on memory work at the expense of logic, had to be completely revised. A revamped arithmetic that fostered rationality through mental discipline had to be simplified so that young children could not only learn it but understand it. Beginning in 1800 several authors tried by piecemeal improvements to overcome the inadequacies of the traditional texts. David Cook, Jr., of New Haven, decided that doing away with fractions altogether would lighten the burden for students and make arithmetic more attractive. He proposed substituting decimals:

> By this method of simplifying fractions, the mind both of the learner and practioner [sic] are freed from the heavy embarrassment of copying therein, such numbers of irregular tables, as they by every other method, are both obliged to learn and retain; by reason of which, multitudes of our fellow citizens, as well as the inhabitants of other countries, have been discouraged in the pursuit of Arithmetic, and thereby rendered incapable of performing those services either to their families or respective countries.[51]

Seven years later, in 1807, a Philadelpia text by Titus Bennett tried to adapt arithmetic to the capacities of young children by simplifying the rules and shortening the examples; the use of federal money in all examples was the key element in his simplification.[52] In 1811 a Massachusetts author predicted that what he called the three basic parts of arithmetic—numeration, operations with simple numbers, and operations with compound numbers—would soon be reduced to two when Americans abandoned the irregular system of weights and measures that formed the substance of compound arithmetic.[53] What need have children to learn wine and beer measure? it was asked.

Postponing vulgar fractions and eliminating the bulk of denominate numbers streamlined the earliest lessons in arithmetic, making it feasible for five- and six-year-olds to concentrate on simple operations with simple numbers. There was still memory work, to be sure, but the memory was now employed in learning number facts, not tables of equivalences. Drill on the four basic operations became a major object of early instruction. Colonial copybooks and texts give no sense that students were ever drilled on basic computations. Between 1800 and 1830, games and prizes for correct recitations of the multiplication table became common. One author recommended that the ultimate goal of drill should be to bypass words and achieve instant recognition of the sum or product of two numbers. That is, instead of learning a singsong "nine times seven is sixty-three" students should learn to glance at a 9 and a 7 and instantly think 63; translating into words was an extra and unnecessary step.[54]

Close on the heels of simplified arithmetic came the idea of teaching beginning arithmetic with tangible objects like counters and bead-frames. The earliest proponent of this was Samuel Goodrich, author of *The Child's Arithmetic,* who in 1818 argued that learning by rules and rote actually prevented children from comprehending arithmetic. Children should instead discover rules by manipulating tangible objects. The idea here was to get children to understand in a physical way what goes on in addition or multiplication (really successive addition) long before they moved on to abstract numbers.[55] Goodrich's idea was taken up and elaborated within a few years by a young Harvard-trained mathematics major who called the new system "mental arithmetic."

"Mental arithmetic" swept the field of mathematics education in the early 1820s. The conventional notion that arithmetic was a memory-based subject fit only for mature minds and chiefly a preparation for business was completely overturned. The young Harvard graduate who inaugurated the revision was Warren Colburn, who in 1821 published *First Lessons, Or Intellectual Arithmetic on the Plan of Pestalozzi.* It contained no rules, no memory work, and was intended for four- and five-year-olds. The *North American Review* prophesied, "We have no doubt that Mr. Colburn's book will do much to effect an important change in the common mode of teaching arithmetic."[56] By 1826 Colburn had published a second edition, a sequel *(Arithmetic upon the Inductive Method of Instruction),* and an algebra text constructed on the same principles. Beginning in 1826, with the first issue of the *American Journal of Education,* reports came flooding in from schools in New England and New York about the great success of Colburn's method.

There were really two related but distinct concepts working behind Colburn's "mental arithmetic." The first was implied in the name: arithmetic done in the mind, without pencil and paper. Colburn proposed to teach very young children to grasp the idea of number by first using tangible objects and then proceeding carefully—and without the use of written symbols—to abstract numbers. Early parts of his texts spelled out numbers as words, as though the arabic symbols were an obstacle to thought: "fifteen and three quarters" made more sense to a beginning student than "$15\frac{3}{4}$," according to Colburn, a notion that underscores the distance between literacy and numeracy in the pre–mental-arithmetic era. Colburn believed that children could develop their own calculative techniques, unhampered by conventional ways of working problems, without the benefit of rules and, apparently, even without the benefit of arabic numerals. Once students developed facility with mental arithmetic, they could then move on to written arithmetic.[57]

The second concept implicit in Colburn's system was inductive reasoning. At the heart of his method was the notion that students would discover the basic rules of arithmetic for themselves by working carefully chosen problems. Set a student to an addition problem, he advised,

> without telling him what to do. He will discover what is to be done, and invent a way to do it. Let him perform several in his own way, and then suggest some method a little different from his, and nearer the common method. If he readily comprehends it, he will be pleased with it, and adopt it. If he does not, his mind is not yet prepared for it, and should be allowed to continue his own way longer, and then it should be suggested again.[58]

The goal was to abandon slavish reliance on rules and memory work. Colburn declared (prematurely, as it developed) that the Rule of Three was dead, since it was worse than useless: it was an obstacle to thought. Children were finally encouraged to think through problems in proportion by using common sense.

The most grandiose claim for "intellectual arithmetic on the inductive plan" was that it permitted students to recapitulate the development of arithmetic as a system of thought; the excitement of discovery would fix the subject in their minds for the rest of their lives. Every child had the potential to be an original mathematical thinker, or so Colburn and his followers thought. In practice, it appears that fewer children than Colburn anticipated had the capacity to be that original; the journal articles of the period never mention the discovery of geniuses as a by-product of the inductive method. Instead, they emphasize the superior logic of Colburn's system as its chief merit. The *American Journal of Education,* for example, characterized the old method of arithmetic as synthetic, proceeding from rule to example, guaranteed to paralyze interest in mathematics, whereas the new method was said to be analytic, working from examples to rules. The teacher still, ultimately, handed down the rules, but now the students would understand them rather than memorize them.[59] The author of "Errors in Common Education" called the new process a movement from the particular to the general, and he added, "I question, if there ever was a boy, who learnt to perform the simple rules of arithmetic, from the directions given in his book, unaided by some visible illustration of the process."[60] But that was the mark of genius in Colburn's system—that within a few years it could seem to be the only way to learn arithmetic.

> The author has heard it objected to his arithmetics by some, that they are too easy. Perhaps the same objection will be made to this treatise on algebra. But in both cases, if they are too easy, it is the fault of the subject, and not of the book.[61]

Why was mental arithmetic so immediately popular in the 1820s? The esteem for rapid mental calculation possibly reflects changed market conditions. If it is true that the market was more free and unfettered in the 1820s and 1830s than it had been before 1800, and if prices fluctuated more in response to short-run conditions, if there were more steps along the way adding value to a product and each step was itself a market calculation of costs and profits, then perhaps mental facility with figures was an adaptive skill. The rapid mental calculator had an advantage in the market, and adults, realizing this, began training their children to compete. But it might equally be true that mental arithmetic was invented by educators as a teaching device, to induce competition in the classroom (like the spelling bee, which we do not ordinarily envision as direct training for some specific adult activity).

The popularity of using arithmetic to foster inductive reasoning makes sense in view of the enormous prestige of inductive reasoning in the early nineteenth century. Here was the link between arithmetic and rational thinking. Students learned to move rigorously from facts to conclusions. This new version of arithmetic disciplined the mind and developed habits of precision, attention to detail and love of exact knowledge. All this was accomplished without abandoning the original mission of preparing youth for participation in the market, since the problems and examples that sharpened inductive thought were still largely drawn from the realm of commerce. Little children may have started out in Colburn, adding apples and oranges or mental quantities, but within a few years they were busy at work on interest questions, which occupied no little space in texts of the antebellum decades.

Colburn did not claim total originality for his method; he gave much credit to common sense.

> The manner of performing examples [i.e., problems] will appear new to many but it will be found much more agreeable to the practice of men of business, and men of science generally, than those commonly found in books. This is the method of those that understand the subject. The others were invented as a substitute for understanding.[62]

However, except for the title of his first book, Colburn did not give credit where it was really due: to Johann Pestalozzi, the Swiss educator who was revolutionizing educational theory with his view that children could take an active part in the learning process.[63] And something more than common sense led to the widespread acceptance of Colburn's adaptation of the Pestalozzian inductive method. In the 1820s people became especially sensitive to the unique nature of childhood. "Mental arithmetic" appeared in the same decade as the introduction of infant schools, Sunday and common schools, a special juvenile literature, and pediatrics as a medical specialty. The same period saw the demise of the theory of infant damnation and the rise of a highly sentimentalized mother-child nexus. Children were no longer perceived as imperfect adults; they had a special psychology, and they passed through stages of intellectual development that were not simply deficient approximations of the adult stage.[64] Colburn's new approach to arithmetic was predicated on the assumption that simple levels of numerical reasoning are appropriate to small children and that more complex levels become comprehensible with the natural unfolding of the human mind. "Our general maxim to be observed with pupils of every age, is never to tell them directly how to perform any example. If a pupil is unable to perform an example, it is generally because he does not fully comprehend the object of it."[65]

Just as the "discovery" of childhood in the 1820s did not necessarily imply an increased solicitude for tender innocents, so Colburn's arithmetic did not necessarily mean an easing of the burden of schoolwork for children.[66] One Connecticut school that used Colburn's second text described the structure of their arithmetic program. Every afternoon the pupils tackled exercises in "mental," "mutual," and "practical" arithmetic. "Mental" problems were done entirely in the head, to teach concentration, discipline, and attention to detail; the school champion could allegedly multiply 314,521,325 by 231,452,153 in his head in five and a half minutes. "Mutual" arithmetic was worked on a blackboard by the whole class, and "practical" arithmetic was done individually on slates.[67] Several "infant schools," with pupils ranging in age from eighteen months to six years, reported success in teaching their charges to enumerate to the millions as well as to add, subtract, multiply, and divide "to a considerable extent. . . . Arithmetic thus taught becomes a fine mental discipline, and strengthens the intellectual powers, instead of resting only in the memory."[68]

Colburn revolutionized the teaching of arithmetic; a biographical portrait of him written in the 1850s claimed that his *First Lessons* was the most successful schoolbook in America up to that time, selling some 100,000 copies a year in that decade alone.[69] By that time, modifications of the inductive method had been instituted in the direction of "the good old fashioned way" of memorization. Even in the 1830s there were some nonbelievers who began to point out that arithmetic was in reality a deductive science and could never be taught inductively.[70] But there was no return to the mindless rules and nonsensical formulations of the commercial texts of the preceding two centuries. Arithmetic had become much more accessible to all schoolboys in the nineteenth century.

Schoolgirls were not excluded from the most elementary levels of mental arithmetic in the 1820s, but neither were they included in the general exaltation of numeracy. Colburn's texts for the very young addressed an audience composed of both sexes, but texts covering material beyond the first four rules were generally aimed at an audience of boys. This was true partly as a matter of custom; for when arithmetic had been deemed suitable only for mature students, adolescents and older, it was correctly assumed that such students would be males. Females rarely progressed beyond a few years of early schooling. In the 1820s, with the spread of the common-school system and the insertion of arithmetic into the elementary curriculum, female pupils for the first time encountered arithmetic, and educators, also for the first time, were forced to articulate the reasons why arithmetic beyond the Rule of Three was inappropriate for girls to learn. A whole corpus of books and articles asserted that it was useless or even impossible to teach girls to reason logically about mathematics. There were some who challenged this view and tried to prove that females could master geometry, but their efforts often met with ridicule or disbelief. It seems supremely ironic that at the precise moment when arithmetic was finally within the reach of the female half of the population, because it was now decently taught in local schools, the stereotype of the nonmathematical feminine mind became dogma.[71]

The stereotype itself was not entirely new in the 1820s. A general association of arithmetic with the masculine sex was part of the English heritage of the colonists. In 1701 John Arbuthnot, the English mathematician, promised a "manly vigour of the mind" to all who studied mathematics, and condemned the "weakness and effeminacy" of those who preferred witty opinions over closely reasoned quantitative arguments.[72] A bit earlier, mercantilist Josiah Child bemoaned the lack of simple arithmetic knowledge among the wives of English merchants, a failing that caused older merchants to withdraw from trade lest their businesses fall into the hands of inept wives. Child claimed that the numerate wives of Holland helped account for that country's mercantile superiority, so it is clear that he did not think that women by nature had no head for figures.[73] He was merely describing the reality of Anglo-American culture, where women had always been less numerate than men, just as they had always had lower literacy rates.

In colonial America too, women were less numerate and literate than men. No one concluded that women individually had more trouble learning to read than males did. It was merely the result of less education and less opportunity to read. Similarly with numeracy: women were rarely taught arithmetic, and so they did not know it. District schools did not teach arithmetic to either sex. Female schools, the few there were, taught reading, writing, and the ornamental arts and ignored the calculating arts altogether. This does not mean that colonial women were totally innumerate, however. Manuscript recipe books handed down from mother to daughter on occasion included arithmetic up to the Rule of Three, since it had some use in altering proportions in recipes. Weaving, knitting, and crochet designs required the use of counting, arithmetic, and geometric progressions and a well-developed sense of spatial relations, all considered today to be part of a mathematical intelligence.[74] But there was no attempt to teach girls written arithmetic, simply because it was assumed that women had no need of it in adult life. Written arithmetic was the tool of commerce and bookkeeping; women did not need this esoteric skill, and indeed many men did not need it either. The critical point is that no one suggested that women *could* not learn it, that they innately had less talent for it than men. The example of the numerate Dutch wife continued to offer a model for calculation in the female sphere. Ben Franklin, for example, was impressed with the business talents of a South Carolina printer's Dutch wife, and he suggested that Americans could benefit from training young girls in arithmetic and accounts so that they could help their husbands in business.[75] But mid-eighteenth-century Americans felt no pressing urgency to educate women at all, whether in numbers or letters.

What was new in the nineteenth century was that a disparity in skills that had arisen out of educational differences was now receiving ideological support from an argument rooted in the idea of natural, unalterable differences between the sexes. As more males became numerate and used their skills to participate in the new republic's commerce and progress, arithmetic, instead of simply being associated with commerce, came to be seen as a masculine skill per se. In theory, females had the opportunity to become numerate too; but if they had become so, that would have required an admission that commerce, progress, and logical reasoning were the domain of women as well as men. Antebellum

Americans were not willing to blur the lines between the sexes in so radical a fashion. It was enough that women were becoming literate on a scale far exceeding the literacy rates of the colonial period, and the great objections that were raised in the 1790s against educating women for literacy had been surmounted only by claims that literate women would make better wives and mothers for republican citizens.[76] But no comparable claim could be made for numeracy. Young sons might well learn moral precepts at their mothers' knees, but Euclid's geometry could come only from Euclid.

The sole justification put forth for teaching girls arithmetic in the new republic was that it prepared them for managing household accounts. "Some knowledge of figures and bookkeeping is absolutely necessary to qualify a young lady for the duties which await her," wrote Benjamin Rush in 1787;[77] one of those duties was to keep household accounts and records of bills, said John Burton in a 1796 New York edition of an English work.[78] The Young Ladies' Academy of Philadelphia, the first female academy in the new republic, demurely justified the study of arithmetic because a knowledge of figures would help young wives "buy or sell advantageously—cast up accounts," and transact such business "as may be found occasionally necessary for yourselves, and as assisting companions to the other sex." A preceptress of a Massachusetts boarding school lectured her pupils in 1798 on the necessity of studying arithmetic in order to keep one's budget well arranged. She illustrated her lesson with the tale of young Lucinda, eldest of six children, whose mother died, causing the distraught father to lose his senses. Trained in arithmetic, Lucinda looked over her father's books, collected debts, bought and sold advantageously, and returned his business to health, delighting the father and restoring him to health as well.[79]

Before the Revolution, American women did not commonly participate in the financial bookkeeping and management of their homes, so these justifications for teaching girls arithmetic were truly breaking new ground. An extensive study of the American Loyalist claims presented in England in the 1770s and 1780s has revealed that female claimants typically could not assess the value of their holdings or testify precisely about the state of their family finances, whereas male claimants could consistently do so, in detail.[80] Probably the inability of the females stemmed as much from their lack of commercial arithmetic knowledge as from a

deep-seated prejudice that labeled family finances the private preserve of men.[81] In the early nineteenth century, when commercial
arithmetic became simplified by decimal money and when commerce itself was spreading so rapidly, pulling more families into
participation in wide markets, it was not unthinkable to award
women the job of family bookkeeper. All they needed was training
in basic computation, and that they could learn in the academies
and common schools of the new republic.

While household accounts and basic computation did not
threaten gender boundaries in the new republic, more elevated
forms of mathematics clearly did. Quantitative reasoning, algebra,
geometry, and trigonometry were of no demonstrable use to
women in their appointed domestic role in life, so they failed to
meet the utilitarian test of proper educational subjects. More significantly, strenuous objections were raised because these subjects supposedly developed and exercised a student's capacity for
logical thought, and that directly conflicted with the idea, then
gaining currency, that women are essentially intuitive, imaginative
beings. An early expression of this conflict appeared in an essay
on female education by the Reverend John Bennett of Massachusetts, who opened his remarks with a declaration of "the
natural equality of women with the other sex." Women were an
"untilled soil," from whom a "great harvest" might be expected;
Bennett was in favor of schooling for girls. But there was such
a thing as going too far. All ancient civilizations had neglected the
education of women except one, the Egyptians, who erred by
going to the other extreme in teaching women science and commercial arithmetic: "It was attempting to make them move in a
sphere, for which Nature never gave them talents, nor Providence
designed them. This people had not discovered, from a rightly
cultivated taste, the true and striking point of female perfection.
The sort of knowledge, which these sages communicated, unmade
the women."[82] So science and arithmetic unmade what Nature
and Providence had tastefully designed. Bennett proved the intentions of Nature by comparing boys and girls at the age of six:
girls were sharper and quicker to a fault, quickness leading to
hasty discrimination and weak judgment. "Gold does not glitter
half so much as tinsel," Bennett pronounced; likening girls to
tinsel was an apt metaphor for the ornamental essence of the
female role. Women were blessed with imagination, men with
judgment. "They cannot, like the men, arrange, combine, ab-

stract, pursue, diversify a long train of ideas,'' as Bennett evidently could. No woman could ever match a Euclid or a Newton.[83]

Bennett's sentiments were echoed with increasing assurance as America entered the nineteenth century, the century that ushered in the cult of domesticity, the sharp division between home and the marketplace, and the separation of the ideal woman from the crass materialism of a commercializing nation.[84] Geometry in particular was identified as the least feminine branch of mathematics, for it epitomized rationality. It was the one branch of mathematics that had never fallen victim to the deadening memory approach of the commercial arithmetic texts. Students learned classical theorems and then applied them in constructing elegant proofs. Logic and spatial relations were requisite to the task; mechanical memory work and mindless computation played no part. It should not be surprising, then, to find that objections were raised whenever girls took up the subject. "Indignation" was aroused when the Greenfield Hill Academy in Connecticut, run by Timothy Dwight of Yale, not only opened its doors to girls around 1800 but put them through the same mathematics courses as were offered to the boys: algebra, geometry, spherics, and calculus. The successful public examination of a female in geometry was belittled by a critic as "pure memory work, for no woman ever had or ever would be able to understand geometry."[85] To the south, the author of a letter to the editor, published in the June 1824 *Philadelphia Portfolio,* felt duty-bound to reveal the shocking news that "the young ladies at a certain school were studying the elements of geometry from a popular treatise of Navigation."

> The proper object of geometry is the development of the abstract properties and relations of space. In this science it cannot be expected that females will make much proficiency. Nor ought geometrical knowledge to be considered as a necessary object of their pursuit.[86]

The purpose of geometry since Greek times, according to the writer, had been to strengthen the rational faculties of youth—and, clearly, "youth" meant only males.[87]

This sort of prejudice served as a challenge to several of the most ambitious advocates of female education. Geometry became the battleground for proving the capacities of women's intelligence. Both Emma Willard and Catharine Beecher included ad-

vanced mathematics in the curricula of their female academies in
the 1820s in order to broaden their students' minds and teach
them to think. Willard came from a Connecticut farm family that
valued ideas, rigorous thinking, and female intelligence. At the
age of thirteen she taught herself geometry and soon embarked
on her long and distinguished career as an educator. After short
stints in district schools, she founded her own Middlebury (Vermont) Female Seminary and emulated the male science and mathematics program of nearby Middlebury College. She later claimed
that "lady-mathematics took its rise" at her Vermont school.
When she opened the Troy Seminary in New York in 1821, she
offered her students geometry, trigonometry, and conic sections.
As at Dwight's Greenfield Hill Academy, the first public performance of a girl on a geometry examination occasioned alarm and
caused the New York legislature to reconsider its financial support
of the Troy Seminary.[88] But Willard insisted on the educational
value of mathematics as an antidote to the mind-contracting qualities of domesticity. Her sister, Almira Lincoln Phelps, developed
the argument at length in an 1830 lecture on females and mathematics. Women, she said, had lively imaginations, which needed
to be tempered by attentive and precise study. Of all subjects,
mathematics most directly required mental discipline and so was
the fastest avenue to stronger reasoning powers. Arithmetic was
now "universally admitted" to be appropriate for girls to learn,
according to Phelps, because it answered both practical and moral
goals. Wives could keep household account books and would
learn to live within their husbands' means: "Many a man has
been ruined, because his wife and daughters have not practised
arithmetic." Algebra and geometry had no immediate practical
applications for women, but they would enhance logic and powers
of observation. Consider a man and woman embarking on a steamboat trip, Phelps suggested; the man, used to observing facts,
would think of the steamboat and its size and velocity, while the
woman would think only of the friends left behind. The goal of
mathematics study was to make the superficial, emotional woman
more observant, practical, and detached.[89]

Catharine Beecher's Hartford Seminary opened in 1823 in Connecticut with a proposed introductory course in arithmetic in the
first year, Euclid in the second and third, and algebra in the last.[90]
This turned out to be rather too ambitious because her pupils,
when they first arrived at her school, were too ill prepared. However, Beecher was confident that they could replicate her own

late-blooming progress in mathematics. Beecher described her father as an "imaginative, impulsive" man, while her mother was "calm, self-possessed, and solved mathematical problems, not only for practical purposes but because she enjoyed that kind of mental effort." She herself, she remarked, took after her father, who had the intellectual habits of a woman, whereas her mother's mind was mathematical and therefore considered masculine. At age twenty-two Catharine Beecher had still not formally studied mathematics; but, since she planned to teach, she took up *Daboll's School-Master's Arithmetic* with the help of a tutor, progressed through Day's *Algebra,* and concluded with a smattering of geometry—all in one winter. She found the study "both the most difficult and most uninteresting," her motivation arising solely from the fact that she was determined to teach the subject to girls.[91]

By her own report, Beecher annoyed her tutor with endless questions about why problems were presented the way they were; Daboll's text omitted all explanations, in true eighteenth-century style. Dissatisfied, Beecher began to write her own text, which was later published under the title *Arithmetic Simplified.* Her innovation was to group all addition problems together—simple and compound addition, and addition of vulgar and decimal fractions—as cases of one general operation and then proceed to subtraction in all forms, and so on. She tested this system at the Hartford Seminary, emphasizing thorough mastery of the principle of operations rather than memorization of countless rules for each type of problem. The pupils had to be able to explain what they were doing, not merely calculate answers. Arithmetic, according to Beecher, "is considered the most difficult and abstruse" subject; the object in studying it "is to *discipline the mind,* and thus prepare it to receive and apply knowledge." No mere facility with computation would satisfy that goal.

But, as Beecher discovered, even a basic facility was lacking in her students. "A large number at entrance do not know the multiplication table. A still larger number have never finished what are called the 'grand rules.' A very few have proceeded to the 'Rule of Three,' and a few, by some unaccountable perseverance, have strolled beyond this almost unfrequented boundary. But as to understanding any one part of arithmetic *thoroughly,* it is very seldom the case an instance can be found." And all these students, she noted, were over the age of twelve, had had

prior schooling, and came from the best New England families.[92]
A year at her school unfortunately did not work dramatic changes.
In an address at the close of the first school year, Beecher com-
mended the students' recitations and studies in all subjects except
arithmetic.

> Many of you seem to be unaware of the importance and benefit
> of this branch of a ladies education. It is not for practical
> purposes only that this study is useful, for in most cases a lady
> finds but little use for any but the simpler rules of arithmetic
> after leaving school. But the chief benefit to be derived from
> attending to both Arithmetic and the higher branches of Math-
> ematics, is the beneficial influence they exert in calling into
> exercise, disciplining, and invigorating the powers of the
> mind.[93]

Already young girls were responding to cultural strictures about
mathematics and femininity.

Beecher confronted the prejudice about the inappropriateness
of mathematics for females when she tried to promote her arithmetic text in the wider world beyond Hartford. A local publisher
had taken the book but had told her that "many narrow-minded
men would not even look at it" because it was written by a
woman; Boston publishers told her the same thing. She toyed
with the idea of writing under a male pseudonym but instead
decided to publish her second text anonymously.[94]

The arguments against teaching girls mathematics in the 1820s
and 1830s took several forms. Some argued that girls had no need
to know much about numbers. The New York legislature objected
to "masculine studies" in Emma Willard's plan for Troy because
they had no bearing on the making of puddings and stockings;
another wag asked, "What need is there of learning how far off
the sun is, when it is near enough to warm us?"[95] This was a
familiar argument that could be used to condemn nearly all
branches of female education, not just mathematics. In 1838 an
extreme version found a forum in the *American Annals of Education,* which permitted one Andrew Wylie to denounce the folly
of teaching a girl languages, painting, music, rhetoric, or poetry,
to say nothing of mechanics, mensuration, trigonometry, astronomy, hydrostatics, optics—(the dash in his text here suggested
a pause, to compound the sense of the ridiculous), chemistry,
physiology, government, politics, economy, logic. All a woman

needed to know, according to Wylie, was how to bake bread, take care of infants, and remain pious.[96] Carried a step further, this line of reasoning led some to predict that educated women would desire to rival men and abandon their wifely duties. "What, will the teacher learn his pupils to make Almanacs?" one said; and, "When girls become scholars, who is to make the puddings and pies?"[97]

These arguments were not entirely persuasive, however, for females in America were finally becoming educated, and there was no noticeable diminution in pudding and pie production. Far more effective were the articles of personal testimony from instructors who were trying, reportedly without much success, to teach girls mathematics. Such evidence advertised and perpetuated the stereotype of women as nonmathematical beings. For example, John Brown, the principal of a female seminary in Buffalo in the 1830s, championed the idea that "Female Instruction Should Be Thorough" in an article of that title. The girls in his primary school were taught reading, spelling, and defining "most thoroughly," and older girls in the seminary learned arithmetic, again thoroughly. No one was allowed to progress without thoroughly understanding what had gone before, and parents were warned not to be disappointed when their daughters were kept long in the introductory text of Emerson's *Arithmetic*.[98] John Brown sounded like a stern taskmaster, but, then (as he seemed to be saying), what could one do with dull students except make them persevere?

In another "Female School," whose "Advanced Department" offered arithmetic, it was reported that "little progress has been made in this department, beyond the simple elements of calculation, few of the pupils having previously undergone the requisite discipline in the mental processes required for mathematical operations."[99] Almira Phelps had a different explanation for this sort of failure. She remarked that an uneducated boy from a farming or artisan background already knew a lot about mechanics and calculation and so naturally had an advantage over untrained girls. Mental discipline would come as a result of mathematics; it was not a prerequisite.[100]

Whether friend or foe to the idea of mathematics for females, all commentators seemed to agree that the subject posed particular difficulties for girls. One sympathetic principal spoke of "that unhappy distaste for Arithmetic, of which so many females so bitterly complain.''[101] As long as the only goal for girls was to be able to maintain household accounts and live within a budget, the amount of arithmetic they had to learn was limited and endurable. The ideas of Willard, Phelps, and Beecher could be safely disregarded because experience showed that few girls were capable of comprehending the higher reaches of mathematics. The irony of this approach became evident only in the 1840s, when feminization of the teaching profession suddenly presented new and compelling reasons for women to become more fully numerate.[102] The attractions of acquiring a less-expensive teaching force required considerable adjustment in the stereotype of women befuddled by simple sums.

Before the American Revolution major obstacles prevented the American population en masse from developing a facility with arithmetic, a facility that was essential to the spread of numeracy. Perhaps the most important obstacle was the close association of arithmetic with commercial concerns. People who were part of a commercial economy, who were oriented toward the marketplace, had an obvious need for basic arithmetic, and so they learned it, usually from masters or from private tutors. But arithmetic was not considered to be part of a general education, and so it was not taught in the public schools except by special arrangement. Neither was arithmetic considered to be appropriate in an elite classical education, and until the late eighteenth century it was relegated to an unimportant part of the colonial college curriculum. For the large proportion of rural Americans, who lived outside the range of the small commercial economy, arithmetic was of little use.

Another obstacle to the diffusion of arithmetic, and of quantitative skills generally, arose from the complexities of the many systems of money, weights, and measures in use before the Revolution. This obstacle was alleviated considerably by the introduction of the decimal system of money and by the imposition of some uniformity (if not simplicity) in weights and measures by the post-Revolutionary government.

As the foregoing discussion of arithmetic teaching has shown, numeracy spread in the early nineteenth century under the influence of two powerful attitudinal changes: the extension of the commercial, or marketplace, frame of mind and the growing dominance of certain ideas associated with the fostering of democracy, especially the notion that rationality in the greatest possible number of people was desirable. As commerce invaded everyday life, more people had somehow to acquire the mental equipment to participate in it. As widespread rational thinking came to be perceived as necessary to the workings of democracy, educators looked to mathematics as the ideal way to prepare a republican citizenry.

Commerce and rationality had long been considered masculine gifts. Hence, as commerce became more pervasive and as rationality was institutionalized in the schools, numeracy—an activity at once commercial and rational—came to be viewed as essentially masculine. The crucial moment when women might have joined men in adapting their minds to quantitative reasoning came and passed, the opportunity missed. A gender boundary in numeracy was erected and defended. In decades to come the boundary moved, under pressure of the need for a cheap pool of "calculators"—that is, clerks who did nothing but tedious calculations.[103] But the boundary was never eradicated. The history of numeracy in the early nineteenth century illuminates the new American division of the sex roles: not only were men everywhere sent into the marketplace while women were isolated within a sentimentalized home, but quantification became masculinized, while its supposed opposite, vague intuition, which resists pinning things down, came to be perceived as a desirable, natural, and exclusive attribute of woman.

5

Statistics
and the State

Political arithmetic in the grand, sprawling tradition of William Petty was reborn in a fad for "statisticks" and "authentic facts" in the 1790s. Petty had advocated the collection of definite facts as an antidote to the wanderings of mutable minds, to mere opinions, and the political culture of the young republic provided a congenial climate for Petty's ideas to blossom. Mutable minds and mere opinions were not sufficient to validate the great experiment in republicanism that Americans had embarked upon; hard data were called for, in the form of "statisticks."

Today the word statistics can refer broadly to any collection of numerical data or to the specialized branch of mathematics that deals with the analysis of aggregate data. But the original sense of the word, the one that prevailed around 1800, was quite different; it meant simply "a statement or view of the civil condition of a people." Dictionaries marked the entries for *statistick* and *statistical* with small pointing hands and distinguished them from *statics*, the art of weighing, and its adjective, *statical;* by contrast, the collection of civil facts "leads to the philosophical weighing of these provincial circumstances, yet certainly the first idea is that of *stating* these circumstances, and therefore these words are formed from the English verb to *state*, and not from *staticks*."[1]

At first statistics did not necessarily entail numbers; any sort of descriptive fact about the civil relations of men could be termed "statistical," for example, a description of state government. Conversely, numerical data were not necessarily statistical. Meteorological records or tables of John Lining's excretions over a year's time, for example, would never have been called "statisticks.'' Men of the new republic limited statistics to definite facts about population, wealth, trade, industry, occupations, and civil and religious institutions, arguing that these were the data most appropriate for assessing the American experiment in republican government.

The compiling of civil facts and figures soon became a common form of reportage that both reflected and promoted a novel way of thinking about society and the state. Statistics were involved in three distinct sorts of endeavors: statistical gazetteers, compiled by private individuals; government projects, chiefly the census; and commercial reference works, such as statistical manuals and almanacs, devoted to disseminating a potpourri of facts. These undertakings testify to the rising appeal of certain kinds of "authentic facts" to men who sought to comprehend and in a measure to direct the social changes of their time. Their evolution, over three decades, into highly quantitative endeavors reveals the interplay between politics and numeracy.

Although the word "statisticks" was not formally inducted into American English until 1803, when it first appeared in a Philadelphia dictionary, "authentic facts" about civil society had been accumulated throughout the 1790s by authors of state and local gazetteers. The infancy of the United States stimulated an outpouring of descriptive books whose purpose was to inform the public, and especially men in public life, about the nature of American society. Neither the state governments nor the federal government as yet felt obliged to engage in broad fact-finding missions, so the task was first taken up by private individuals.

The forerunners of the gazetteers were works of geography, travel, and natural and civil history by such authors as William Douglass, Peter Kalm, and Thomas Jefferson.[2] But the gazetteers produced after 1790 departed from their precursors in significant ways. The earlier works might mention quantified facts about society, most typically population, but they were casual and imprecise. Even Jefferson's *Notes on Virginia* was surprisingly unburdened with numbers, and some parts of it were quite speculative. The gazetteers of the 1790s, in contrast, emphasized definite facts. Sets of facts about population and trade were set forth to provide a picture of trends. Implicit in the new style was an assumption of historical progress: the facts of today were important to know because they presaged the improvements of tomorrow. The emphasis on sets of facts turned large sections of civil histories into dry reference works, and the driest of them assumed the title "gazetteer" or, after 1803, "statistical view" or "statistical account."[3]

Authors of gazetteers often called attention to features that set their volumes apart from earlier works of description and travel. Some apologized for the dull prose that the new factual approach obliged them to adopt. Others explained their innovative methods of collecting data. And, in what became a constant refrain, almost all of them proudly proclaimed that only "authentic facts," unsullied by personal opinion, were admitted to their texts. For example, Samuel Williams, a Vermont clergyman and almanac writer, warned readers of his *Natural and Civil History of Vermont* that they would find in it

> a minuteness of dates, facts, and circumstances, not common in European productions; and not very entertaining in itself. This method was adopted with choice, and by design. Persuaded that the American commonwealth is yet in the early years of its infancy, and unable to comprehend to what extent, magnitude, and dignity it may arise; the author of these sheets views the history of a particular state, rather as a collection of facts, circumstances, and records, than as a compleat and finished historical production. The more important the *United States* shall become in the future periods of time, of the more importance it will be to be able to find a minute and authentic account of the facts, proceedings, and transactions, from whence the grand fabric arose. To collect and record such facts and proceedings . . . is what I have attempted.[4]

Williams did not discuss his method for collecting facts, but other authors did. Jeremy Belknap devoted the final volume of his three-volume *History of New Hampshire* to a compendium of the facts he had gathered by an intensive one-man investigation. The book was brimming with quantitative measurements: New Hampshire's situation, extent, boundaries, climate, topography, mountains, rivers, lakes, and roads were all noted, along with commentary on the sizes of trees and animals, the value of soils, population growth, mortality, imports and exports, and prices, wages, and taxes. In order to collect all this information, Belknap had scoured the countryside, talked to prominent local people, searched public record offices, sometimes surveyed land himself, and circulated a letter of inquiry to local clergymen and "other gentlemen of public character," so "that no source of information might be left unexplored." The response to his letter was not gratifying, Belknap admitted, but the idea of sending out questionnaires to solicit factual information was so new in 1792 that it was unreasonable to expect many replies. Quite possibly the surveyed gentlemen had never thought about the kinds of questions Belknap asked, or perhaps they had no way of assembling factual answers. There was one squire who caught the spirit of the inquiry; he contributed an elaborate table showing, for 1773, the ratio of tax monies paid to the number of representatives in the general assembly for each district in New Hampshire. Presumably his intent was to comment on the nature of pre-Revolutionary representation, suggesting that elected men represented money rather than people. But neither he nor Belknap pointed that out, leaving it to the reader to puzzle out the table's meaning.[5]

In South Carolina, later in the decade, David Ramsay encountered similar difficulties with the same method of collecting data. In 1798 he began circulating inquiries to elderly people in his state to secure information he feared was "fast hastening to oblivion." It was not unique personal histories he sought but detailed accounts of population growth and economic development in the informant's area. One reply to his survey was so thorough that Ramsay printed it as a thirty-page appendix to his *History of South Carolina,* intending it to serve as an inspirational model. Coauthored by a clergyman and a physician, the "Statistical Account of Edistoe Island" was nothing if not compendious; it described the situation, soil, and settlement of their island; the major crops and rate of cultivation per field hand; the current prices of land and labor; a census of inhabitants, conducted epecially for the occasion; and a register of white births, deaths, and marriages over sixteen years and a similar register for slave births on one plantation. Ramsay promised to devote a book to the statistics of the entire state if other volunteers would furnish similar data: "If this proposal should be carried into effect, a collection of facts useful to philosophers, legislators, physicians, and divines, would be brought to light."[6] His project did not materialize until nearly two decades later, when Robert Mills circularized leading South Carolina gentlemen and assembled the results in a book designed to inform politicians as well as to attract immigrants to the state.

By then the method pioneered by Belknap and Ramsay, that of asking local men of substance for first-hand information, had become much more familiar and successful.[7] The unquestioned assumption that leading gentlemen were the best sources of accurate statistical information indicates only that local elites dominated the civil relations of their communities, not that they were necessarily the most numerate people in town.

Claims to complete accuracy appear in the prefaces to many of these local histories. Authors of gazetteers took pains to assure readers that only "authentic facts," facts that had been verified, were fit for inclusion in their books. Facts were carefully distinguished from opinions and estimates, and several authors presented wildly eclectic data as if to prove that no preconceived theory dictated their selection. Some compilers went so far as to boast that they had eliminated commentary altogether: facts should be permitted to speak for themselves, without interpretation or amplification. "In composing a work like the present," wrote James Mease in *The Picture of Philadelphia* (1811), "the author is of opinion that the chief object ought to be the multiplication of facts, and that the reflections arising out of them, should be left to the reader." Mease offered such information as the number of gallons of oil used in city lamps per year (14,355) and the number of printed sheets put out by the eight daily newspapers (8,328), the latter number set alongside the number put out by the nine weekly papers (7,058). His readers were left perfectly free to draw their own conclusions from these facts. Rodolphus Dickinson boasted of the "merit of impartiality" conferred by the facts and numbers in his *Geographical and Statistical View of Massachusetts Proper* (1813), and David Warden asserted that he had "seldom indulged in discussion or speculation" in his ambitious three-volume work, *A Statistical, Political and Historical Account of the United States of North America* (1819), as if such indulgence were a vice. Rather, he wanted "to put his readers in possession of a full and authentic collection of the most interesting facts regarding the population, industry, wealth, power and resources of the United States."[8] Facts had come to be seen as anterior, indeed antithetical, to opinions and theories. Facts were objective and indisputable; opinions were idiosyncratic and debatable.

An extension of this respect for facts was the idea that if only enough facts were known, disagreement on public issues would end. "Whence arises the diversity of opinion?" asked the editor of the *Literary Magazine and American Register* in an article published in 1804. The answer lay in indolence, dogmatism, and "a want of certain data": "Did all men know alike, though imperfectly, their opinions must be the same"—apparently a mark and desideratum of a healthy society.[9] Social facts and figures took on critical political importance in the 1790s, when sharp differences of opinion split Congress into a worrisome division that verged on being a party system.

Political parties were unwelcome in the 1790s because they were thought to violate the ideal of virtuous, impartial solons legislating for the common good. Granted that the country was large and diverse; still, commitment lingered to the norm of a single public interest, a general public happiness. A major Antifederalist worry at the time of the ratification of the Constitution was that a homogeneous common good would be difficult to obtain in so large a country; the Federalist response was not to welcome fractures in the body politic but to keep dissident factions small and out of power. Both sides agreed on the existence of a transcendent common good. To square the recognized reality of social heterogeneity with that older norm of an all-embracing common good, proponents of statistics argued that a comprehensive knowledge of general social facts could be the new foundation of politics. Knowing the exact dimensions of heterogeneity would compensate for the lack of homogeneity in the diverse United States. If only lawmakers knew enough facts, differences of opinion would evaporate and the correct course of action would be clear. Facts would dispel the factious spirit.[10]

"Authentic facts" were thus held to be the essential foundation of good government. Authors of gazetteers and statistical accounts constantly advertised the value of their works for the makers of public law and policy. Wise governmental actions would flow from certain knowledge, whereas uncertain, speculative, or theoretical assertions led inevitably to conflicts of opinion. Noah Webster spelled out this difference between facts and factions in 1794:

> Another cause of violent parties is frequently a difference of opinion on *speculative* questions, or those whose real tendency to secure public happiness is *equivocal*.—When measures are obviously good, and clearly tend to advance the public weal,

there will seldom be much division of opinion on the propriety
of adopting them. All parties unite in pursuing the public interest, when it is clearly visible. But when it is doubtful what
will be the ultimate effect of a measure, men will differ in
opinion.[11]

Like Webster, Timothy Dwight of Yale assumed that the common
good could be agreed upon and advanced by the use of statistics.
In a sermon of 1795, entitled *The True Means of Establishing
Public Happiness,* he maintained that to "promote the general
good" men must have knowledge derived from close observation
of facts. Webster, Dwight, and other statistical writers appealed
to facts to bury the doctrinal political disputes of the 1780s and
1790s and to create consensus on the principles of public happiness and the means of pursuing it.[12]

Dwight's own statistical work illustrated one way by which
numbers could promote unity. In 1796 he began collecting materials for a descriptive guidebook of the Northeast, which was
published in four volumes after his death. His goal was to assemble data that would mark the improvements of the age; growth
of population, career opportunities for Yale graduates, the price
of food in New Haven—all answered his purpose. The minuteness
of detail "in all probability may be disagreeable to a considerable
class of readers," he politely conceded, perhaps in reference to
the ladies; but another group, so described that most patriotic
male readers would recognize themselves in it, was bound to be
enthusiastic: "Men, who unite curiosity with expansive views,
usually find not a little pleasure in comparing the different degrees
of improvement, which a country attains at different states of its
history."[13] Thus it was not only the *certainty* of facts about society
that allowed men to reach agreement, as Dwight had argued in
his sermon. Consensus would also be aided by the particular kinds
of facts that men like Dwight were likely to discover when they
went out with notebooks in hand. Dwight's facts indicated improvement and expansion and very often took a quantitative form.
Men of expansive views took pleasure in statistics, according to
Dwight; they found personal happiness in contemplating the rising
state of public happiness.

Dwight and Webster joined forces in the most ambitious of the
privately undertaken statistical surveys in the young republic.
Both were members of the newly formed Connecticut Academy

of Arts and Sciences; under their prompting, the academy sent
a circular letter to every town in the state requesting quantitative
answers to thirty-two "heads of inquiry."[14] The questions included not only predictable ones about population, number of
houses and other buildings, and manufactures but also inquiries
about "instances of suicide in the last twenty years," the number
of clergymen and the amount of their salaries, and the number
of carriages and coaches. The academy's grand yet vague purpose
was to contribute "to the collection and propagation of useful
knowledge" by publishing a multivolume statistical history of
Connecticut. After ten years, however, only thirty towns had
returned answers, of varying quality and utility, and the two volumes that finally saw print sold so few copies that the series was
discontinued. Dwight himself was the author of one of the two
completed books, *A Statistical Account of the City of New-Haven.*[15] But, surprisingly, this long-time champion of empirical fact-
gathering confessed to encountering difficulties in carrying out his
assignment:

> The public will naturally ask why the answer has been so long
> delayed. The true reason is, that every man, here, is closely
> engaged in his own business; and that no man of business is,
> ordinarily, willing to write on subjects, unconnected with his
> personal concerns. My own situation, to those who know it,
> would fairly excuse me from the undertaking. I have made the
> attempt, because I was convinced, that it would be made by
> no other person. As this account is drawn up in circumstances
> of extreme inconvenience, the Academy will, I doubt not,
> readily excuse its imperfections.[16]

Dwight had discovered that systematic collection of data is an
onerous and time-consuming task and that not one other person
in New Haven could be persuaded that it was worth doing. Love
of statistics was clearly not yet a widespread phenomenon. In
view of the difficulties that beset even the most dedicated vol-
untary efforts, political men began to suggest that government
take on the job. If facts were essential to good government, if
certain knowledge promised to restore political harmony, then
governments should conduct inquiries of their own.

A merican "statists"—a common synonym for statesman in the early republic—were, of course, familiar with official censuses and trade statistics. Throughout the second century of colonial rule, Britain's Board of Trade had repeatedly requested reports on population and foreign trade, and colonial governors and customs officials had tried valiantly to supply the numbers in the face of frequent opposition from colonial subjects, who worried that the figures would be used to measure military strength or to exact taxes. Trade statistics, a by-product of the collecting of customs duties, were seriously deficient owing to tax evasion and smuggling. Yet, however inaccurate the numbers might be, Americans at least knew that modern states considered it important to gauge the size of their population and the extent of their foreign trade.

Accordingly, the new federal government paid attention to only those two sorts of statistical information. A law of 1789 required customs officials to record the volume and dollar value of trade crossing the national boundaries, and this information was again chiefly the by-product of the system of import and export duties. And the new Constitution mandated a periodic count of free and enslaved persons, the express purpose of which was to determine the numerical basis for representation in the lower house of Congress.[17]

The founders of the republic took little interest in expanding the scope of economic statistics. From 1791 on, the Treasury Department aggregated customs records for the use of Congress but made no attempt to monitor the internal trade and manufacturing of the United States. Even among the leading proponents of commercial development in the 1790s—that group of nationally minded men among whom one would most expect to find a well-developed taste for and grasp of facts and figures—there was no one who yet saw a need for systematic collection of data. Tench Coxe was probably the most sophisticated political economist in the federal government, and, as Alexander Hamilton's right-hand man, he was in a position to appreciate the utility of quantitative economic facts. Periodically he issued reports and papers on the state of the economy for the use of Congress, sprinkling them so liberally with numbers and quantities (culled mostly from import and export records) that his work has been characterized as betraying "more than a trace of fact-benumbed pedantry."[18] But the close reader of these reports will detect a substantial amount of hypothesis, unsupported generalization, and guesswork beneath the superficial glitter of definite numbers. Coxe studded his writings with numerical tidbits to support sweeping statements about the progress of manufactures and the balance of trade, but the numbers were often meager and random (he presented, for example, a survey of the home manufactures of twenty Virginia families, taken "indiscriminately," and a count of manufacturing establishments in one Pennsylvania town.)[19] His political opponents could thus claim that he had not left the realm of mere opinion.[20] Political economy would not acquire a strong empirical bent until 1810, when the first census of manufactures was taken.[21]

In contrast, a few congressmen immediately appreciated the decennial census as a tool for gathering facts about the civil relations of Americans. Information about people, rather than products, seemed to them the means for achieving consensus on national political goals and measures, but others in Congress disagreed and thwarted their efforts. The debates on the censuses of 1790 and 1800 show how controversial the statistical approach to government was.[22]

The foremost advocate of expanding the census in 1790 beyond the basic constitutional stipulation was James Madison, at that time a strongly nationalist representative from Virginia. Madison served on the committee responsible for drawing up the "enumeration bill" and got a more detailed census schedule onto the House floor for debate. His proposal called for classifying the population into five categories—free white males, subdivided into those over and under the age of sixteen, free white females, free blacks, and slaves—and for identifying each working person by occupation. These categories were hardly an unusual or sophisticated way of classifying the population, for many colonial censuses ordered by the Board of Trade had sought as much or more. Separating free persons from slaves was essential, since a slave was only three-fifths of a person for purposes of representation in Congress. But the rest was more than the Constitution required. Distinguishing free blacks from whites, females from males, and boys from men, as Madison proposed, had the effect of identifying and isolating the group that most mattered, the free adult white males—in other words, the workers, voters, and soldiers of the nation. Congress agreed with Madison on these priorities and wrote the five categories into the first census.

Madison's proposal to report occupations, however, encountered stiff resistance. Madison offered in its defense what probably seemed to him to be a simple truism: "In order to accommodate our laws to the real situation of our constituents, we ought to be acquainted with that situation." He reminded his colleagues that in earlier debates on bills that concerned the agricultural, commercial, and manufacturing interests, "did they not wish then to know the relative proportion of each, and the exact number of every division, in order that they might rest their arguments on facts, instead of assertions and conjectures? Will any gentleman pretend to doubt, but our regulations would have been better accommodated to the real state of the society than they are?"[23]

House members did in fact profess that doubt. Samuel Livermore of New Hampshire raised serious questions about the feasibility of a census of occupations, protesting that it would be very difficult to decide exactly what occupation many people had. His constituents, for example, often had two or three, depending on the season. Livermore "was confident the distinction which the gentleman wished to make, could not be performed," and he opposed the extra expense and labor. Worse, he "apprehended it would excite the jealousy of the people; they would suspect that government was so particular, in order to learn their ability to bear the burthen of direct or other taxes," and so they would refuse to cooperate. Another critic, John Page of Virginia, also thought the proposed census would "occasion an alarm" among the people, for "they would suppose the government intended something, by putting the union to this additional expence, beside gratifying an idle curiosity." Page contended that even if congressmen were "acquainted with the minutiae, they would not be benefited by it."[24]

Over such resistance the House passed Madison's plan intact, but the Senate approved only the five basic categories of sex and race as legitimate objects of inquiry.[25] Lacking a report of Senate debates comparable to the *Congressional Register* transcript for the House, we have no record of specific objections to the tally of occupations. Virtually the only source for Senate debates in the First Congress, the journal of Senator William Maclay of Pennsylvania, treats the enumeration bill more as a vehicle for expressing personal enmity than as an issue of substance in its own right. Maclay moved to reject the entire proposed "lengthy

schedule," for reasons undisclosed. The debate focused on a trivial detail, and in the end the bill was consigned to committee.
"The debate was scarce worth mentioning," Maclay said, except
insofar as the debaters scored points for parliamentary prowess.
When the bill emerged from committee, the tally of occupations
was gone.[26]

In a bitter letter to Jefferson, Madison stated that his plan "was
thrown out by the Senate as a waste of trouble and supplying
materials for idle people to make a book." Along with these objections to the count of occupations as trivial and useless, he
identified an antiquantitative strain in the negative vote. He
warned Jefferson to "judge by this little experiment of the re-
ception likely to be given to so great an idea as that explained in
your letter of September," a reference to Jefferson's developing
ideas on the illegitimacy of one generation's binding future generations to political contracts—ideas rooted in tenuous mathematical extrapolations from death data reported in bills of
mortality.[27] The Senate was barely able to grasp the advantage of
knowing the number of men over the age of sixteen and could
find no value in a census of occupations. The idea that political
theory could be mathematically constructed from demographic
observation was sure to be greeted with scorn, as Madison suspected.[28]

When Congress designed the census of 1800, efforts were made
to transform it into an unprecedentedly ambitious social survey.
Madison had once suggested merely adding occupations and had
been called visionary for his trouble; proponents now evinced a
heady enthusiasm for inquiring into other characteristics of the
population: age, nativity, and marital status, as well as occupation.
Belief in the necessity and appropriateness of "authentic facts"
for comprehending America had grown during the previous decade. Statistically minded men now felt encouraged to appeal to
the government to conduct a fact-gathering foray into every home
in the republic. Two learned societies each petitioned Congress
to serve science by enlarging the census. Dwight, speaking for
the Connecticut Academy of Arts and Sciences, and Jefferson,
as president of the American Philosophical Society, each submitted memorials elaborating on the value of diverse quantitative
facts about the population. "To present and future generations,"
Dwight contended, "it will be highly gratifying to observe the
progress of population in this country, and to be able to trace the

proportion of its increase from native Americans, and from foreigners emigrating at successive periods; to observe the progress or decline of various occupations; the effects of population, luxury, mechanic arts, the cultivation of lands, and the draining of marshes, on the health and longevity of the citizens of the United States."[29] Congress, however, was not convinced that future generations would be gratified to have such information. The 1800 census differed from its predecessor only in refining the age classification of the free white population into five categories for both sexes, and this format was used for the 1810 census as well. That no one was interested in learning either the sex or ages of black Americans, whether slave or free, testifies to the relative unimportance of blacks in the social hierarchy and in the eyes of science.

Why did all but a few congressmen in 1790 and in the early 1800s fail to see an opportunity in the census? In the midst of a developing cluster of ideas associating good government and knowledge of the common good with facts and statistics, why did they refuse to take advantage of an information-gathering mechanism that could have yielded a wealth of facts? The reasons can be found in the statements of the legislators themselves. Many of them believed that Congress had no authority to collect more than the most basic fact of the numbers of free and other persons, and that was certainly a legitimate sentiment at a time when the limits of governmental power were still under exploration. Alexander White of Virginia felt compelled to reject a plunge into social research, however attractive the possibilities, simply because the Constitution did not expressly authorize such activity. Another Virginian, John Page, held that this sort of knowledge was the appropriate province of historians and philosophers, not of politicians, who were concerned with immediate policy. Page thought a census of occupations worse than useless because it would spark alarm among the people, who would naturally imagine a sinister purpose behind it. Livermore agreed: "so particular a detail might excite some disagreeable ideas in the minds of the people." Americans' experience with colonial censuses had shown that a distant government could use information in ways adverse to the public interest. Members of Congress understandably wanted to exercise caution; only a few shared Madison's enthusiasm for "marking the progress of society."[30]

Even if most congressmen could accept Madison's observation that, to legislate wisely for the people, Congress must know their true situation, it still did not follow that a division of the people into the categories Madison had chosen—the agricultural, commercial, and manufacturing interests—was appropriate. One representative, Theodore Sedgwick of Massachusetts, wanted to expand the list to include the learned professions, particularly lawyers, as a distinct class. Madison professed agreement but pointed out that the learned professions could never properly be "objects of legislative attention" in the way his three basic categories presumably were. Others, like Livermore, wanted to abandon the list of occupations, because they were persuaded that no such distinctions could be drawn. It is, in fact, true that the boundaries dividing agriculture, commerce, and manufacturing were often vague and overlapping in the eighteenth century. The activity of a Chesapeake tobacco-grower was at once agricultural and commercial; a New England farmer who made shoes in winter was both a farmer and a manufacturer. While Madison spoke of measuring "the growth of every interest," Livermore denied that separate interests could be distinguished.[31]

Clashing here were two notions of the common good. The opponents of a census of occupations did not see a need to determine the relative weights of economic interests; the very idea conflicted with the traditional principle of a common good that embraced the entire community. The object of wise governmental policy was to foster the happiness of society as a harmonious whole, a notion that arose from eighteenth-century ideas of an organic society. Madison, on the other hand, thought a census revealing the "several classes" of America would allow Congress to adapt legislation to reality. In his view, the common good could no longer be known solely through the ability of talented leaders to divine, somehow, the genius of the people. Statistical writers of the 1790s echoed Madison's idea that empirical knowledge was now essential for determining the common good. For example, Timothy Dwight, in his sermon of 1795, expressed no doubt about the existence of one overarching public happiness, which he thought could be served by collecting statistics. By insisting on the value of survey data, men like Madison and Dwight were subtly shifting the grounds underlying the traditional idea of a common good. It was a short step from Dwight's position to the idea that public happiness was best thought of as the sum of many individual happinesses, that the common good was really the greatest good of the greatest number.[32]

That step was not taken in the 1790s. In arguing for a census of occupations, Madison approached the position that the interests and strengths of competing groups should be weighed before legislation was enacted. But the imprecise boundaries of the groups he named prevented him from following through with the logic of an empirically determined common good. There were other ways to classify the population by economic interest; categories like relative wealth, debtors and creditors, employers and employees would find favor with political economists in later times, when the empirical common good had been transformed into the majoritarian version, the greatest good of the greatest number. This view, which became an aphorism in mid-nineteenth-century political thought, implied a quantitative assessment of a measured good that benefited some known proportion of the population. Madison's census of occupations would reveal the proportions of competing groups only if it were decided that agriculture, commerce, and manufacturing were in fact separable groups constituting the most meaningful distinctions in the social order. In 1820 that step was finally taken; the federal census of that year required that each household be labeled as belonging to one and only one sector of the economy. The common good was being broken into constituent parts, and the social order could now be comprehended through arithmetic.

How had this change come about? One answer that satisfies common sense is that the occupation categories of the census directly reflected the increasing specialization of economic activity in the country; one person could no longer be both a farmer and a shoemaker when shoemaking ceased being a cottage industry, moving first into the workshop and then into factory production. But more was at work here to encourage a mathematical approach to politics. People do not count occupations merely because there are now discrete occupations waiting to be counted. By 1820 the perception had grown that distinct classes existed and mattered. Thus an anonymous writer in the *North American Review* in 1816, commenting on Moses Greenleaf's *Statistical View of the District of Maine*, remarked that in times past

little information was sufficient, to provide for the wants and
exigencies of the community, as men were not divided into so
many classes, having distinct interests, as they are at the present day. . . . A nation composed of wood-cutters and farmers
. . . could have no *time* for such inquiries and speculations, no
means of improving their condition much by them, and very
little occasion to think of them.[33]

The emergence of such interests, together with the government's
increasing acceptance of responsibility for fostering economic
growth, demanded that accurate and comprehensive statistics be
made available in readily accessible form. The form these facts
took was increasingly quantitative.

Writers began to talk about perfecting a "science of statistics,"
in which unimpeachable data would reveal the laws of political
action.[34] Journals like *Niles' Weekly Register* made statistical tables a regular feature from 1811 on, declaring such quantitative
displays to be "among the most useful and interesting articles we
can possibly insert."[35] Between 1810 and 1820 the output of state
gazetteers rose sharply, and by the 1820s a book that claimed to
be statistical without being quantitative was heavily criticized for
misrepresenting its contents and for containing no useful knowledge.[36] Almanacs, the staple of every man's reading, began to be
garnished with facts and figures in the 1810s. One almanac of 1817
even suggested that the owner add to his own copy statistics on
the local price of labor, the value of his produce, and the expenses
of living, and it reminded him that "fact, accuracy & conciseness
are requisite." The series of almanacs, sewn together, would form
a personal quantitative record of one's life, most appropriately
shelved next to the family Bible, with its personal record of vital
events.[37]

This movement to comprehend society through quantitative
facts accelerated in precisely the same decade in which arithmetic
instruction in the schools was being thoroughly revamped. Americans in the 1820s were receptive to quantitative facts more than
ever before, and educators responded to that interest by emphasizing numeracy training in the schools. Arithmetic not only improved the logical faculties of the mind and prepared young boys
for commerce; it also opened the doors to useful political knowledge in the form of statistics. An early assertion of this idea came
in 1804, when a Philadelphia publication, *The Literary Magazine
and American Register,* printed a fold-out table entitled "A Sta-

tistical View of the United States of America," showing each
state's total area, population by race, ratio of blacks to whites,
persons per square mile, chief towns and their populations, and
the value of exports. The accompanying text recommended that
the table be "gotten by rote by every scholar between twelve and
fifteen years of age."[38] A children's board game, dating from 1806,
encouraged memorization of quantitative statistics; a map provided the playing field, and players moved from state to state,
garnering electoral votes for answering factual questions about
population, commerce, and government, the answers to be
checked in a forty-three-page reference booklet. The object of
the game was to win the presidency; the lesson of the game was
that statistical knowledge leads to political power.[39]

If statistics were really all that important, then adults as well
as children would want easy access to systematic reference works
in addition to the miscellaneous tables that cropped up in the
periodical literature of the day. The statistical manual, a new sort
of book intended to satisfy the public's appetite for facts and
figures, made its appearance in 1806 and was perfected by 1818,
perfection being defined as strict adherence to the objectivity of
bare numbers. Three such works were published during that period. The first was Samuel Blodget, Jr.'s, *Economica: A Statistical
Manual for the United States,* published in the nation's capital.
Blodget, an erstwhile insurance man with interests in Washington
real estate, announced that his book would "embrace every statistical point yet in our power"; but his "points" turned out to
be only those few statistics collected by the federal government,
for he compiled them solely from census reports and Treasury
documents on exports and imports.[40] What he offered was no
more than a convenient collection of existing data.

That in itself was sufficient justification for the book, for in 1806
there was no other even remotely comparable compilation. But
Blodget's work was flawed in the eyes of his contemporaries by
the dogmatic and opinionated text that accompanied, but made
little reference to, the numerical data. Blodget had emphatic views
on such subjects as the public debt, narcotic drinks, southern
indolence, the fair sex, and slavery, and he argued these with
slight regard to quantitative facts. For example, he presented
figures comparing the price of a slave to the worth of a free person
but observed that "this estimate, as far as it is opposed to slavery,
corresponds with that of every other rational calculating econo-

mist. But is this a subject for cold calculation? No, it is the cause
of feeling! of humanity! of virtue!''[41] While Blodget's was by no
means an unusual view of slavery in 1806, it was thought to be
out of place in a book that claimed to be a "statistical manual."
Though credited as a pioneer by other statistical writers of the
1810s, Blodget was sharply criticized by them for being inexact
and inaccurate. One writer observed that he had an "ardent" and
"speculative" mind and that, consequently, his statistics were
imprecise and his conception of the subject was indistinct and
undiscriminating. Another complained that Blodget was "deficient in the details" and gave too many of his own estimates.[42]

The next quantitative manual, Timothy Pitkin's *Statistical View
of the Commerce of the United States of America,* published in
1816, proposed to remedy the deficiencies of its ill-fated predecessor. Pitkin, a congressman from Connecticut, intended his
compilation primarily for the use of merchants and statists but
maintained that anyone could peruse it with profit, for "every
individual must feel an interest, in obtaining a knowledge of the
wealth and resources of his own country."[43] This confidence that
commercial statistics commanded universal appeal marks a new
development in social thought, and the theme was picked up and
elaborated on by the anonymous reviewer of Pitkin's manual in
the *North American Review.* The reviewer argued that the growing complexity and interdependence of society demanded accurate statistical information. Formerly a few great men had
determined the course of history, and the rest of the population—
huntsmen, fishermen, shepherds—was inconsequential, but now,
under the post-Revolutionary "arrangements of society," the
mass of men, with their combined "intellectual, moral, and physical powers," set the direction and pace of progress. Here he
meant more than the notion that political democracy results in
shared power; he was saying that the complexity of the economy
makes one man's actions have an impact on other people's lives.
The impact was not made equally by all, however. There was
inequality in economic power, resulting from the growth of commerce and the concomitant concentration of wealth, and that
meant that the "general will" had to be studied in its component
parts. Manuals like Pitkin's, the reviewer declared, admirably
revealed the component parts, "the internal proportions of power
and of influence" in the body politic. They should therefore "be
studied by all who aspire to regulate, or improve the state of the

nation; and even by all who would judge rightly of their duties
as citizens." The benefits of such books of "Political Arithmetick,"
as the reviewer termed it, lay in the harmony of thought they
would promote: "As men approximate towards certainty in their
judgments concerning the facts which indicate the condition of
the nation, parties will be likely to draw nearer to each other in
their plans of policy." In view of their social and political utility,
such compilations amounted to "something more than the gratification of mere curiosity" (the charge leveled by Madison's opponents nearly thirty years earlier); they should be required
reading for citizens, legislators, and commercial men alike, because statistics had become essential for calculating "the force
of the nation."[44]

Two years later, Adam Seybert, a Pennsylvania physician and,
like Pitkin, a member of Congress, published his *Statistical Annals*. Noting that Pitkin's book was excellent yet limited, Seybert
pushed beyond the realm of commerce to include detailed data
on population, the public lands, the post office, and the military.
In a further improvement, he often transformed sets of large numbers into ratios, such as the proportion of free persons to slaves
or of males to females, an innovation that the *North American
Review* hailed as a great boon to memory and understanding.[45]

Seybert addressed his "authentic book of reference" to two
sets of readers. First were the legislators (to whom he dedicated
the book), who not only would learn the facts they needed in
order to govern well but also would read in the statistics the
measure of their success:

> The state of civilized society and the resources of nations, are
> the tests by which we can ascertain the tendency of the gov-
> ernment. It is to the condition of the people, in relation to their
> increase, their moral and physical circumstances, their hap-
> piness and comfort, their genius and industry, that we must
> look for the proofs of a mild and free, or of a cruel and despotic
> government.[46]

The other audience consisted of those people, both in the United
States and abroad, who entertained "errors and misrepresenta-
tions" about the condition and progress of the country and who
needed to be set straight. Perhaps with this readership in mind,
Seybert managed to get the book circulated in Britain and translated into French in 1820.

The prestigious *Edinburgh Review* rendered a mixed verdict on Seybert's volume in a lengthy article in 1820. The critic credited it with giving "a pretty complete picture of America" but complained that the book had a disagreeably chauvinistic air; its boasts were, in his view, unwarranted. Since Seybert's book contained very little textual commentary, the charge related to the contents of the tables, which featured standard statistics of growth and progress. The critic challenged whether records of population, imports and exports, taxes, and the like could justify national pride when culture, genius, science, and art were missing not only in the statistical tables but in American society. The typical American, according to the *Review,* was "vulgar and arithmetical" and was in danger of becoming vain if he took these quantitative boasts seriously, for in fact they were "unspeakably ludicrous."[47]

The American press, by contrast, viewed Seybert's work as a monumental tribute to the virtues and accomplishments of America.[48] Seybert did not need to wave the flag; his facts spoke for themselves, communicating national pride to native and foreign reader alike. While the Scottish critic thought that Seybert's measurements constituted a false claim to greatness, American proponents of statistics agreed that grandeur could be captured by numbers. Statistics signaled America's rising power and glory; numbers commanded respect because they measured and weighed the very aspects of American life of which the people of the republic were most proud. Statists in the 1810s valued data that revealed material growth, progress, improvement, and abundance. Their choice of statistical facts was informed by a quantitative notion of achievement: more people, more trade, more daily newspapers, more gallons of lamp oil. No opinionated comment was necessary because the choice of facts already carried the assumption that *more* meant *better.*

There were, of course, many countable social facts whose growth and augmentation would not have been matters of pride to Americans. The statistics of pauperism, for example, might not have been something to brag about in the 1820s. Around 1820 there began a wave of reform movements in America, touched off by the evangelical Second Great Awakening. Many private agencies and volunteer groups with reformist agendas adopted the statistical approach to social facts in order to document the dimensions of the problems they were dedicated to eradicating.

They turned to numbers for the same reasons the early statistical writers had championed them: numbers were impressive because they were objective; quantitative statistics constituted proof of their claim (whatever the claim) and would persuade others to join with them; certain knowledge was the basis for automatic agreement. But these groups represent a new departure, for, unlike the early statistical writers, in applying numerical measurement to social problems they were exposing the quantum of unhappiness rather than the sum of happiness in society.

The earliest examples enlisting statistics in the cause of reform date from the late 1810s. In 1816, for example, the Philadelphia Society for Alleviating the Miseries of Public Prisons appointed a committee to prepare a statistical overview of the miseries of prisons; a year later the committee's report was presented to the public in the form of a pamphlet. It contained tables showing numbers of convictions per year for certain crimes in relation to liberalized laws on capital punishment, types of crimes, by year, and the race and sex of prisoners. In the text accompanying one table, which displayed the awesome and growing number of prisoners in jail still awaiting trial for each of five recent years, the committee observed that "having presented these reflections and truths to public notice, and beseeching a particular regard to their importance, we leave the subject to a virtuous community."[49] The facts spoke for themselves; no further commentary was necessary. The committee assumed that the virtuous public was also numerate and able to interpret the tables without difficulty.

The Massachusetts Society for the Suppression of Intemperance inaugurated statistical argument in 1816, in its fourth year of existence. Up to then the society had relied on morality and sermonizing to carry its temperance message, an approach it did not, of course, abandon, but the 1816 report emphasized that "facts and calculations" were the chief justification for the society's very existence. In this report the authenticity of the numerical facts was more asserted than proved, since the source of the data was not identified and the reader had to take it on faith that $33 million was spent on liquor, that 6,000 persons died annually of it, and that seven-eighths of the poorhouse inhabitants were intemperate. The report also charged that alcohol shortened life but conceded that it was "impossible to make any *accurate* calculation here"—the emphasis being added to lend an air of accuracy to the *asserted* facts.[50] By the early 1830s the temperance

advocates had made considerable leaps in numerical sophistication, for documentation of facts was now requisite. Temperance
reformers scouted jails and almshouses to count the intemperate
inmates. Their method of counting—asking the overseer of the
poor or the jailer—left something to be desired, but at least they
considered the problem of observer bias (and concluded that the
overseer's opinion was more valid than their own observation of
the inmates). However, they never managed to distinguish between correlation and causation in their statistics. Another eager
quantifier sent a questionnaire to Congregational and Presbyterian
ministers in New England, New York, New Jersey, Pennsylvania,
and Ohio to learn the extent of intemperance in another sort of
institution, the church. Ministers were asked to consult church
records of confessions and excommunications to see how many
of the total disciplinary actions involved alcohol. One hundred
thirty-five ministers managed to respond (even three self-reported
inebriates), and the quantifier thought this was a large enough
group to represent all churches. (Random sampling was a concept
unknown in 1831.) Data on over 1,600 church members over periods of time ranging up to fifty years boiled down to one authentic
fact: half of all sin was caused by intemperance.[51] A national
temperance convention in 1833 resolved that full and accurate
statistics should be the object of intense investigation and that
every local society should submit information on such points as
the population of their town, the number belonging to the temperance society, the number of groceries and taverns that refused
to sell spirits, the number of reformed drunkards, the number of
distilleries closed down, and the number of deaths, paupers, and
crimes attributable to drink.[52] In the mid- to late 1830s special
temperance almanacs publicized such statistics to promote the
cause.

Numbers were especially attractive to temperance groups because of the strategic importance of arguing that alcohol abuse
was a growing, not a constant, problem in the nineteenth century.
Alcoholic beverages had long been an acceptable form of drink
in America; what was new, they said, was overindulgence and
the resulting social costs. Temperance reformers found it easier
to claim that a new vice stalked the land, bringing destruction,
rather than to argue that a centuries-old practice, tolerated by
distinguished ancestors, was suddenly to be regarded as wrong.
The contemporary quest for quantification, coupled with an utter

lack of statistics for the prior era, allowed them to sustain their argument about growing abuse.[53] Numbers justified their society's existence, and numbers would supply the proof of the success of their efforts.

A third early example of statistics-gathering in the interest of public policy issues cropped up in 1817, when the Boston School Committee conducted an unprecedented ward-by-ward survey of children both in and out of school to see whether Boston's educational facilities matched the number of potential scholars. The committee found that only a very small fraction of the children of the town were attending school, a result that was both surprising and deflating to them.[54] The unusual aspect of this survey was that the results did not validate the preexisting views of the School Committee. The potential for pre-1840 quantitative survey research to surprise the investigators was predictably low, given the crude state of methods together with the unchallenged assumption that any number represented objective truth. A few years later, in 1821, the Massachusetts legislature appointed a committee to survey the condition of the state's paupers, expecting to find many of them languishing in custodial care that was not cost-effective. And that is just what they claimed to find; the committee complied with an exactness on the number of poor and the sums spent for poor relief that set a model for future investigations. Just three years later the New York legislature copied the Massachusetts survey by polling almshouses and sending questionnaires to the overseers of the poor.[55] One historian who has studied the reports has called them "path-forging" and "exceptionally thorough" in their empiricism, but he notes one oddity: despite the claim that legions of poor had been discovered, in fact the actual number was not large, perhaps 2 percent of the population. The reports established hard facts, but the meaning of those facts was submerged in the general rush to discredit the old method of handling pauperism.

Social problems and political issues had become part of the domain of number, and religion soon joined them. In 1817 the Boston Society for the Moral and Religious Instruction of the Poor surveyed the dimensions of irreligion in Boston by sending gentlemen to impoverished abodes to inquire how many attended public worship and how many owned Bibles. The findings convinced many citizens to subscribe to the society's program for distributing Bibles and setting up Sunday schools. In 1818 the society proudly reported on the number of new pupils, the average attendance at the Sunday schools, and the scriptural verses, hymns, and catechisms the pauper children had committed to memory since the preceding February: 54,029 verses, 1,899 hymns, and 17,779 answers to catechisms.[56] A way had been found to quantify piety.

T he rising popularity of statistics in the new republic allows a fresh angle of vision on the question of how Americans confronted the economic expansion that quickened after political independence was gained. In the 1790s, statistical thought offered a way to mediate between political ideas based on a homogeneous social order and economic realities that were fast undermining homogeneity. Inventories of descriptive facts about society were touted as providing an authentic, objective basis for ascertaining the common good. Complete possession of the facts, it was hoped, would eliminate factionalism and allow government to rule in the best interest of the public. Further, collections of social data were thought to constitute the proper scientific proof that the new experiment in republicanism did indeed benefit all citizens. By 1820 the subject matter of statistics had shifted somewhat, indicating alterations in the conception of the common good and in the proof of the republican pudding. Statistical information took on a specifically quantitative connotation and narrowed its focus to measurable facts about society. This meant that the benefits of republicanism were now most readily demonstrated by appeals to quantifiable facts, notably of demographic or economic character. The celebration of growth, so evident in statistical manuals like Pitkin's and Seybert's, thus became closely tied to the celebration of republican institutions. At this very time, however, statistical writers abandoned the idea that they were elucidating a single common good and moved toward an acceptance of competing economic interests. Avid collectors of statistics had come to recognize that distinctions and divisions in American society legitimately existed and had to be reckoned with. The particular distinctions they made—for example, between agriculture, commerce, and manufacturing—they regarded as inherent in their social order; empiricism, they insisted, was objective and value-free. But of course their empiricism was freighted with unacknowledged values. They counted acres of land and export tonnage, miles of road built and postage stamps sold, the inebriate poor and hymns memorized. The kinds of things they did *not* count and calculate in the 1820s—for instance, the number of slaveowners, black mortality, female illiteracy—tells as much about them and their society as the things they chose to notice.

6

The Census of 1840

In the early 1830s an English traveler, Thomas Hamilton, toured America and noted with distaste the natives' preoccupation with punctuality, measurement, and calculation, which he felt permeated life in the United States. For example, Americans seemed to be acutely aware of each other's financial status, and Hamilton reported uncomfortably that "I am already well informed as to the reputed resources of every gentleman of my acquaintance, and the annual amount of his disbursements." Among New Englanders, Hamilton observed, "Arithmetic, I presume comes by instinct among this guessing, reckoning, expecting, and calculating people." In New York he learned the high value set on punctuality and about the speed of American eating habits, and he warned that "no man should travel in the United States without one of Baraud's best chronometers in his fob. In no other country can a slight miscalculation of time be productive of so much mischief. Woe to him whose steps have been delayed by pleasure or business, till the fatal hour has elapsed, and the dinner-cloth removed." Philadelphia, with its grid pattern of streets, struck him as "mediocrity personified in brick and mortar. It is a city laid down by square and rule, a sort of habitable problem, —a mathematical infringement on the rights of individual eccentricity, —a rigid and prosaic despotism of right angles and parallelograms." With eccentricity eradicated by uniform city blocks, individuality distinguished primarily by income rank, and meals bolted so that this "calculating people" could return quickly to the countinghouse, it is no wonder that Hamilton was scornful of what he identified as an American absorption with numbers and quantities. In his eyes, and in the eyes of other

foreign travelers in the 1830s, an important aspect of the character
of American life had finally crystallized.[1]

European countries in the 1830s were of course not strangers
to modern calculation. In fact, academic and bureaucratic statistics in countries like England, Belgium, and Prussia quickly over-
shadowed American statistical efforts, and all of the major
developments in the mathematical theory of statistics in the nineteenth century originated in Europe.[2] But what struck foreign
travelers in America was the extent to which the ordinary inhabitants had incorporated and internalized a tendency to measure,
count, and calculate. With decimal currency and the newly popular double-entry bookkeeping, men of business in the 1830s were
accustomed to reckoning their financial worth with speed and
ease.[3] In the new pediatric-advice manuals, mothers could peruse
a table of distributions of 7,077 neonatal weights to see how their
own newborn babes measured up.[4] Even children might encounter
statistics in the pages of *Parley's Magazine,* where an 1835 article
conjured up rows of black children, ten abreast, stretching forty
miles in the distance, to represent vividly the vast numbers of
enslaved children in the South, as an illustration of the meaning
of statistics.[5] The many statistical presentations in newspapers,
periodicals, almanacs, and pamphlets of the Jacksonian years
demonstrate that there was a keen popular concern to know how
many paupers and how many millionaires there were, how many
drunks and how many prostitutes, how many scholars and how
many lunatics, how many Democrats and how many Whigs.[6] And
everywhere the rule of the clock had permeated American life;
cheap, mass-produced wooden clocks became standard household fixtures even in remote areas, forcing almanacs to abandon
the unevenness of solar time for the fiction of uniform days and
"mean" time.[7]

This full flowering of the quantitative mentality created buoyant
expectations for the upcoming decennial census of 1840. Proponents of statistics wanted to seize the opportunity to produce a
landmark statement of the progress and accomplishments of
America after fifty years of enlightened government. The preceding five federal censuses had gradually departed from the Constitution's bare requirement to count the total population, first by
creating, then by progressively refining, categories based on age,
sex, and color and, second, by including broad inquiries about
occupation and occasionally about the extent of manufactures—

information presumed to be useful in formulating legislation. But in the mid-1830s the idea took hold in several quarters that the census could become a full-dress inventory of the greatness of America and that even statistical information that had no conceivable bearing on potential legislation could legitimately be collected. The cause of national harmony would be served, it was argued, by displaying the vast interrelations of all sections of the country. The census of 1840 held promise of being a federal action that was both nonpartisan and nonsectional—something of a rarity in the 1830s. Census results, it was hoped, would unite calculating Americans in proud contemplation of their country.

As it happened, the census of 1840 turned out to be a complete fiasco. From its beginning in 1839, when Congress set up the machinery to carry out the enumeration, to its unsettling and inconclusive end in various congressional hearings, which dragged on into the 1850s, the census of 1840 engendered controversy, hard feelings, and angry dispute. The scope of the census was expanded, as many had hoped, to capture the grandeur of America, but assistant marshals in the field complained that their pay was too low, given the size of their territories and the length of the census schedules. People in several localities absolutely refused to answer the new questions until they could be assured by the secretary of state that the government had no malevolent purpose in asking them. Two antagonistic printers in Washington, D.C., each laid claim to the contract for printing the statistical compendium of the census, and each went ahead and printed it and presented Congress with inflated bills for the work. The final versions they printed did not lead Americans to join hands in nationalistic pride; instead, the census fed the fires of sectional conflict. The most controversial "finding" was that the black population of the North appeared to be beset with epidemic rates of insanity, which suggested to some that "science," as revealed by tables of figures, had proved freedom to be detrimental to blacks. To others these figures proved only that the entire census must be officially and entirely repudiated, to prevent America from becoming a laughingstock in the eyes of the European scientific and statistical community.[8]

It is one of those savory ironies of history that the census of 1840 turned out to be a landmark event after all, although not of the sort anticipated by the statistically minded men of the 1830s.[9] The commotion it created, both in the buoyant expectations it excited and in the angry aftermath, filled with disappointment and dispute, marks a turning point in the level of sophistication Americans had reached with respect to quantitative discourse. Skepticism about the reliability of numbers replaced the earlier naive view that all numerical facts were sacrosanct. No longer was it possible to maintain that agreement on facts would lead to political agreement, as men in the early years of the republic had thought. The errors, frauds, and political machinations surrounding the 1840 census also paved the way for the introduction of "experts" into government service for the taking of the 1850 census, when control of the enumeration was removed from the hands of unemployed diplomats, and the clerks were placed under more stringent supervision.

Because it proved to be so controversial, the census of 1840 illuminates in dramatic fashion the range of prevailing beliefs about quantitative rationality and numerical gullibility in antebellum America. The cast of characters in the episode was large and varied. It included politicians in the national arena, most of whom were bent on denying that slavery and sectionalism could be divisive federal issues and who looked to the census to sustain those views. It included a small circle of statistical experts, mostly educated men affiliated with the American Statistical Association, founded in Boston in 1839, or with academic institutions. These men yearned for international recognition of United States statistics, and they feared that European governments—not simply Belgium and Prussia but even France and Italy—were rapidly advancing beyond the United States by establishing official bureaus of statistics, a development that would be hard to reconcile with the supposed natural affinity of democratic republics for data about the people's general welfare. A third set of characters was drawn from the medical world of the 1840s, consisting of physicians who had been making assiduous private efforts to find correlations that would explain the rising insanity rate and who were outraged by the findings of the census. Another group was composed of proslavery apologists, who greeted the census results with glee. Finally, there was the clerical staff in Washington who had charge of the census, operating under the aegis of the Department of State. They were no mere recorders of an event played out on a larger stage; they were, it appears, quite central to the dramatic action.

The person most responsible for expanding the scope of the 1840 census was Joseph E. Worcester, a lexicographer and gazetteer-writer from Massachusetts, who for fourteen years, starting in 1831, edited *The American Almanac and Repository of Useful Knowledge*. From its beginning, the *Almanac* had championed the cause of statistics, which Worcester broadly defined as "an account of whatever influences the condition of the inhabitants, or the operations of government on the welfare of men in promoting the ends of social being, and the best interest of communities."[10] Year by year Worcester published a miscellany of statistical tables, on population and commerce, banks and schools, cotton production and canals—seemingly whatever quantitative snippets came his way. In the preface to his 1838 edition, written in the fall of 1837, he argued that a great mass of statistical information, regularly gathered, would be "attended with the most salutary consequences" for government and citizens alike, inasmuch as it would "advance the moral civilization and improvement" of the country. In particular, Worcester envisioned tomes full of data about the major economic interests of commerce, manufacturing, mining, and agriculture. His own experience with the *Almanac* had made it clear to him that data collection on this scale was beyond the capacities of individuals or even private associations, and so he recommended that the federal government transform the next census into an all-encompassing survey.[11]

Worcester's comments apparently came directly to the attention of President Martin Van Buren, who himself had conducted the 1830 census when he was secretary of state under Andrew Jackson. Van Buren was impressed with the suggestions and passed them along to his secretary of state, John Forsyth of Virginia. When Forsyth was later asked to explain to some uneasy citizens why there was a new raft of questions beyond the basic head count, he credited them to the influence of the editor of the *American Almanac* on the president.[12]

There were other men also trying to move the federal government into statistical work. In 1836 Francis Lieber, professor at South Carolina College, had presented a memorial to Congress pointing out that many European governments had statistical departments for the regular collection and classification of facts and that the United States should hardly do less. Lieber took it for granted that the audience for his memorial shared a common belief about the superiority of inductive reasoning: "It may be consid-

ered as one of the characteristic traits of our times, that, with
regard to many branches of importance to the well-being of society, a careful collection of detailed facts, and the endeavour to
arrive at general results by a comprehensive view and judicious
combination of them, have been substituted for mere theorizing."
What he was pushing for was a commitment by the federal government to underwrite the regular collection of facts, since the
scope of the project lay beyond the powers of individual citizens.
Congress took no action on Lieber's memorial, but his arguments
might well have helped smooth the way for an easy passage of
the census act two years later.[13]

A third figure who tried to exercise influence over the 1840
census was Archibald Russell, a twenty-eight-year-old New York
lawyer and reformer newly arrived in America from Edinburgh.
Russell wrote a lengthy book, *The Principles of Statistical Inquiry*
(1839), the subtitle of which made clear his intent: *As Illustrated
in Proposals for Uniting an Examination into the Resources of
the United States with the Census to be Taken in 1840*. In more
than a dozen chapters he expounded the virtue of statistics as a
way to assess the effects of rapidly advancing civilization. His
prediction that future historians would want and need this sort
of information was on the mark. "However advanced we may
appear in the arrangements for promoting the physical comforts
of all classes of the community, the details of our present social
organization are utterly unknown, and the writer in another century, who wishes to draw an accurate picture of our present condition, must pursue the same means as we have now to use in
depicting the manners of the 18th century." Russell proposed
adding to the census questions about the volume and value of
manufactures and agriculture, occupations and nativity, vital statistics, the dependent classes, education, religion, and taxation.
He even produced a sample of printed schedules. It is as if he
were angling for appointment as census superintendent by writing
a book that already did half the job. A decade later Russell did
have a hand in drawing up the 1850 census schedule, but what
his motivations were in 1839 is entirely cloudy.[14]

A distinguishing feature of Russell's book was his recognition
that numbers, for all their seeming clarity and precision, are not
always reliable, are not always "facts." He chastised other "vo-
taries of this science" for presenting numbers "decked out in all
the imposing business-like aspect of tabular views" so that they

intimidated readers from questioning them. Figures are not facts until it is ascertained that they are absolutely correct, Russell pointed out. With even the smallest errors, "arithmetical reasoning" leads to fallacious results, especially when estimates are multiplied by estimates. In demonstrating this kind of sensible caution, Russell not only removed himself from the general culture's enthusiasm for everything numerical but perhaps removed himself also from playing any larger role in the coming census.[15]

Worcester and Lieber soon joined with others to form a network of men with similar interests in statistics. Both were charter members of the American Statistical Association, headquartered in Boston. This organization had grown from a meeting of five friends in November, 1839, to a national organization a few months later, complete with constitution, bylaws, a publication, and fifty-four local members from New England, thirty-six honorary members, mostly public officials, and fifteen corresponding members, from as far away as Louisville and Little Rock.[16] At the founding meeting, almost no notice was taken of the 1840 census, slated to begin four months later. The apparent initial intent of the group was to foster private efforts to collect and diffuse statistical knowledge; they modeled themselves on the London Statistical Society, a private association founded in 1829.[17]

Quite a few of the members of the American Statistical Association were local historians and antiquarians, some of them leading members of the Massachusetts Historical and Genealogical Society or officers of the American Antiquarian Society. The somewhat parochial interests of this subgroup might have deflected the organization in its early years away from making pleas to the federal government, like the ones made by Lieber, Worcester, and Russell, for these were men who relished painstaking individual labors on narrow topics. Other founding members more clearly had quantitative interests and skills in their backgrounds. Lemuel Shattuck, the man who called together the first group of five, had once written a local history of his town, but by the late 1830s he was intensely interested in questions of public health and the registration of vital events.[18] He, more than anyone, steered the group into the mainstream of the international statistics community, toward government-sponsored public health surveys, and away from the sorts of topics that interested the antiquarians, whose concept of statistics led to projects to determine the number of carriages in Massachusetts in 1756 or the expenses of Governor Winslow's funeral in 1680.[19] Another fourteen of the fifty-four local members were medical doctors, several with publications on mortality or epidemiology. A few were men who had already participated in special state commissions to collect particular sorts of statistics, while others were prominent in reform movements of the day.[20]

Although the American Statistical Association did not begin life as a pressure group to lobby the federal government, it was soon forced to take on that role when the errors of the 1840 census surfaced. The significance of the ASA's founding in 1839–40 is that a network of skilled experts had just materialized, men who were temperamentally suited to the task of sifting through volumes of tables and who were competent to criticize the results of the census. They were also in touch with the European community of statisticians, and this made them sensitive to the repercussions a bad census would have on America's reputation abroad. To protect that reputation, and to establish their own as well, they were ready to spring into action.

Politicians in Congress in the late 1830s were receptive to the coming census, but they were not at all inclined to spring into action to implement it. A January 1839 article in the *United States Magazine and Democratic Review* on "The Approaching Census" wondered why, when the advantages of an expanded census were exciting general interest, Congress had "unaccountably neglected," thus far, to pass a census act. Although the Constitution directed that a census be taken every ten years, the practice in Congress had always been to pass a formal bill anew each decade, ordaining a particular mechanism for taking each census. (As an alternative, they might have handed the job over, for all time, to a continuously existing department.) But in the winter of 1838–39, other hot issues in the House—the Maine boundary dispute and a nasty and persistent disagreement over the use of public funds to purchase books for congressmen—pushed the census to the sidelines. The *United States Magazine and Democratic Review* praised the census extravagantly as a "neutral ground" on which warring parties could agree: "For the sake of variety, it will be quite refreshing to meet in truce on such a common ground, undistracted by a jealousy, an alarm, or an interest, of a partisan character."[21] It was precisely this that allowed Congress to feel confident that the passage of the census act could be handled with dispatch, and so the debate was put off until the very end of the final session of the Twenty-fifth Congress.

The committee that drafted the enumeration bill, as it was called, did not bring to its task much fresh thought about the census. The lengthy bill repeated the 1830 census act with only three changes, and it is very likely that two of these were added by amendment after the bill had reached the House floor.[22] The one change whose origins remain mysterious was the additional direction to count the insane and idiots, distinguished by race and by mode of support, whether public or private. The 1830 census had asked about the numbers of blind, deaf, and dumb, and it is possible that whoever drew up the bill in 1839 simply thought the same logic should be extended to another dependent class. Joseph Worcester had not suggested counting the insane; Archibald Russell had mentioned the possibility only briefly, in a discussion of pauperism, and in any case his book was published after the enumeration bill had been drawn up. However, Russell's reasoning for inquiring about the insane might well have been the same as the committee's: if government ought to provide support for paupers who could not support themselves, then it would be useful to know just how many such indigents there were who were truly dependent and not just lazy.[23] Thus the context for the whole group of questions about the handicapped was the issue of government welfare support and the work ethic. There is no evidence that medical specialists who dealt with the insane and who were following the fashion of quantitative analysis to discover the causes of insanity had any input at all on the enumeration bill.

The two other changes almost certainly added by the process of amendment appear at the very end of the act, following five pages of elaborate details about required oaths, double copies, mailing directions, and pay scales. Section 13 directed that a census of pensioners should also be taken, with names and ages of each former soldier, and that "statistical tables" should also be returned, containing "all such information in relation to mines, agriculture, commerce, manufactures, and schools, as will exhibit a full view of the pursuits, industry, education, and resources of the country." The survey of pensioners had specifically been requested by the president, in a message to Congress on the day the bill came to the final vote. His purpose was clear: the War Department wanted to purge the pension rolls of deceased pensioners and stop impersonators from defrauding the government.[24]

It was the second item in this section, calling for blanket statistics on America, that was breathtaking in its ambitiousness, naiveté, and vagueness. In contrast to the earlier part of the bill, which spelled out with great specificity the facts to be ascertained about the population, this final section in one quick half-sentence handed over an unprecedented authority to the State Department to inquire into nearly anything that could be construed as bearing on the economy and resources of the country. That the House did not trouble to define its desires for statistical information more clearly indicates either that its members did not realize the complexity of their order or that they trusted the State Department's judgment completely. Or perhaps it was simply that time was short and they really did not care.

No one in Congress was in the least disturbed by the precedent they had just established. The debate was consigned to the Committee of the Whole late in the afternoon of February 28, 1839, a decision that freed most members to take a long lunch and rest before the evening session; it also concealed from the eyes of posterity whatever discussion there might have been on Section 13, since debate in committee is not a matter of public record. When the evening session resumed, several more amendments were considered, and their substance indicates something of the state of mind of the Congress about statistical inquiries. The *Congressional Globe* reported that "Mr. Loomis moved an amendment, proposing to add certain items to the returns of the marshals relating to the ages of unmarried persons. It excited no little merriment in the committee, and was rejected." It is a trifle hard to recapture Loomis's humor, 140 years later, but possibly his joke had sexual innuendos, enhanced by a sense that the subdivisions of the enumeration schedule for the white population had reached a ridiculous intricacy. The House considered changing the day the census was to begin, lengthening the span of time for conducting it, and raising the pay for assistant marshals—none of them subjects likely to generate the kind of enthusiasm that Loomis's idea had. A more controversial issue was raised by a Vermont representative, who proposed a more "minute classification of the colored population as to age, &c., &c.; but it was rejected without a count." No one was willing to allow that the age structure of the black population should command as much attention as the one for whites. Since the 1820 census, blacks had been classified into six age groups bounded by the ages 10, 24,

36, 55, and 100. Archibald Russell complained that these categories were very unsatisfactory because they precluded any comparison with the white age structure, which was defined by different categories. The Scotsman was fresh from university and interested in scientific questions. He did not notice that the age boundaries for the black enumeration marked out convenient categories for assessing the economic utility of a labor force. Russell was keen to compare the mortality experiences of the two races in America; Congress, with the possible exception of the Vermont representative who raised the point, decidedly was not keen to facilitate such an inquiry.[25]

Congress adjourned, and its members returned home, probably satisfied that their decennial constitutional obligation had been properly fulfilled and that the census would proceed along the traditional lines. But for reasons unknown, Secretary of State Forsyth decided he would hire a chief clerk to superintend the census instead of doing it himself, as Van Buren had done in 1830 and John Quincy Adams had in 1820, when he was secretary of state under James Monroe. In mid-March, 1839, Forsyth hired William A. Weaver, a forty-two-year-old fellow Virginian with a rather spotty record in government service.

Weaver had entered the United States Navy at the age of fourteen and had seen battle in the War of 1812. For the next decade he followed a naval career, rising through the ranks with appointments in the Mediterranean. In 1824 he was cashiered, or, in the polite words of the *National Cyclopedia of American Biography,* he was "obliged to abandon service due to a misunderstanding." Thereafter he unsuccessfully sought employment with the State Department at diplomatic consulates in Havana and the Balearic Islands. For a brief time he worked for the Patent Office but lost that job after some dispute, of uncertain circumstances, in 1833. He then served on a claims commission to Mexico in 1834, and his letter of recommendation following that job praised him for being a hard worker who knew Spanish and could do "laborious accounts." This seems to be the only item, in an otherwise undistinguished dossier, that recommended him for the task of organizing and running the 1840 census.[26]

Weaver lost no time in hiring some help; within a month he had added to the payroll his brother, James G. Weaver, and a youthful relative of the State Department's bookkeeper. Instructions were sent to the federal marshals of each state and territory to begin the search for assistant marshals to be employed for taking the census. From April to December, 1839, Weaver and his two helpers planned all the questions and forms to be used in the census, secured the approval of the president, and printed and began to distribute the forms to the marshals.[27]

The forms Weaver devised generally showed good intentions in interpreting the census act, but they fell far short of perfection. The population schedule exactly followed the law's specifications for questions about age, race, sex, and the dependent classes, and to these inquiries Weaver added others, which would answer the purposes of Section 13 and which seemed logical to ask in the process of a house-to-house survey. To get statistics on the different sectors of the economy, Weaver provided seven columns for the enumerator to use to record the various employments of the population. The 1820 census had provided a precedent for this in asking about employment classified as agriculture, commerce, or manufacture. Weaver used the language of the 1839 census act for five of his categories—mining, agriculture, commerce, manufacturing, and the learned professions—and added two more, perhaps best understood as the inspiration of a former Navy man: ocean navigators and navigators on rivers. Right in the middle of the schedule he put the president's question on pensioners, with a wide column for the name of each person and a space for each age. Toward the end of the schedule he put in columns for recording information on schools, colleges, and universities and the numbers of their students. The final question, on literacy, asked for the numbers of white persons over twenty who could neither read nor write. Each question by itself represented an intelligent response to the mandate to collect general statistics, but taken all together, along with twenty-six columns for recording the white population, twelve for the free colored, twelve for slaves, and ten for the dependent classes, the extra questions turned Weaver's version of the census schedule into a nightmare for anyone with less than perfect vision. Each schedule contained seventy-four columns, with headings in microscopic type printed across the tops of two pages. It did not occur to Weaver that the format of the printed schedule might pose problems.[28]

An additional schedule devised by Weaver to yield statistics on the resources of the country further burdened the assistant marshals. It contained 214 inquiries, usually asking for the dollar amounts of capital invested and the dollar value of the end product for a long series of different economic endeavors. Less often, questions about the numbers employed and the quantity of production were inserted. Weaver probably had in mind neat tables that would facilitate comparison of the different interests by reducing them to the common currency, but instead he greatly complicated the survey of resources by emphasizing *value* instead of *quantity*. A farming family might engage in home production of cloth or shoes but find it difficult to set a dollar value on it. A tanner might know the number of saddles his saddlery turned out, but it required a second step to calculate the aggregate value of his output, especially if the market price changed during the year. And while the farmer and tanner stopped to figure, they might also wonder why the government wanted this information. By asking for dollar values, the census encouraged a suspicion that government taxation might be one consequence; after all, import and export records were entered as dollar values because of their relation to a customs duty. Perhaps Weaver thought this schedule would be easy for most Americans, for the reason pointed out by the foreign traveler Thomas Hamilton, that Americans appeared to have knowledge of their incomes and financial resources always at the tips of their tongues. If so, Weaver failed to appreciate that there might be a vast difference between the accurate numerical facts that statisticians desired and the easy quantitative bragging that Europeans found characteristic of Americans.[29]

In December, 1839, Secretary Forsyth submitted a progress report to both houses when the Twenty-sixth Congress opened. He suggested several sensible amendments to the census act, two of which have bearing on the controversy that later developed. As passed the previous March, the census act stipulated that the assistant marshals were to make two clean copies of their enumerations, post them in two prominent places for public inspection, and then turn them over to their marshals. The marshals were directed to send one copy to the Department of State and another to the clerk of the district's superior court, along with an attested copy of "the aggregate amount of each description of persons" to each place.[30] The court clerk's role was to lay the returns before a grand jury, but only so that the jury could make sure that they were done on time; the jury had no charge to inspect for accuracy. After that, the clerk was to send the enumeration and the aggregate totals to the secretary of state, who would print

them in 10,000 copies. Forsyth suggested changing this complicated process at two points. He recommended that the second
manuscript copy remain in the hands of the clerks, for safekeep-
ing; one copy sent to Washington was enough. And he further
suggested that the final printed version be a corrected copy of the
aggregate returns. In 1830 the State Department had checked the
addition of the marshals and found it occasionally in error, but
both the original and the corrected versions had been printed, he
claimed, because the law designated that the marshal's returns
be printed, making no allowance for arithmetic mistakes.[31] Forsyth secured agreement from Congress that the State Department
had the right to make corrections, both in addition and in classification of the population, and that the corrected version would
stand as the official version.[32] The result of these amendments
was that tampering would be hard to detect from the printed
version alone. That criminal thought undoubtedly did not cross
Forsyth's mind; otherwise he would not have suggested leaving
one of the two original copies in each state.

Between December, 1839, and June 1, 1840, when the census
was to begin, William Weaver apparently felt he had little to do.
In February he received official status as "superintending clerk,"
along with a raise in pay and raises for his staff, which now
numbered three, with the addition of another Weaver, his son.
But Weaver was restless and ill informed about the nature of his
job, for in May he applied for a post as secretary of the Mexican
Claims Commission on the surprising grounds that his work with
the census was nearly done. The laborious business of aggregating
the returns—the very work Weaver was said to be good at—
seemed unimportant to him, something that could be left to subordinates. That the superintendent of the census could be so offhand about the job did not bode well for the quality of the final
product. Weaver's resignation was not accepted by Forsyth.[33]

Even when the returns began to arrive, Weaver showed reluctance to dig into his work. The earliest returns came from Maine
and New Hampshire in the late summer, but it was not until the
end of November, 1840, that Weaver officially promulgated instructions to his clerks about the procedures to use in correcting
returns.[34] In February, 1841, the Senate passed a resolution de-
manding a progress report from the State Department. Weaver's
reply—which in effect constituted the department's report—fas-
tened on delays from the field and delays by the printers in getting

the right kind of typeface.[35] Displaying an attention to detail that
came to the fore whenever he felt challenged, Weaver included
in his report two tables showing the stage of preparation for each
of the forty-one census districts and also lumped in all the cor-
respondence between himself and the printers, the firm of Blair
& Rives, about completion timetables, bindings, type styles, and
paper quality.

Francis P. Blair and John Rives were the official printers to
Congress. They were entitled to print all the documents emanating
from Congress as well as to prepare the *Congressional Globe*, a
weekly journal of the proceedings of both houses. Kentucky men,
they had been brought to Washington by Andrew Jackson in 1830,
and their Democratic sympathies did not prevent them from getting government contracts as long as the Democrats were in
power. The census act had specified that the official printers to
Congress would be awarded the job of printing the enumeration
of inhabitants, and Weaver had duly handed the work to Blair
& Rives. The census act said nothing, however, about who should
print the added statistical compendium; it is clear from Weaver's
progress report to the Senate, of February, 1841, that he was
proceeding on the assumption that Blair & Rives would naturally
do that job as well. However, a week and a half later, a Whig
administration was inaugurated in Washington, and Weaver's new
boss, Daniel Webster, secretary of state to William Henry Harrison, was not so friendly to Blair & Rives. Out of this combination
of ingredients the printing-contract controversy was born.

It should be noted at the outset that the imbroglio over the
printing of the census was very far from the center of the political
stage in Washington in 1841. The sudden death of President Harrison, the *Armistad* incident, the conflict between the new president, John Tyler, and Congress over bank vetoes, the mass
resignation of the cabinet, all created an atmosphere in which the
census was dwarfed in importance. Further, the swift stream of
commanding political events helps explain why, in hearings on
the census in 1842 and again in 1844, the memories of witnesses
tended to be very hazy and incorrect.[36] The census simply was
not important to Daniel Webster in 1841, aside from his interest
in seeing a printer friendly to the administration reap the rewards
of printing it. For the next six months he left the whole matter
to Weaver and his staff, which had now grown to include two

more Weavers—females this time—and a clerk named
J. E. Weems.[37]

Perhaps the only person in Washington who cared much at all
about the census in the summer of 1841 was John Quincy Adams.
Adams wanted to procure the aggregate returns as soon as possible so that he could pass them on to a constituent and friend,
Joseph E. Worcester of the *American Almanac*. The *Almanac*
usually went to press in September, so in early summer Adams
dropped by the State Department one day to inquire about the
returns. Webster told him that they were not quite finished, and
then apparently he put pressure on Weaver's staff, for the next
morning clerk Weems called on Adams and gave him a brief table
of total population by states and territories. That afternoon Adams
presented a resolution in the House calling for the returns, officially, and a few days later Weaver complied, presenting the same
brief table. Adams, however, knew that Worcester wanted more
detailed data for his *Almanac,* so he kept after Webster, asking
for the loose sheets of the official printed version as soon as they
came off the press. In early October, 1841, Adams conveyed to
Worcester the loose sheets in unopened packages; he had not
been interested enough to look at them himself. Worcester rushed
them into print in his 1842 *Almanac* with the general comment
that the sixth census was an improvement over the last but was
still far from perfect; it needed to be "better digested," he said.
But he did not have time to scrutinize the results.[38]

Meanwhile, in Washington, Webster began to assert his authority over Weaver for the first time. An act of Congress on
September 1 directed Webster to produce the statistical-compen-
dium part of the census, beginning with the taking of bids for the
job. Webster ordered Weaver to contact Thomas Allen, printer
of *The Madisonian,* a paper soon to be the official organ of the
administration. Weaver stalled, objecting that Blair & Rives had
already begun the work. Webster's authority prevailed, however,
and at the end of September Weaver wrote Allen to award him
the job officially. By the law of September 1, the secretary of
state, not Weaver, clearly had the legal right to award the job; on
the other hand, Webster did not take bids on it, as required. Thus
both printers felt they had strong legal grounds for claiming that
the other's contract was void, and both proceeded to print the
compendium. Weaver stood to profit from the Blair & Rives contract, since he held the copyright on their edition and expected

financial gain from their printing, so he continued to supply them with copy. Webster plumped for Allen because of political connections and because he was angry at Blair & Rives for leveling charges of corruption against him in the *Globe* in the summer of 1841. That the whole dispute consumed Weaver's attention but hardly fazed Webster is not surprising, since the latter was a prominent man with many issues claiming his time, while the former was a subordinate clerk whose family enterprise was in danger.[39] Weaver began to fret over his pay and submitted an ingenious claim for a 900 percent raise, based on a comparison to Tench Coxe's salary for the 1810 census of manufactures: the sum Coxe received, divided by the number of ems of type used in printing the 1810 volume, yielded an unusual wage rate that would reward Weaver handsomely, in view of the much larger number of ems of type he anticipated the 1840 compendium would require. Webster, unimpressed with this ridiculous application of the Rule of Three, asked the attorney general to prosecute Weaver. In the spring of 1842 the feud reached its final stages in congressional hearing rooms, and Weaver finally resigned.[40]

The whole sorry dispute over the printing contract did not resolve any problems for the principals, but it does resolve some key questions for historians interested in what went wrong with the 1840 census. Because the competing claims of the printers led to a series of congressional hearings, and because each hearing generated a report with supporting documentation, we have an abundance of information about how the 1840 census was conducted that would otherwise have been irretrievably lost. The committee reports make it clear that the clerical work of correcting the census proceeded in an atmosphere of hostility and ill will. Demonstrating the grandeur of America with science was not uppermost in the minds of the Weaver family. They were mainly interested in getting the job done and getting it to the favored printer. It becomes easier to understand how egregious errors could have slipped by them.

The first person to call public attention to the possibility of errors in the census of 1840 was Edward Jarvis, a Massachusetts medical man and specialist on the subject of insanity.[41] Jarvis was living in Louisville, Kentucky, in the summer of 1842, when the Blair & Rives printed edition of the enumeration came into his hands. The first thing he noted was that the total number of insane persons and idiots fell short of what he believed to be the actual

numbers, based on several prior state surveys and his contacts
with various lunatic asylums. But what appeared even more extraordinary to Jarvis was that the returns showed that the black
population in the North suffered from insanity at a rate more than
ten times greater than blacks in the South. Jarvis calculated the
proportion by dividing the numbers of black insane and idiots in
each state by the total black population of the state, and he found
that an astonishing gradient seemed to exist: the further north
one went, the likelier it became for blacks to be insane. Maine
topped the list, with 1 in every 14 black persons so designated;
in Louisiana only 1 in every 5,650 was returned as insane. Over
all, in the North, 1 in 162.4 blacks was insane or an idiot, while,
in the South, the ratio was 1 in 1,558. Insanity among the white
population exhibited a fairly even prevalence, Jarvis said, with
ratios of 1 in 970 in the North and one in 945.3 in the South. In
his first musings on the subject, published in a September issue
of the *Boston Medical and Surgical Journal,* Jarvis fell back on
the popular association between rising insanity and the worries
and burden of life in a rapidly commercializing economy: slavery,
while "refusing man many of the hopes and responsibilities which
the free, self-thinking and self-acting enjoy and sustain, of course
. . . saves him from some of the liabilities and dangers of active
self-direction."[42]

Not content with his own explanation, Jarvis continued to puzzle over the meaning of the numbers, and two months later he
published another communication in the *Boston Medical and Surgical Journal,* virtually retracting his first article. In his first calculations he had noted one large error in the census for Worcester,
Massachusetts, and had corrected it, because he was familiar with
the lunatic asylum there and knew that the inmates were white,
whereas the census reported 133 black lunatics. This error, so
patent, prompted him to wonder whether there might be other
errors of the same type for Maine, the state with the highest ratio
of insane blacks, so he began to look over the printed tables with
more care. The Worcester error had been easy to spot, since it
was a large number transposed into the wrong column by one
simple error and easily verified as untrue. But in Maine there
were no large concentrations of insane persons. The insane and
idiot blacks were scattered throughout the state, one in one town
and two or three in another, for a grand total of ninety-four. So
Jarvis checked for internal consistency and was mortified to find

that many of the towns reported to harbor insane blacks in fact
had no black population at all! A study of the printed statistics
of other northern states turned up the same pattern: towns all
over the North with completely white populations were stealthily,
incrementally swelling the total of insane and idiot blacks in that
far right-hand column of Weaver's census schedule. "How far
these reports should impair our confidence in the other parts of
the statistical report, I leave to the reader to determine for himself," Jarvis said, with restraint. But he was not averse to pointing
a finger of blame. "I have no doubt that these errors must have
arisen at Washington, in the arrangement and condensation of the
thousand reports from as many different marshals." Indeed, there
seemed no other way to explain such extensive errors. Jarvis
hoped that the original manuscript returns could be reexamined
and the errors corrected.[43]

Others besides Jarvis had begun to notice peculiarities in the
printed versions of the census. George Tucker, professor of political economy at the University of Virginia, had embarked on
a lengthy analysis of the census in serial installments in *Hunt's
Merchants' Magazine* in July, 1842. In the first few articles he
discussed the history and purpose of the United States census
and the general population increase of the preceding fifty years.
In the third installment, of September, 1842, he compared the
increase of whites and blacks since 1830 and found the rate for
whites to be much greater—34.66 percent as compared to 23.4
percent for blacks—over the space of a decade. "These differences are so great, compared with any before experienced, as to
cast a shade of suspicion over the accuracy of the last enumeration, if they were not capable of explanation." Tucker then proceeded to try to explain it, but despite his heroic efforts, invoking
forced emigration of slaves to Texas, higher black mortality, and
even abolitionism, he could not satisfy himself that he had accounted for the deceleration in the rate of black population
growth.[44]

Tucker did not notice anything strange about the statistics on
insanity. In his fifth installment, published in January, 1843, he
passed over the question quickly because he computed ratios for
the entire country by race instead of looking at insanity state by
state or region by region. Over all, 1 in 978 blacks was said to be
insane; this was almost exactly the same as the ratio for whites,
1 in 977. Tucker's oversight was remedied in the March issue of

Hunt's, when an anonymous writer contributed a "Table of Lunacy in the United States" based on the figures given in Tucker's article which Tucker himself had failed to analyze. This table arranged the states from North to South and displayed the eerie gradient in the ratio between black insane and black population, just as Jarvis had done. But this author worked independently of Jarvis, for he made one consistent error. He neglected to add the black male and female population together to get the total denominator of his ratio (it was another failing of the Weaver census schedule that nowhere was the total black population given), and so this writer's ratios were double those that Jarvis had arrived at. Having calculated fantastic ratios, such as 1 in 6.7 for Maine, the author coolly suggested that these were "remarkable" statistics and drew no further conclusions. In the May issue of *Hunt's* yet another anonymous author pointed out the error in the denominator of the previous contributor's calculation and presented corrected figures. Still, caution was the keyword in interpreting these findings: the author worried that the census, "that most valuable document, will be wrested from its proper purpose to give a currency to error, by lending to it the seeming sanction of mathematical reasoning." It would be well, he concluded, "to suspend our opinion, until we have further evidence or explanation."[45]

Such restraint was not shared by all members of the popular press. In June, 1843, the *Southern Literary Messenger* presented a disturbing image of mentally crazed blacks running amok all over America. The *Messenger's* ratios for insanity varied somewhat from Jarvis's and from the piece in *Hunt's,* supporting the editors' contention that they had independently arrived at their conclusions, which, they said, were based on the official version of the census and its replication in the 1842 *American Almanac.* (The capacity of even highly educated nineteenth-century men to produce original quotients, given the same set of data for numerator and demoninator, produces lucky clues for those who trace chains of influence from one statistical author to another.) In great detail the article justified its belief that the census had uncovered a fundamental truth about the races in America. How could there be collusion among a thousand assistant marshals in the field? The uniformity of the results fitted well with other statistical facts about free blacks—their high rates of incarceration in jails and prisons, their high mortality, and their pauperism.

"The free negroes of the northern states are the most vicious persons on this continent, perhaps on the earth," said the *Southern Literary Messenger*. It was perfectly understandable why the New England states had the most vicious and crazed blacks: these were the hotbeds of abolitionism and the refuges of runaway slaves. Southern slaves were happy and carefree—their rates of mental stability attested to that—and fugitives had to be somewhat crazed to want to leave.[46]

The material on insanity from the census had enormous appeal for proslavery advocates like the *Southern Literary Messenger*. Not only did it appear to substantiate the argument that slavery was good for the blacks; it also called up vivid images of maniacs at every northern crossroads and lent itself perfectly to the kind of emotional hyperbole that was so often employed by defenders of slavery. The *Messenger* article did not fail to take advantage of the extravagant possibilities in the data, but what is of interest here is that, by marshaling additional quantitative arguments to allay suspicions about the accuracy of the census, the article marked a new stage in the slavery debate. In the 1830s, abolitionists and their opponents for the most part stood on moral and emotional grounds in their arguments, with personal testimony about slavery the backbone of their proof; after the early 1840s, verbal duelers increasingly chose as their weapons quantitative facts taken from the public record or from institutional records. Moralism and sentiment did not disappear, as the popularity of *Uncle Tom's Cabin* attests, but they were joined by hard-nosed statistics offered by both sides. Preachers and orators mounted platforms with notes on homicide rates, army desertions, per capita income, illegitimacy, and bank-failure rates to bolster assertions about the comparative virtues of the North and the South.[47] The growing use of statistics to defend or attack slavery paralleled the emergence of slavery as a central and acknowledged political issue.

The point of view expressed by the *Southern Literary Messenger* received widespread attention in late 1843, prompting Edward Jarvis to write another, more comprehensive, rebuttal to the census findings on insanity. His piece, published in the January, 1844, issue of the *American Journal of the Medical Sciences,* essentially repeated the charges of inaccuracy published earlier in the *Boston Medical and Surgical Journal,* where his proof rested on the internal inconsistencies of the printed version of the census. In deference to "the honour of our country, to medical science, and to truth," Jarvis suggested that Congress investigate the handling of the returns at the State Department, in order to locate and correct the errors.[48]

In order to speed the process, Jarvis, now back in Boston, joined with a few other members of the American Statistical Association to prepare a careful memorial to Congress, identifying the causes of their concern and calling for an investigation. This time, however, he went a step further in locating the problems. He visited the Massachusetts clerk's office to consult the local copy of the original manuscript returns. For the first time he had a clue that the errors might not have been made in Washington, for the manuscript returns revealed that the individual assistant marshals had indeed entered digits in the columns for "insane and idiot" blacks in families where there were no blacks. In their memorial, Jarvis and his coauthors specified several such errors, naming the families and the assistant marshals involved, and demanded to know how this perplexing error could have happened.[49]

The purpose of memorializing Congress was to put that body on notice that the census contained errors. The American Statistical Association did not presume that the federal government could uncover the error by itself. Jarvis and several other members of the ASA were also members of the Massachusetts Medical Society, and it occurred to them that their network of medical men throughout the state might prove useful in getting to the bottom of the mystery. So in May, 1844, at the biannual business meeting of that group, a committee was appointed to study the census error on insanity. Over the summer the committee sent circular letters to physicians, clergymen, and postmasters in each Massachusetts town said to contain insane blacks. According to the manuscript census, these towns contained 173 insane and idiot blacks; according to the answers to their survey, only 21 such people had existed in 1840. Further, they inquired about each individual family, and they were informed that "many" had insane or idiot *white* members *not* recorded by the census. In other words, in these households the error had been caused by entering the insane white in the wrong column, just as had happened in the case of the inmates of the Worcester asylum.[50]

But the question remained: how could this error have been committed all over the North, with especial frequency in New England, and by so many assistant marshals operating independently? Why were there not similar errors in the South? To get answers to these questions, a full investigation of all the states' manuscript returns was needed.

All Jarvis needed was one sympathetic congressman to introduce the subject of the census, and he had one in John Quincy Adams. Adams was deeply concerned about the proslavery uses to which the census was being put, and so on February 26, 1844, he moved in the House to ask the secretary of state to look into the allegations of errors in the returns "as corrected by the Department of State." In his diary Adams confided, "I expected objection to this call, but there was none." In general, the mood of the congressmen was favorable to the promotion of statistics; just a month earlier they had established a Select Committee on Statistics to look into the feasibility of creating a permanent Bureau of Statistics in the Treasury Department. Whoever might conceivably have had reservations about Adams's motion, as he proposed it, would certainly have had no quarrel with the way it was finally worded on the printed resolution sent to the secretary of state. A typographical error changed the date in the phrase "as corrected at the Department of State in 1841" to 1843, allowing a loophole, which the secretary, now John C. Calhoun, slipped through. In May, Calhoun replied, informing the House in one pithy paragraph that, since no census returns had been corrected in 1843, there was nothing for him to investigate.[51] Adams, outraged, tried to mobilize the House into a debate on the census, but he failed. Within a few days he brought in the memorial from the American Statistical Association, prepared by Jarvis, explaining the errors on insanity and pointing to other errors as well, but he failed to get the necessary two-thirds vote to present the memorial to the House. The best he could do was to secure a promise from the clerk of the House that the memorial would be looked over by the new Select Committee on Statistics. Adams was not satisfied, and, even though the chairman of the committee was a New York man, he worried that "the slave oligarchy will yet prevail to suppress this document."[52]

He was right. The findings about blacks in the census were simply too useful to southerners to repudiate. Calhoun had already made good use of them in April, 1844, when he defended the annexation of Texas as a slave state against European critics with the argument that slavery, much as it distressed whites, was actually a blessing to blacks, as the United States census demonstrated. When he wanted to, Calhoun could appear to take the census very seriously and present himself as a disciple of statistics, ready to base his faith and his political life on a foundation of quantitative facts. In private, when Adams confronted him personally about his views on the census, Calhoun tossed off the subject by saying, according to Adams, that, "where there were so many errors, they balanced one another, and led to the same conclusion as if they were all correct." Adams was stunned, seeing Calhoun as devoid either of "honesty or of mental sanity." He determined to pursue the investigation further.[53]

His pursuit lasted nearly a year, and it always hit dead ends. The Select Committee on Statistics went nowhere with it and offered the bland opinion that a Bureau of Statistics would heal the wounds of the 1840 census by producing facts to make the country feel proud and unified. Just how the proposed bureau would avoid the problems of the census was nowhere discussed. (The bureau was established soon after, in 1845, and, in the two short years that it existed, it produced two hefty volumes, consisting chiefly of financial statements from every bank in the country.)[54] The Senate was prodded to consider the memorial of the ASA, and its Library Committee, to whom the matter was referred, sleepily reported that, whatever the problems might have been in 1840, they hoped they would not be repeated in 1850.[55] Adams managed to get another select committee appointed in the House, in early 1845, with himself as chair, to consider directly the memorial of the American Statistical Association. About half the members of the committee were total newcomers to Congress, some having arrived just the week before. They did not show up for the meetings of the committee at all or else came so late that there was no time for business. Adams gave up, especially after the State Department issued its report, which was lengthy.

The State Department's report promised to produce the most substantial progress yet in the investigation. In January, 1845, the House again voted to ask Calhoun to investigate the census, recommending that he appoint a "thorough" investigator, and he did—he chose William A. Weaver, indeed a thorough man. Oddly, the very reasons one would think would disqualify Weaver from the job were the ones Calhoun praised in asking him to do it. As the man who had been in charge, Weaver was the most likely person to know what had gone wrong. That much was certainly true, but whether Weaver would be willing to admit it was another question—one that Calhoun may or may not have considered.

Weaver defended his census, of course, with the tiresome thoroughness that other House investigating committees involved in the printing-contract dispute had come to expect of him.[56] He combed through the ASA memorial, jumping on every doubtful statement he could find, cautioning the critics to be more tolerant of small errors, since they themselves were prone to err. For example, he suggested that they erred in assuming that the manuscript census at the clerk's office in Boston was a legitimate source; since it was not the "corrected" copy, it was therefore not official and not reliable. He neatly overlooked the point that not all the "corrections" might have been warranted. To prove his point, he added up the number of red marks that had been made by the correctors in Washington on the Massachusetts census and found an astonishing 20,350. That did not mean that that many separate errors had been made; the true number of errors in Massachusetts was only 233. But any error caught on one page of a township's enumeration had to be carried over in the addition of all successive pages of that town; this was what had led to the proliferation of red marks. Weaver was a tricky fellow when it came to beating the quantifiers at their own game.[57]

Weaver's basic defense of the prevalence of black insanity was based on what he claimed were legitimate ambiguities in the assistant marshal's instructions. Vagrants and transients in each district were supposed to be recorded by name in the list of householders, even though they had no household. But since they had no fixed residence, they could be recorded anywhere in the district, even at the end of the entire schedule. In Weaver's view, the crazed blacks of the North were very likely to be vagrants; when the enumerator encountered one, he would record him in the column for his disease, but he might easily forget to enter him in the householders' list, or he might enter him only at the end of the district. Thus the only proper denominator for computing the proportion of insane blacks was the total black population of the entire district, not the total for each town, which Jarvis had used. Weaver's logic in the whole vagrancy argument could make sense only to someone who had never consulted a census schedule. To enter an insane or idiot person anywhere in the course of canvassing the district, an enumerator had to place him in the context of *some* household.

Weaver passed over the difficulty of that problem and moved on to demolish another objection. The household investigation carried out by the Massachusetts Medical Society was invalid, according to Weaver, because it was entirely possible that some insane blacks had been entered a line or two above their proper household because the long schedule was printed on two sides of one large sheet of paper, causing a break in the row for each household. To Weaver these were errors of no consequence, since the desired information was simply the total number of such people; the government did not need to know what particular household each was lodged in. A similar ambiguity occurred in the column on scholars, although Weaver did not point this out. Some enumerators asked for the numbers of scholars in each household and entered it in that column, but others waited until they came to a schoolmaster's house and entered his total number of pupils in the row for his household, even though they did not live there. To Weaver, this sort of difference was immaterial.[58]

To defend the thoroughness of the census, Weaver included in his report the instructions given to the enumerators, the oaths they took, the procedures for verification and transmission of copies, and the policies on red-ink corrections at the State Department. A final precaution there, instituted by Weaver, was that a coterie of "diligent" clerks should double-check a fixed proportion of each parcel of returns for errors committed by the first team of examiners, and pay had been withheld from careless clerks who let errors slip by, leading to "loud and denunciatory complaints" to the secretary of state. (It is not hard to imagine which team the Weaver family was on.) The effect of this section of the report was to make Weaver look like a competent and sure-handed administrator.[59]

A last section of Weaver's defense consisted of further statistics of the sort put forward by the *Southern Literary Messenger,* which supported the view that northern blacks were more vicious, criminal, and disabled than either northern whites or southern blacks. A comparison of the ratios of deaf, dumb, and blind blacks in the 1830 and 1840 censuses demonstrated the same consistent gradient, from Maine to Louisiana, and prison statistics told the same story of abundant black vice. Faced with such unarguable evidence, why should anyone doubt that insanity and idiocy could follow the same remarkable pattern?[60]

Weaver could not resist taking a few parting shots at Massachusetts in his closing paragraph. Why was only this one state complaining? No one else found anything objectionable in the census. He implied that the memorialists were a small group of cranks, not worthy of further notice. And what matter if the 133 lunatics in Worcester were black or white: "They are entered in the appropriate columns according to their sex, age, and condition, and of course"—the final insult—"are represented in the legislature."[61] This sort of elegant jab, suggesting obliquely that the Massachusetts legislature represented idiots, and, indeed, the cleverness of the whole report reveal Weaver as a man of more ability than his prior record of service would lead one to think. Forsyth probably did not overestimate him in choosing him to head the census. The caustic humor that surfaced in this document might also explain why Weaver had such a poor track record at keeping jobs.

Weaver's report brought the official investigation to a close. Jarvis and his networks of statists and doctors ceased to pursue the matter, as did John Quincy Adams. In the early 1850s a rediscovery of the lunacy statistics, published anew, led Jarvis to construct a final statement on the matter, summarizing his earlier descriptions of the error in Massachusetts and offering the explanation for it that seemed most reasonable to him. Two factors accounted for the error, in his mind. The chief cause was the fact that the column for insane and idiot whites was right next to the one for blacks; it was therefore easy, in such a lengthy schedule, for someone to transpose numbers either way. A secondary cause was that the census passed through five stages of copying, from the original returns to the final printed version, and at each stage errors could be, and were, made.[62]

Historians have been content with Jarvis's explanation. He had investigated the error more thoroughly than anyone. He had begun with the presumption that the guilt lay in the State Department but had changed his mind about that after seeing the original returns. His revised explanation sounds very plausible and charitable, and further suspicion at this late date might appear to be otiose, while the work involved in checking out suspicions would be time-consuming.

Nevertheless, questions remain. Why the uniform gradient from North to South? Why that particular transposition of columns, and always in the direction of white to black?

Now that the manuscript census returns are widely available on microfilm, Jarvis's approach to the problem can be tested on states besides Massachusetts. It is impossible, of course, to duplicate the town-by-town survey conducted by the Massachusetts Medical Society, to learn the truth about the actual existence of insanity in each family listed as having an insane black inhabitant. But a study of the returns for several key New England counties suggests some answers to the mystery. Films for Oxford and Lincoln counties in Maine and for New London county in Connecticut were made from the copy of the census located in the National Archives, and they contain the assistant marshal's lists, the signed testimonials by the proper sequence of local authorities, an aggregate page for each town, and the corrections made by the State Department clerks.

Four striking facts emerge from a study of these films. First, in all cases, the insane and idiot blacks were listed in all-white households, and there were no vagrant free blacks listed within that enumerator's district to validate Weaver's overly generous scenario of what might have happened. Second, in more than half the households in question there were aged whites—males or females aged 70 to 79, 80 to 89, and 90 to 99. Possibly some of these elderly people were senile and therefore candidates for the label "idiot." Third, the headings of the columns in the enumerator's printed tally sheets differ from the headings in the editions of the census printed by Blair & Rives and by Thomas Allen. The meaning of the headings was the same, but the way the type was set up on the schedule made it very easy for idiot whites to be recorded in the insane and idiot blacks column. On the tally sheet the word "idiot" was not included in the second tier of headings for whites, and the enumerator's eye might easily have traveled on to the next place on the second tier where the word "idiot" appeared, failing to notice the word "colored" (i.e., black) in the heading above. Fourth, it appears that the returns from the Maine counties were not checked over as carefully as the ones from Connecticut. They were the first to arrive at the State Department, and it was several months before Weaver issued his correction procedures.[63] On some returns there are no signs of correction at all; on others the addition has been corrected but other errors still remain. For example, in the town of Nobleborough, in Lincoln County, the addition on one page of the return was found to contain four errors, and the aggregate page was adjusted accordingly; however, the corrector did not notice that four idiot and insane blacks appeared on the aggregate page also, whereas no one of that description was recorded anywhere in the listing by household. The Maine returns are also lacking the signed statements of certification that are scrawled all over the returns for Connecticut, Massachusetts, and presumably other states as well. The returns for Scituate, Massachusetts, for example, bear these notes: "Examined, J. E. Weems"; "Reexamined and found many errors. D. H."; and "Corrected, J. E. W." In being the first state census to be completed and corrected without well-developed procedures, Maine's is likely to have contained more than the average numbers of errors.

Suppose, then, that a certain number of senile whites were considered idiots in the common parlance but not insane; suppose that some fraction of them were entered in the column for insane and idiot blacks merely because the word "idiot" was not prominent in the section for whites, while the word "colored" was not prominent in the section for blacks. It stands to reason, then, that a series of ratios comparing insane blacks to the total black population would exhibit an interesting gradient from North to South and from East to West, because there was an excess of elderly people in the East and a deficiency of black people—the denominator of the ratio—in the North. In regions with large black populations, such as the South, the small numbers of errors recording senile whites would fade into insignificance. In regions with just a handful of blacks, a similarly small number of such errors would boost the ratios of insanity to alarming proportions.

That no one in the 1840s offered this explanation in all the commotion over the census shows something about the degree of quantitative sophistication they all shared. Instead, the grounds of their debate centered on the trustworthiness of quantitative facts: were these true facts, or had a fraud been perpetrated in the Department of State? Weaver claimed they were true because there had been no fraud, because other quantitative facts supported the substance of the charge, and because it was politically expedient for him to please John C. Calhoun, who hired him to do the investigation and who certainly found the official results of the census useful in foreign diplomacy. Men like Adams and Jarvis thought that either fraud or gross carelessness had occurred, and that the "slave oligarchy" was now deliberately covering it up. Once Jarvis learned that the errors appeared in the original returns, he was content to resort to a random-error argument, resulting from multiple copies and fluttering eyes. No one studied the statistics to see whether some systematic error, unrelated to the morals of blacks, could account for the apparent proportions of black lunacy. Also, no one challenged the criminal statistics about blacks by offering alternate explanations for the high rates of incarceration of blacks, based on mathematical quirks. There were still very real limits to the quantitative abilities of even some of the most acute quantifiers in the 1840s; in this case the limits were imposed by an inability to move beyond a moral framework in interpreting statistics about blacks.

The story of the census of 1840 is a story of innocence lost. Out of it arose a more general recognition that statistics could sometimes lie. Practitioners of the science of statistics had to adopt a defensive posture and a measure of caution about numbers, for they now knew that their numbers could be challenged by other sets of numbers.

Conclusion

By the mid-nineteenth century the prestige of quantification was in the ascendant. Counting was presumed to advance knowledge, because knowledge was composed of facts and counting led to the most reliable and objective form of fact there was, the hard number. The errors of the 1840 census did nothing to diminish the infatuation with numbers. To critics and apologists alike, the errors had arisen from mistakes in counting or recording data, and so the proper response was to improve the technique of counting. No one questioned the assumptions on which the whole enterprise had been founded. For example, no one wondered whether distinguishing lunatics by race was the most meaningful way to organize data on lunacy. Indeed, no one (except, perhaps, the underpaid and complaining census enumerators) wondered whether counting lunatics contributed at all to the perplexing study of mental illness. Counting was an end in itself; it needed no further justification.

Why was there such broad agreement on the benefits of quantification? In view of the fact that twentieth-century men and women are still enamored of numbers, this may at first seem like a hard question to answer, for it forces us to step outside ourselves and take an outsider's look at an ingrained habit. We ourselves so completely accept the benefits of counting that we seldom question the practice. In the mid-nineteenth century, the habit was still new enough that the devotees of numbers were conscious of the particular appeal that quantification had for them. "The human mind swells with satisfaction upon ascertained results, and finds pure enjoyment in the contemplation of truths which evince a progressive knowledge respecting the real condition of the human family," said census official Joseph C. G. Kennedy in an 1859 address entitled *The Progress of Statistics.*[1] Statistical knowledge was deeply gratifying because it was presumed to be objective, unimpeachable truth. It met an inner need for certainty. No other form of knowledge promised to be so clean and unambiguous. "Numbers are the only perfect instruments we can handle, and the only means of ascertaining the true effect of any given cause," wrote an author in justifying yet another improved arithmetic text.[2]

When wielded properly, these perfect instruments could be powerful, and that naturally enhanced their attractiveness. Mere opinion, it was thought, would wither on the vine when challenged by the superior force of exact data. The staunchest advocates optimistically maintained that numbers might even solve the most serious political crisis of America.

> Few persons have an adequate idea of the important part the cardinal numbers are now playing in the cause of Liberty. They are working wonders in the South. . . . Those unique, mysterious little Arabic sentinels on the watch-towers of political economy, 1, 2, 3, 4, 5, 6, 7, 8, 9, 0, have joined forces, allied themselves to the powers of freedom, and are hemming and combatting the institution [of slavery] with the most signal success. If let alone, we have no doubt the digits themselves would soon terminate the existence of slavery.[3]

Numbers would do this by proving beyond a doubt that slavery was unprofitable and had caused the South to lag behind the North in every way familiar to and measurable by people of the nineteenth century.

The popularity of quantification in the nineteenth century tells us much about American culture. *What* people chose to count and measure reveals not only what was important to them but what they wanted to understand and, often, what they wanted to control. Further, *how* people counted and measured reveals underlying assumptions about the subject under study, assumptions ranging from plain old bias—the historian's easy target, when it is detected—to ideas about the structure of society and of knowledge. In some cases, the activity of counting and measuring itself altered the way people thought about what they were quantifying: numeracy could be an agent of change. In this final chapter I shall elaborate on and illustrate these assertions in an effort to explain the interplay between numeracy and American culture.

In the nineteenth century, what was counted was what counted; the play on words drives home the point that people generally count only the things that matter. Each new instance of enumeration testifies to a concern about the prevalence of what is counted, and the concern is often linked to a belief that the prevalence has been or can be altered. For example, a society does not collect statistics on infant mortality until someone develops a concern about dead infants and a sense that the frequency of their deaths is variable and perhaps manipulable. The fact that a new enumeration appears signals a concern to give definite form to something that before was formless, or inexact, or perhaps not even noticed. At a later time, when that particular form of enumeration has become accepted, familiar, and established, it is harder to read its meaning than at the time of its origin, since it may be the case that statistics go on being collected out of bureaucratic inertia. Therefore, it is important to lay bare the historical roots of any particular instance of quantification, to understand how the concerns of the moment led to the reformulation, along numerical lines, of a subject that people were once content to be imprecise about, if, indeed, they noticed it at all.

A few examples will clarify this point. Prostitutes had probably always existed in American cities, but it was not until the 1830s that someone attempted to specify the dimensions of the problem of prostitution. The New York Moral Reform Society was an evangelical benevolence group formed in 1834 to attack the problem of rising male licentiousness and its destructive effect on women. Several factors sparked the forming of the organization: the evangelical and perfectionist religious ideas of the Second Great Awakening, a changing ethos about female sexuality, and a labor-market shift of young men and women from countryside to city, where they took up work and residence without the protections of family life. The Moral Reformers were alarmed, and one way they chose to communicate that alarm was through statistics. Their publication, *The Advocate of Moral Reform,* informed readers that in the United States there were as many as 12,000 brothels, 75,000 to 120,000 harlots, 500,000 licentious

wicked men, and 50 shops selling evil books, pictures, and "the
paraphernalia of destruction." Twenty thousand females died annually as a result of prostitution, they claimed.[4] Clearly, their
figures were estimates, and there was no way the reader could
evaluate them. But that was less important than the shock value
of such large numbers. The numbers focused attention on the
magnitude of the problem and thereby made distinct what had
before been indistinct or unacknowledged.

It is important to realize that the numbers signify nothing about
the changing incidence of male licentiousness, even though that
is exactly what the Moral Reformers thought they were documenting. Minimum-level fornication rates have been adduced for
the eighteenth century based on data on prenuptial pregnancy,
that is, suspiciously early births to newly married couples, and
the figures suggest that somewhere between 30 and 45 percent of
New England brides were well along in pregnancy at the time of
their marriage.[5] It could be that what had changed between the
eighteenth and the early nineteenth century was not the frequency
of fornication but rather a growing inability of the family to command marriage between errant sons and ruined daughters. The
ruined daughters, cast out of their homes, fled to the anonymity
of urban life, where they could secure women's work at women's
wages. Their collective presence in cities like New York and
Boston as a sexually and economically exploitable pool of laborers
awakened the evangelical reformers to their mission and led them
to conclude that rising male licentiousness was the cause of the
trouble.

Temperance statistics are another example of how the inauguration of quantification corresponds to a new sensitivity to
something that had existed before but that now was seen as something necessary to control. Excessive drinking was not new in the
1830s, but the urgency to control it was. Moral arguments against
drink were supplanted by statistical arguments because of the
presumed power of numbers to reflect objective reality. Temperance conventions sent out the call for all local societies to collect
statistics; annual reports were replete with compilations of these
reports. Almanacs were enlisted in the temperance cause, an apt
conjunction, expressing the idea that excessive drink was an in-
disputably real and daily fact of life, appropriately linked to a
daily calendar with its usual innocuous lists of presidents' terms
and state capitals.

The total effect of enumerating tipplers, drunks, breweries, and grog shops was to lend greater reality to the claim that drinking had become excessive. Someone had counted and measured, and so it must be true. Whether or not it really had become more excessive than in the eighteenth century is a question that may not finally be answerable, given the lack of statistics for the earlier time period and the doubtful authenticity of the temperance advocates' data. One suspects that the increasing presence of English and Irish immigrants in the 1830s had a good deal to do with alarm over drink and that the new work habits required by a factory organization of labor also contributed to the redefinition of intemperance. A once-tolerated level of drinking was redefined as excessive when it was manifested in an unwelcome group of people and when it conflicted with disciplined work.

But temperance statisticians never focused on drinking by ethnic group or within the laboring class alone. They opted for numbers that were as general as possible, numbers that implicated everyone, so that everyone's moral sense would be touched. Indeed, there was a recognition that, to maximize their impact, statistics should be brought as close to home as possible. That is why temperance-society conventions encouraged the local chapters to collect and submit statistics; not only would the national society get the big picture that way, but their own little picture would be brought into sharp focus for local temperance societies to contemplate. A temperance tract published in Hartford, Connecticut, made the point explicitly: "Facts and statistics brought from a distance . . . are much less regarded and have much less influence" than those collected in one's own community. The Hartford temperance society therefore published only Hartford County statistics, town by town, so that local people could absorb the full force of the numbers and translate them into known people when they read the exact numbers of drunkards, tipplers, and children suffering as the result of intemperate parents in their town. Lists of town figures also allowed comparisons, so that townspeople could experience pride or shame when they saw how their town stacked up against the town down the road. The statistics were at once the means of defining the problem and the measure of success in the work of reform.[6]

Sexual license and excessive drinking became amenable to quantification once they were identified as undesirable behaviors whose frequency could be controlled if only the entire community

could become aware of the extent of the problem. Statistics crystallized that awareness. But, obviously, simple concern over undesirable behaviors was not by itself sufficient to trigger counting.
Seventeenth-century Puritans were greatly concerned about the
proper conduct of sexual relations: sexual excess was bad, and
the individual, or, if need be, the community, was responsible for
curbing licentiousness. But they did not advertise moral failings
with statistics. Instead, they used public humiliation and punishment of individuals to bring community attention to lapses from
good behavior. Numbers were not a pervasive part of their universe and so would not have been an effective method for crys-
tallizing public opinion.

What had changed by the early nineteenth century was that
numeracy had become common because of arithmetic education
and the spread of a market economy. Now reformers could employ numbers to communicate concern to a numerate public. One
temperance almanac directly affirmed the utility of school-learned
numeracy for comprehending temperance by printing a roster of
classic arithmetic problems with contents all drawn from the temperance lexicon. The first of these twenty "Curious and Instructive Arithmetical Questions and Answers" was a straightforward
practical problem using Reduction and the Rule of Three Inverse:
If each individual in the United States (population 13 million) has
one half-gill of whiskey per day, how many gallons would be
consumed in a year? (Answer: 74,140,625 gallons.) Another dozen
questions followed, raising temperance consciousness while they
sharpened arithmetic skill. The last few questions drifted off into
a parody of the genre, as if to suggest that even exalted arithmetic
could not entirely capture the magnitude of alcohol abuse. "How
many tears have the wives of drunkards shed in the United States
since 1790, supposing the number of drunken husbands to be
15,000 per year? Ans: Enough to float the US Navy."[7]

In the rush to parade statistics, other methods of raising public
consciousness, akin to the Puritans' public humiliation of individual sinners, were not neglected. The touching case history of
the seduced and abandoned maiden and the picture of the weeping
child plucking the sleeve of a besotted father continued to play
an important part in moral-reform and temperance literature. Such
stories made their appeal at an emotional level. Statistics, on the
other hand, were thought to appeal on a rational level. Antislavery
writer Hinton Rowan Helper compared his book of slavery sta-

tistics to Harriet Beecher Stowe's *Uncle Tom's Cabin,* which he agreed was a highly effective abolitionist tract: "It is all well enough for women to give the fictions of slavery; men should give the facts."[8] Human stories were fictions, numbers were facts. Both conveyed information, both could be persuasive, but in different ways. The illuminating anecdote evoked sympathy, outrage, scorn, or some other feeling toward the person in the anecdote and his or her predicament; statistics, on the other hand, communicated the size, frequency, or prevalence of some issue or problem. Individuals faded into anonymity when taken in the aggregate; statistics put distance between the person counting and the persons counted.

How people count and measure embodies certain assumptions about the thing they are counting; this was true in the nineteenth century, and it is equally true today. The preexisting concern about the subject being studied inevitably shapes the method of enumerating. Any instance of counting reveals not only the mere fact of concern about the subject but the assumptions already built into the way people think about the subject. The assumptions easiest to spot are the ones that have led to biased results, and examples abound in the historical record. (It should be remembered that we become alert to the possibility of biased results mainly when the results conflict with our notions of what the data should show. When results confirm our notions, we are not so apt to scrutinize the procedures by which the data were obtained.) Well into the nineteenth century, the novelty of numbers, and especially their concreteness, conferred such reality on quantitative data that few people were moved to examine the process by which they had been generated. The specificity of numbers was mistaken for accuracy and exactitude.

A priori assumptions affect data collection at many levels. How one identifies the subject being counted, how one constructs categories for classifying data, how one labels data, all involve judgment. Some things are harder to count than others. Most counters would have little trouble enumerating males and females in a community, but what about tipplers and drunkards? By what characteristics are they defined and distinguished?

Temperance reformers used such terms as "tippler" and "drunkard" as though they had concrete, unambiguous meaning

and never specified protocols for counting either one. Even Samuel Chipman—the man who visited jails and poorhouses in four
states in the 1830s but asked the jailers to apply the labels of
"temperate" and "intemperate" to the inmates so that his own
judgment would not contaminate the data—did not consider that
lack of clarity in the label itself could skew his results. He described his method as one of "extreme caution." "As I was asking
for information, I could not, of course, dictate the answer that
should be given—especially as my object was not to obtain some
general expression of opinion, but an official certificate—one
which it was understood was to be published, and which the
person giving it would meet in his own county, where any error
or mis-statement might be detected and exposed." Chipman's
check on bias was to make results public, thus preventing jailers
from lying. If they did not lie and they counted case by case, then
his results had to be absolutely certain and objective. He never
worried that "intemperate" might itself be an imprecise and
value-laden term, subject to interpretation.[9]

The problem of imprecise terminology was magnified when legions of counters, armed with their individual interpretations of
labels, contributed to a large-scale enumeration. One man's tippler might be another man's drunkard. The census classification
of the population by race suffered from this problem when it
began adding "mulatto" as a possible category in the 1850 census,
forcing enumerators to make a judgment based on inspection of
skin color. For the rest of the nineteenth century, confusion
reigned over this part of the census, and anyone who has tried
to trace individual Negroes through successive censuses discov-
ers the results of quantifying an ambiguous entity: not a few
people mysteriously change skin color from decade to decade.
Eventually the designation "mulatto" was dropped. Whether that
happened because the data were recognized to be flawed or because racial amalgamation had become a subject best left imprecise or, even better, forgotten in the turn-of-the-century days of
Old Jim Crow is hard to say.

Another problem involved in identifying and classifying data
has to do with the choice of variables by which the data are sorted.
In the 1840 census the insane and idiots were sorted into black
and white, as was everything else the census collected in the way
of personal characteristics, because it was assumed that race was
the most salient division of the population. Separating lunacy by

race was not compelled by the politically necessary distinction between free and slave or by the socially sanctioned tradition of distinguishing free blacks from whites. The lunacy column appeared on the second page of the schedule and was not part of the first page's classification of sexes and ages by race. Also, the 1840 census took the household, not the individual, as its unit of analysis, so the linking of race and lunacy was no mere by-product of the method of data collection. It was consciously chosen over other variables that might arguably have been just as important: age, sex, class. Medical specialists in the mid-1840s and 1850s sometimes did separate lunacy data by sex, class, or nativity, and, when they did, they generally found differences, however small, that they thought were worth commenting on. It is as though the decision to adopt the particular type of classification of data arose out of a prior suspicion that there might actually be interesting differences between rates of insanity for blacks and whites, males and females, paupers and nonpaupers, native-borns and foreigners.

In the 1830s, sex and race were the most commonly used variables, which was fitting for a culture with a heightened sensitivity to gender and racial differences. Temperance and moral-reform statistics were collected with nary a concern for ethnicity, not because there were no ethnic differences but because those differences were not seen to be important. By the 1850s, nativity had become a commonly used variable, reflecting the worries that native Americans had developed not only about the immigration of foreigners but about the internal migrations that had occurred between the 1830s and the 1850s. William Sanger's landmark study of prostitutes, conducted in New York City in 1856, pinned down the ethnic background of 2,000 women in the trade and found that over 700 of them came from Ireland. That did not surprise him nearly so much as the finding that more than twice as many came from Maine as came from Virginia, even though, he observed, both states were equidistant from New York City and Virginia had a much larger population. Sanger could come up with an explanation, of course; a man who could write a 600-page book in less than a year was not a man at a loss for words. It was Maine's low-wage manufacturing that encouraged prostitution, he concluded. He did not consider that the smallness of the actual numbers (24 from Maine and 9 from Virginia out of

2,000 surveyed) might render his conclusion close to meaning-less.[10]

A few nineteenth-century statistical writers expressed concern about the quantification of imprecise categories. In an 1855 review of Edward Jarvis's *Report on Insanity and Idiocy in Massachusetts,* Isaac Ray proclaimed that statistics rightly conceived could be based only on discrete, precise facts, not on anything that had its ultimate source in opinions or guesses. He illustrated his point with mortality statistics. The number of deaths in a community was a concrete fact, potentially ascertainable with complete accuracy; by contrast, statistics on the causes of death were based on "diverse and variable" opinions. The same was true for the causes of insanity, he said, and "to give them a statistical form is to make no real advance in knowledge." This was a caution that few enthusiasts cared to take into account when they launched a statistical survey. Isaac Ray criticized the quantification of opinion on the grounds that "an accumulation of errors can never lead to the development of truth." Opinions were subjective and could as easily be erroneous as true, whereas clear and distinct facts that could be numbered, measured, and classed were objective and would by their very nature lead to truth. Having made this point, Ray quickly succumbed to the glorification of objective numbers, generated by counting and measurement, in his next sentence. Errors of pure measurement, he claimed, were not serious compared to the error of quantifying opinion, for "in a mere matter of quantity, the errors on one side generally balance the errors on the other, and thus the value of the result is not materially affected."[11]

Ray's faith notwithstanding, it is quite true that errors can creep into even the most direct and concrete enumeration in ways that bias the outcome. All errors are not random. Counting people, for example, would seem to be an entirely straightforward task, since people are clearly distinguishable from dogs, trees, and other things, and about the only problematic decision having to do with identifying the class to be enumerated would arise in the question of whether or not to count a person who died on the day of the census. Yet clarity of identification does not preclude other systematic errors. Sometimes it happens that the rewards for census-takers are inconsistent with the goal of an accurate census. If the man in the field is paid according to the number of persons enumerated, there exists a distinct incentive to inflate the data.

The first United States censuses tried to check that tendency by requiring the census roll to be posted in a public place so that local people could attest to its accuracy; but later the right to privacy took precedence, and this emboldened one Boston enumerator in 1840 to list several thousand people as inhabitants of a single apartment building in his district. Too low a pay rate in relation to the effort required encourages imaginative responses rather than house-to-house calls. A hostile population—one, for example, that feared the census would result in increased taxes or military duty—might also create skewed results by hiding from the census-taker or by frightening him so that his zeal for thorough counting would diminish.

These three examples all illustrate the way that decisions about *how* to measure include built-in assumptions that can alter the results. Setting a rate of pay is one decision, and a related one is choosing the sort of person who will be hired to do the counting. Sending marginal types of people—students, retired persons, the unemployed—at a low wage into dangerous, tough neighborhoods to cense will produce materially different error rates from sending highly paid social workers into middle-class neighborhoods. In the seventeenth century, censuses were conducted by the leading gentleman, minister, or military captain of each precinct, since these were the men most likely to be numerate and knowledgeable about their neighbors and authoritative enough to demand information. There were consequences to this decision too, for leading men might be less inclined to go from door to door in bad weather than some subaltern ordered to do the job. Through much of the nineteenth century, federal marshals had charge of the United States census. They often delegated the work to assistants or to temporary workers, but the finished schedules passed through their hands. Marshals were law-enforcement men in the employ of the federal judicial branch. It is reasonable to suspect that their control of the census inhibited in some instances the honest reporting of family and financial information. A man contemplating bankruptcy would think twice before reporting all of his true wealth to the man whose job it was to seize property in bankruptcy proceedings. An 1870 congressional report recommended that the use of marshals be discontinued for this reason.[12]

William Sanger turned to captains of each police precinct in New York for his census of prostitutes, and they in turn farmed the work out to ordinary uniformed policemen. Sanger's census had official sanction but no budget, so who better was there to do the work than city employees already on the payroll? Policemen were familiar with local vice and thus in a good position to identify the target population, which was not so easy to count as butchers or bakers. But the particular choice of policemen almost certainly altered Sanger's survey results from what he would have got by using the middle-class evangelical Christian women who ran homes for destitute women and unwed mothers. The general point here is that decisions about how to count and measure inevitably have an impact on the data collected.

A particularly clear-cut instance of how assumptions can subvert measurement occurred in the 1840s when American scientists fervently pursued craniology, the measurement of skulls, in an effort to quantify human intelligence. Samuel George Morton of Philadelphia measured the volume of some 600 skulls and found, to no one's surprise, that, on the average, whites' skulls were larger than Indians' skulls, and Indians' were larger than blacks'. The theory that informed his work was that skull size was an indication of intelligence, and his conclusion was that big skulls, and therefore superior intelligence, belonged to white males. What could be more straightforward than comparing the volume of two vessels? And yet, as Stephen Jay Gould has shown in his book on the reification and measurement of intelligence, Morton and his colleagues committed at least three types of fundamental error. There were plain arithmetic errors made in figuring the averages, as Gould discovered when he recalculated the sums, and the errors all magnified racial differences. Second, judgments were made about which skulls to include in calculating the averages; these judgments were inconsistently applied, and they always worked in favor of augmenting the average for white skulls in comparison to Indians and blacks. Third, the very method of measuring the skulls was subject to some variability. Morton first chose mustard seed as his medium; he poured it into each skull until the skull was full and then transferred it to a graduated cylinder to measure it. Mustard seeds are not perfectly regular and can vary in settling, depending on how much they are agitated. Morton discovered this himself when the same skull, remeasured, yielded different results. He later switched to using small lead shot to achieve greater consistency. The data derived from the seed measurements deviated from the lead-shot measurements in a pattern that exaggerated the racial differences in brain size.

Gould conjures up an image of Morton in the lab, funneling mustard seed into skulls and unconsciously giving the known white men's skulls a few extra shakes to accommodate the maximum amount of seed. There was no deliberate fraud here, no intent to fake data. The prior assumption of white superior intelligence was so powerful and strong that it manifested itself at every step of the investigation and ultimately controlled the conclusions.[13]

How quantifiers handled the problem of data that did not fit their preconceived ideas reveals the very real limits of inductive thinking in the nineteenth century, despite the popularity it commanded. Morton and other craniologists devoted very close attention to any data that seemed to equalize brain sizes, but they did so in order to explain away such surprises. One only wishes that the level of analysis they brought to bear in that effort could have been applied to their whole undertaking. Sanger confronted a similar problem when his policemen-interviewers came back with figures showing that 513 of the 2,000 prostitutes reported "inclination" as the cause of their taking up the sinful life. That cause was second only to "destitution," which 524 claimed, and far ahead of the third most frequent cause, "seduced and abandoned," named by 258. To Sanger, "inclination" could mean only base gratification of sexual passion, for he said so; it is not known what it meant to the policemen or to the women themselves. "In itself such an answer would imply innate depravity, a want of true womanly feeling, which is actually incredible." Sanger could not believe this particular answer because it did not fit with his notion of women's sexuality. He therefore reclassified the answer in a more acceptable form. "The force of desire can be neither denied nor disputed, but still in the bosoms of most females that force exists in a slumbering state until aroused by outside influences." The real cause was therefore presumed to fall under other categories on the list: the influence of bad company, seduction, or drink.[14]

In point of fact, Sanger was not entirely wrong to reassign the data. His reasons were wrong, since his prejudices dictated the adjustment in the statistics; but the data were flawed because the categories of response to the question were neither precise nor mutually exclusive. How did "inclination" differ from attraction to the "easy life"? How did "bad company" differ from "seduction" or "persuaded by prostitutes"? Since Sanger supplied his interviewers only with questions, not with possible answers, it seems likely that the prostitutes gave open-ended answers and that the policemen developed their own scheme for categorizing the responses. The list of twelve answers is not very uniform, ranging from a general "destitution" to the narrow "seduced in an emigrant ship." Sanger probably compiled the results, according to his best lights, collapsing some categories but not others, and in doing this he established his right to take liberties with the classification system. The problem, of course, was that the liberties he took had no relation to the meanings the responses had had for the people who made them and to those who collected them.

Reclassification of data was routine at the census office in the nineteenth century. The Weaver family with their red pens claimed the right to correct errors, but who was to define error? Mistakes in simple addition constitute one sort of error on which there would be general agreement, but what about errors of inclusion or exclusion or errors of categorization? The Weavers decided that insane and idiot blacks entered in households where there were no black residents did not constitute an error, and they defended that position vociferously. Had Edward Jarvis been running the census, those data would have been moved three columns to the left. In later decades, census officials routinely corrected similar sorts of errors, where the markings made in the field contradicted common sense. The problem became most serious after the introduction of machine-readable coding cards in the 1890 and 1900 censuses, according to historian Margo Conk. This was the first time that explicit procedures were developed for checking the quality of coding by monitoring for internal consistency. A coded card that showed a female or a person of color in a high-status occupation was automatically subject to review, thus creating a subtle pressure for coders to alter the data so that their work would escape criticism. Several times in the twentieth century, Census Bureau officials actually changed age and occupation data when they encountered anomalies. On one occasion, over 6,000 female workers in railroad and fire-fighting occupations were arbitrarily reclassified into other skilled jobs in order to create consistency with earlier census publications. In the course of using occupational sex segregation as a check on accuracy, the Census Bureau in effect perpetuated sex segregation by erasing from the record the deviant cases that challenged the system.[15]

Unmasking the assumptions that have exerted an influence on counting and measurement is only one of the ways that historians can find out something about the past from historical statistics. It is also possible to regard statistics as a form of communication and to ask the question, on what basis do the statistics persuade? What attitudes or assumptions does the statistics-collector tap by choosing to quantify information, and to quantify it in particular ways, so that it will communicate his message?

On the most general level, we can observe that a familiarity with numbers in both statistician and audience is requisite to the act of communication by numbers. In the seventeenth century, John Smith asked the Indians how many fish they caught daily, and they could not give him a numerical answer. A century later Dr. Zabdiel Boylston tried, with statistics, to prove to Bostonians that inoculation was efficacious, but no one heeded him. In the First Congress, Madison proposed an enlarged census, but few of his colleagues could see any use in it. It was not until the early nineteenth century, when education reform put basic numeracy within the reach of all schoolchildren, that quantitative discourse on the level of descriptive statistics could become commonplace.

In addition to sharing a set of basic skills, users of statistics also shared the belief that quantities were more exact than qualities—that they were less subject to the uncertainty and caprice of personal judgment. Something that was counted or measured was known. Someone else could count it and get the same result. The exactness and objectivity of numbers meant that quantified information was a more truthful form of information than opinion, intuition, or judgment.

The nineteenth-century collector of statistics, assured of an audience that would understand his numerical message and accord it a superior credibility, had only to choose the exact form his data would take. The choice was governed by what was available, what was possible to collect, and what his particular audience would best respond to. Temperance, economic, and slavery statistics offer three illustrations of how social values were embodied in specific sorts of statistics.

Temperance statistics took a variety of forms, reflecting someone's assessment of what arrangement of data would have the most impact. Advocates might emphasize the numbers of drunkards, which, if high, would create an impression on people who before did not think the problem was widespread. Or they could

choose, instead, to publicize the number of women and children
made miserable by drunken fathers, a choice encouraged by nineteenth-century sensibilities about dependent childhood and ro-
mantic womanhood. On a less emotional level, they sometimes
publicized statistics on the quantities of spirits sold and the number of acres of grain devoted to alcohol production, a line of
argument persuasive to people who preferred to think about economic waste rather than human misery. Samuel Chipman elaborated on this point in defense of his figures on the costs of confining
the intemperate in jails and poorhouses:

> The pecuniary considerations connected with the subject of
> temperance, are absolutely so contemptible, when compared
> with those of a moral nature, that it is humiliating to be obliged
> to give the former so great a prominence when presenting mo-
> tives designed to influence the minds of our fellow-men; still,
> if there are those that cannot be affected except by the love
> of gain—if there is no chord in their hearts that can be touched
> by representations of domestic misery—of bodily and mental
> suffering—and even the everlasting displeasure of their Maker,
> we must, however humiliating and revolting to our feelings, let
> dollars and cents, the god of this world, make their appeal.[16]

Chipman was right to distrust pecuniary arguments, for it was
rather easy for opponents to construct counterarguments, also
quantitative; by contrast, it was difficult to argue that society
could tolerate *any* number of miserable, destitute wives and children. A representative of the United States Brewers' Association,
for example, pointed out that the dollars and cents cost of pauperism should be seen in relation to the revenue the government
derived from liquor taxes. Not that he agreed, of course, that
pauperism or any part of it was *caused* by drink; if there was any
relation at all, he suspected the reverse to be true. (This champion
of the brewers was less successful in combatting the temperance
advocates' statistics on crime and liquor. Property crimes, he
said, were based on calculation, not inebriation, and he flatly
asserted that crimes of passion were caused by women, not alcohol: "In my opinion women are [at] the bottom of a great
number of crimes." In a book brimming with statistics and hard
facts, this gratuitous dig at womanhood seems out of place. Unable to sustain his point about crime and liquor with quantitative

proof, the author took refuge in insulting women, the backbone of the temperance crusade.)[17]

Another example of how statistical discourse illuminates social values lies in the prolific generation of economic and trade statistics, which graced almanacs and periodicals from about 1810 onward. Obviously, such information was useful; it helped farmers, merchants, bankers, shippers, planters, and manufacturers to know the shape and scope of the market they were dealing with. But, once generated, such statistics took on an emblematic life of their own. They became a shorthand message about the state of America. Someone in the insurance business might have sound financial reasons for wanting to know how many steamboats there were (as well as how many had exploded) on American rivers in 1833, but a statistic like this had meaning to a far wider audience because it symbolized the growing greatness of America. The number of steamboats indexed the much-vaunted industry and innovative genius of the country. So did the number of bales of cotton produced, the yards of cloth manufactured, the miles of railroad track laid, the rate of population increase. The popularity of economic statistics derived from their ability to tell Americans what they wanted to hear. The creators and consumers of these numbers shared a social vision that associated bigness with being the best. "By these [statistics], and these alone, we can trace the progress of society and civilization; or, in other words, measure a nation's moral and religious improvement; its health, wealth, strength, and safety," said Virginian George Tucker in his prospectus for a nationwide General Statistical Society in 1847. America's greatness was measurable and, therefore, indisputable and objective.[18]

Men like Tucker talked as though the only important things about America were things that were measurable. The idea that national health, wealth, strength, safety, progress, and morality could be traced only by statistics meant that things inherently nonquantifiable were set aside, no longer to be regarded as important factors. The numerical versions of strength and safety, for example, would stress quantities like the size of the army, the number of young men, the quantity of arms and ammunition, the distance from enemy borders. But what of courage, determination, or paranoia? Such qualities surely have a decisive effect on national safety or strength, but, since there was no way to measure them, they were filtered out by the arithmetical approach so esteemed by Tucker.

A third example of the way in which underlying social values are communicated by statistics can be seen in the arguments used by those who claimed that numbers could settle the crisis of slavery. North Carolinian Hinton Rowen Helper amassed statistics to show how the South trailed the North in every measurable aspect. In so doing, he was building on the work of others, who for two decades had been accumulating statistical material relating to the slavery debate. Helper compared population growth rates, statistics of commerce, agricultural productivity, and education and literacy rates and found the South deficient in every particular. "Figures shall show the facts," he maintained. "Properly the South has nothing left to boast of; the North has surpassed her in everything, and is going farther and farther ahead of her every day."[19] Helper was sure that his figures carried conviction and that anyone who paid attention to his tables would have to agree that slavery was the ruin of the South. His object was to get nonslaveholding southerners, men like himself, to unite in political action to abolish slavery peacefully. Only that would reverse the downward trend of statistics. On what basis did he expect his statistics to persuade?

Helper assumed that the reader of his book would be the proverbial rational man who puts economic arguments ahead of all else and who would therefore agree to scrap slavery if it could be shown that it hurt the pocketbook. He also assumed that aggregate measures of wealth and productivity were the best way to convince people that slavery hurt the pocketbook (this in turn suggests that people would agree that their own fortunes were tied to their state's economic climate). He further assumed that the miserable state of the South's economy, once demonstrated statistically, would naturally be attributed to the mere existence of slavery rather than to mismanagement of the South's economic system, or to climate, or to Providence.

It is quite possible that Helper was wrong in none of these assumptions (although there was no mass rising of nonslaveholding whites against slavery in the wake of his book). The point is that they were assumptions about what form an argument had to take to be convincing. There are many other ways one could choose to contrast two cultures as dissimilar as the North and the South were in 1857. Ideas about race, religion, morality, work, violence, legal systems, and kinship and family patterns are but a few of the alternate ways to approach a North-South comparison. Not all of these ideas were overlooked at the time, since the sectional crisis was all-consuming in the 1850s and hardly a difference between North and South went unremarked. But none of these approaches could wrap themselves in the mantle of authenticity the way numbers could. Appeals to sentiment or emotion might be effective, but they did not appear invincible.[20]

Actually, the numerical argument about slavery appeared invincible mainly because there was a paucity of southern statisticians to combat it. Helper and others drew on the census of 1850, which had been run by a southerner, J. D. B. DeBow of Louisiana, but had been designed by four northern members of the American Statistical Association, chosen to redeem the census in the eyes of the professional statistical community after the fiasco of 1840.[21] The census data were not collected with the idea of highlighting North-South differences. In order to get data that would vindicate the South, DeBow said that there would have to be southern-generated data—as clear a statement as any of the connection between a data-collector's purpose and his resulting figures.

> They [the northern states] have all the statisticians to themselves and all the statistical reports. They have used them as powerful implements of aggression, and the South, having nothing to show in return, has been compelled to see her cause greatly prejudiced. Until almost the present day none of the southern states have regarded it at all important to secure records and returns of population and wealth. Not one periodical devoted itself to these subjects, though the North had many. We were taunted with our comparative weakness, poverty, insecurity, decay, and told that they were the natural results of our slavery. Having no facts, to oppose, we were passive, and for the most part admitted the justice of the charge.[22]

Once a southerner with some numerical sophistication went to work on the pro-North statistical comparisons, it was not hard to pick holes in the fabric of the argument. Helper had compared the total wealth, real and personal, of the North and the South and declared that the results, which showed the North more wealthy by $1,166 million, were the "irrefragable evidence of the unequaled efficacy and grandeur of free institutions!"[23] But what

about comparing per capita wealth instead of total wealth? Would
slaves then be counted as population, in the denominator, or as
wealth, in the numerator? In raising this sort of question, DeBow
was educating his readership on the inherent flexibility of statistics
and the way that their arrangement can alter the message they
impart even when the numbers themselves are not false.[24] What
one wished to demonstrate with numbers dictated the arrangement of the data. Social values left their imprint on supposedly
objective empirical facts.

Numbers have immeasurably altered the character of American society. One has only to ask where we would be without numbers to realize how much of what we identify as
modern civilization was created by numerate people using numerical skills. We inhabit a highly technical society: the very
structures and machines around us reflect and perpetuate our
dependence on numbers. Once bridges were overbuilt or else
were built and then gingerly tested by inching a heavy vehicle out
onto them; the mathematics of engineering has now replaced trial-
and-error construction. We have a complicated economy, the
product of billions of individual calculating acts. We quantify
those acts and project them into the future, making predictions,
constructing trends and indices, that in themselves then exert a
powerful influence on future individual calculating acts. We reduce the complexity of the economy to a few key indicators, like
the GNP, the Consumer Price Index, and the unemployment rate,
and we reify the social welfare of the nation with measures like
the infant mortality rate. Public opinion surveys now play a vital
role in politics that could never have been imagined by the framers
of our democratic government. Probability theory and sampling
techniques have greatly refined the measurement of social facts,
lending credence to the idea that there might genuinely be a science of human society. Baseball has its batting averages, education is ruled by scores on achievement tests, and even sex has
had its Alfred Kinsey to measure frequency of coition over the
life-cycle. Computers, fast becoming commonplace, will only
speed this invasion of numbers, which has been under way for
the past two hundred years.

The history of numeracy suggests that new forms of quantification of social phenomena will change the way we think about

those phenomena. The statistical champions of the mid-nineteenth century were fairly clear about what they regarded as the effects of quantification on social thought. Enumeration focused concern on an issue, accurately described its dimensions, and suggested the proper course of action to be taken. Without quantitative facts there might be no agreement on the nature of the problem, and so no course of action would be apparent. Without numbers there would be no sure way of evaluating the course of action afterwards, to see whether it had had the desired result. The proper object of statistics, said Joseph Kennedy of the census office in 1859, "is the amelioration of man's condition by the exhibition of facts whereby the administrative powers are guided and controlled by the lights of reason, and the impulses of humanity impelled to throb in the right direction." Statistics would point the way to right action. Moral statistics "have accomplished more in the last half century for the alleviation of misery, the prolongation of life, and the elevation of humanity, than all other agencies combined—they are the practical workings of an elevated Christianity." Kennedy went so far as to compare the mission of statistics to the mission of the Savior and suggested that statistics could cause the blind to read and the "deaf and dumb to express themselves."[25] His general point was that the act of quantifying led inexorably to the proper response. The measure of a problem was also the measure of its solution. There is a striking element of hubris in nineteenth-century statistical thought, a hubris that is still at work in the twentieth. To measure is to initiate a cure.

Our modern reliance on numbers and quantification was born and nurtured in the scientific and commercial worlds of the seventeenth century and grew in scope in the early nineteenth century, under the twin impact of republican ideology and economic development. Numbers were celebrated because they were genuinely useful, because they were thought to discipline the mind, because they marked the progress of the era, and because they were reputedly objective and precise and hence tantamount to truth. Numerical facts trounced opinions and were supposed to foster community consensus, because all thinking people would naturally agree if they possessed total and accurate information. The United States in its first half-century of existence provided fertile ground for numeracy, and mass education ensured its healthy growth.

Early statistical thinking was flawed by unsophisticated techniques and time-bound sentiments that now, in retrospect, are not hard to detect. Yet even with our more sophisticated mathematical foundations, we continue to live within the framework of ideas about numbers that developed in the early nineteenth century. Numbers still compel, and they still suggest objectivity and rationality, the opposites of feeling, passion, and intuitive judgment. Numbers define problems and dictate solutions, and we become ever more ingenious in discovering ways to quantify what was once thought to be beyond the realm of the measurable or the countable. The domain of number continues to spread, and it does so as much because of the historic allure of numbers as because of any inherent benefits of counting.

Notes

Introduction

1. Alexis de Tocqueville, *Democracy in America,* ed. J. P. Mayer and Max Lerner, trans. George Lawrence (New York: Harper & Row, 1966), pp. 262–63, 508–10.

2. William A. Alcott, *The Young Man's Guide,* 2d ed. (Boston: Lilly, Wait, Coleman & Holden, 1834), pp. 34, 42, 108–10, 198.

3. James Hall, *Statistics of the West, at the Close of the Year 1836* (Cincinnati: J. A. James, 1836), p. 213; Thomas Hamilton, *Men and Manners in America* (1833) (reprint ed., New York: A. M. Kelley, 1968), p. 222. Several recent works that characterize Americans of the 1830s as "calculating" are Daniel Calhoun, *The Intelligence of a People* (Princeton: Princeton University Press, 1973), pp. 99–108; John R. Howe, *From the Revolution through the Age of Jackson* (Englewood Cliffs, N.J.: Prentice-Hall, 1973), pp. 122–23; and Ralph Lerner, "Commerce and Character: The Anglo-American as a New-Model Man," *William and Mary Quarterly* 3d ser. 34 (1979): 10.

4. Cf. Jack Goody, ed., *Literacy in Traditional Societies* (Cambridge, Eng.: At the University Press, 1968); David Cressy, *Literacy and the Social Order: Reading and Writing in Tudor and Stuart England* (New York: Cambridge University Press, 1980); Kenneth Lockridge, *Literacy in Colonial New England* (New York: Norton, 1974); and Harvey J. Graff, *The Literacy Myth: Literacy and Social Structure in the Nineteenth-Century City* (New York: Academic Press, 1979).

5. See Claudia Zaslavsky, *Africa Counts: Number and Pattern in African Culture* (Boston: Prindle, Weber & Schmidt, 1973); Karl Menninger, *Number Words and Number Symbols: A Cultural History of Numbers,* trans. Paul Broneer (Cambridge, Mass.: MIT Press, 1969) (German ed., 1958). On the slow rise of numeracy in the European Middle Ages, from nothingness to a bit of numeracy lodged in calendar reckoners and merchant houses, see Alexander Murray, *Reason and Society in the Middle Ages* (Oxford: Clarendon Press, 1978), chaps. 6, 7, and 8.

6. John Arbuthnot, "An Essay on the Usefulness of Mathematical Learning," in *The Life and Works of John Arbuthnot,* ed. George Atherton Aitken (Oxford: Clarendon Press, 1892), p. 421.

227

Chapter 1 • Numeracy in Seventeenth-Century England

1. For example, see the title pages and prefaces of William Leybourn, *The Art of Measuring, or the Carpenter's New Rule* (London, 1669), and John Smith, *Stereometrie: Or, the Art of Practical Gauging* (London, 1673), p. iv.

2. See Lucas N. H. Bunt, Phillip S. Jones, and Jack D. Bedient, *The Historical Roots of Elementary Mathematics* (Englewood Cliffs, N.J.: Prentice-Hall, 1976), pp. 223–24, 227–28; Florian Cajori, *A History of Elementary Mathematics* (New York: Macmillan, 1896; 2d ed., 1917), pp. 119–21; Karl Menninger, *Number Words and Number Symbols: A Cultural History of Numbers,* trans. Paul Broneer (Cambridge, Mass.: MIT Press, 1969), p. 425.

3. Cajori, *Elementary Mathematics,* p. 121.

4. Some texts followed Recorde's model to the point of plagiarism. For example, Thomas Hill's book of 1600 included whole sections taken verbatim from Recorde.

5. Augustus de Morgan, *Arithmetical Books from the Invention of Printing to the Present Time* (London: Taylor & Walton, 1847), is a helpful annotated bibliography listing multiple editions of each work.

6. See E. G. R. Taylor's introduction to William Bourne, *A Regiment for the Sea* (1588) (reprint ed., Cambridge, Eng.: Hakluyt Society, 1963), pp. 1–2, 7–8. See also D. W. Waters, *The Art of Navigation in England in Elizabethan and Early Stuart Times*(New Haven: Yale University Press, 1958), pp. 340–401, where the period from 1594 to 1631 is identified as the time of greatest advance in arithmetical navigation.

7. One historian has suggested that the grid–like conception of geography parallels the development of painting in the Renaissance: the canvas is divided into small blocks that interrelate according to the rules of perspective. In contrast, medieval maps depicted a symbolic arrangement of the world around Jerusalem, and medieval painting ordered subjects according to a theological hierarchy. See A. C. Crombie, "Quantification in Medieval Physics," in Sylvia L. Thrupp, ed., *Change in Medieval Society* (New York: Appleton-Century-Crofts, 1964), pp. 188–207.

8. Waters, *Art of Navigation,* p. 50.

9. Richard Norwood, *Trigonometrie, Or, The Doctrine of Triangles, with an Annexation on Navigation* (London, 1631), p. 82.

10. Leonard Digges, *A Geometrical Practise, named Pantometria* (London, 1571), preface.

11. William Leybourn, *Cursus Mathematicus: Mathematical Sciences, in Nine Books* (London, 1690), preface, p. vi.

12. Samuel Sturmy, *The Mariners Magazine, stor'd with Mathematical Arts* (London, 1669; 3d ed., 1684), book 5, pp. 18–20. According to modern measurement, the height of the peak of Teneriffe is 3,718 meters, or 2.3 miles, using the same mile (5,280 feet) that Sturmy used.

13. E. G. R. Taylor, *Late Tudor and Early Stuart Geography, 1583–1650* (New York: Octagon Books, 1934; 2d ed. 1968), p. 159.

14. An early example of a publication giving distances along the roads from London is *A New Almanacke and Prognostication for the Yeere of our Redemption 1631* by John Smith, "Wel-willer to the Mathematicks."

15. Many seventeenth- and eighteenth-century arithmetics gave page after page of equivalences. For example, Thomas Dilworth, *The Schoolmaster's Assistant* (London, 1743), pp. 13–22, distinguished a firkin of butter (56 pounds) from a

firkin of soap (64 pounds) to lead off ten pages of such terminology. Ronald Edward Zupko, *A Dictionary of English Weights and Measures from Anglo-Saxon Times to the Nineteenth Century* (Madison: University of Wisconsin Press, 1968), is a valuable guide.

16. Smith, *Stereometrie,* preface. Two other titles published around the same time as Smith's book reflect the new interest in accurate measurement of containers: Robert Anderson, *Stereometrical Propositions* (London, 1668), and Thomas Everard, *Stereometry Made Easie* (London, 1684).

17. The shift to commercial texts has been noted and documented by Cajori, *Elementary Mathematics,* and by David Eugene Smith, *A History of Mathematics,* 2 vols. (Boston: Ginn, 1923).

18. Cajori, *Elementary Mathematics,* pp. 190–91; George Emery Littlefield, *Early Schools and School-Books of New England* (1905) (reprint ed., New York: Russell & Russell, 1965), p. 173.

19. James Hodder, *Hodder's Arithmetick: or, that Necessary Art Made Easy* (Boston, 1719), preface.

20. Dilworth, *Schoolmaster's Assistant,* p. 2.

21. George Fisher, *The American Instructor, or, Young Man's Best Companion, Containing Spelling, Reading, Writing, and Arithmetick,* 9th ed. (Philadelphia, 1748), pp. 56–57. Actually, this definition was a garbled version of what Recorde had written in 1543: "Every figure hath two values: One alwates [*sic*] certayne that it signifieth properly, which it hath of its forme, and the other uncertaine, whiche he taketh of his place." See Recorde, *The Grounde of Arts* (London, 1543), "numeration."

22. Lest this seem completely bizarre and irrational, it should be noted that some modern-day students stumble over the idea that multiplication and division of fractions are the same operations as multiplication and division of integers. In ordinary speech, multiplication means increase, and division suggests a breaking into smaller parts. Yet multiplication by proper fractions yields smaller numbers, and division leads to increase. See Sheila Tobias, *Overcoming Math Anxiety* (New York: Norton, 1978), p. 49.

23. Edward Cocker, *Arithmetick* (London, 1677), p. 2.

24. John Bonnycastle, *The Scholar's Guide to Arithmetic* (London, 1780), preface.

25. Cajori, *Elementary Mathematics,* p. 207.

26. *Diary of Samuel Pepys,* ed. Robert Latham and William Matthews, 9 vols. (Berkeley and Los Angeles: University of California Press, 1970), 3:134; see also pp. 131, 135, 137.

27. Titles of ready reckoners are listed in David Murray, *Chapters in the History of Bookkeeping, Accountancy, and Commercial Arithmetic* (Glasgow: Jackson, Wylie, 1930), pp. 296–301.

28. Hugh Oldcastle, *A Briefe Instruction and Maner How to Keepe Bookes of Accompts* (London, 1543); the first original book in English was John Mellis's *A Briefe Instruction and Maner how to Keepe Bookes of Accompts after the Order of Debitor and Creditor* (London, 1588).

29. James D. Edwards, "Early Bookkeeping and Its Development into Accounting," *Business History Review* 34 (1960): 446–59; B. S. Yamey and A. C. Littleton, eds., *Studies in the History of Accounting* (London: Sweet & Maxwell, 1956).

30. B. S. Yamey, "Scientific Bookkeeping and the Rise of Capitalism," *Economic History Review* 2d ser. 1 (1949): 99–113.

31. See Joyce Oldham Appleby, *Economic Thought and Ideology in Seventeenth-Century England* (Princeton: Princeton University Press, 1978).

32. John Arbuthnot, "Essay on the Usefulness of Mathematical Learning," in *The Life and Works of John Arbuthnot,* ed. George A. Aitken (Oxford: Clarendon Press, 1892), pp. 421–22.

33. Some historians have suggested that there was a direct parallel between the balance of trade and the balance of account books in the double-entry system; see C. H. Wilson, "Trade, Society, and the State," in E. E. Rich and C. H. Wilson, eds., *The Cambridge Economic History of Europe,* 7 vols. (Cambridge, Eng.: At the University Press, 1967), 4:500.

34. G. N. Clark, *Guide to English Commercial Statistics, 1696–1782* (London: Royal Historical Society, 1938), p. xii; Edward Misselden, *The Circle of Commerce Or the Ballance of Trade* (London, 1623), pp. 127–30.

35. John Collins is discussed by William Letwin, *The Origins of Scientific Economics: English Economic Thought, 1660–1776* (London: Methuen, 1963), pp. 99–113. Collins wrote books on quadrants and navigation, dialing, gauging, interest rates, and decimal arithmetic. He was a frequent correspondent of Isaac Newton and nearly a dozen other eminent mathematicians and was knowledgeable about the latest developments in calculus and algebra. He reported to a friend that he belonged to a mathematical club "consisting of divers ingenious mechanics, gaugers, carpenters, shipwrights, some seamen, lightermen, etc., whose whole discourse is about equations" (quoted by Letwin, p. 109). In 1667 he was invited to join the Royal Society. Collins is a prime example of the man whose delight in mathematics led him to apply it in many diverse areas.

36. "Numerist," according to seventeenth-century dictionaries, meant "he that numbreth"; it is derived from the title of the Roman officer who kept registers. "Numbrist" was a variant. See Elisha Coles, *An English Dictionary* (London, 1677), and Thomas Blount, *Glossographia, or a Dictionary* (London, 1656).

37. William Petty, *Political Arithmetick* (London, 1690), reprinted in Charles Henry Hull, ed., *The Economic Writings of Sir William Petty,* 2 vols. (Cambridge, Eng.: At the University Press, 1899), 1:244.

38. Biographical facts about Petty's life are taken from E. Strauss, *Sir William Petty: Portrait of a Genius* (Glencoe, Ill.: The Free Press, 1954), and Letwin, *Origins of Scientific Economics,* pp. 114–46.

39. In his will, Petty boasted of the mathematical skill he had attained by the age of twenty and claimed that no one else at that age had known more than he. See Strauss, *Sir William Petty,* p. 183.

40. Hull, ed., *Economic Writings of Sir William Petty,* 1:256–57.

41. Charles Davenant, *Discourses on the Publick Revenues* (London, 1698); Gregory King, *Two Tracts: Natural and Political Observations and Conclusions upon the State and Condition of England (1696) and Of the Naval Trade of English Anno 1688 and the National Profit then arising thereby,* ed. George E. Barnett (Baltimore: Johns Hopkins University Press, 1936); Edmund Halley, *Two Papers on the Degrees of Mortality in Mankind,* ed. Lowell J. Reed (Baltimore: Johns Hopkins University Press, 1942); John Arbuthnot, "An Argument for Divine Providence, taken from the constant Regularity observ'd in the Births of both Sexes," Royal Society, *Philosophical Transactions* 27 (1711): 186–90.

42. Arbuthnot, "Usefulness of Mathematical Learning," p. 422.

43. Adam Smith, *An Inquiry into the Nature and Causes of the Wealth of Nations,* ed. Edwin Cannan, with an Introduction by Max Lerner (New York: Random House, 1937), p. 501.

44. An early occupant of the office was Charles Davenant, who greatly admired Petty's political arithmetic. See Clark, *Guide to English Commercial Statistics,* pp. 12–19.

45. See ibid., pp. 2–3, 33–42; Peter Laslett, "John Locke and the Origins of the Board of Trade, 1695–1698," *William and Mary Quarterly* 3d ser. 14 (1957): 370–95.

46. D. V. Glass, *London Inhabitants within the Walls, 1695* (London: London Record Society, 1966), pp. ix–x.

47. Sweden was the first country to institute regular censuses, in 1749. For a survey of early census-taking, see T. H. Hollingsworth, *Historical Demography* (Ithaca: Cornell University Press, 1969), chap. 3, "Population Counts," and David S. Landes, "Statistics as a Source for the History of Economic Development in Western Europe: The Protostatistical Era," in Val R. Lorwin and Jacob M. Price, eds., *The Dimensions of the Past* (New Haven: Yale University Press, 1972), pp. 53–91.

48. Glass, in *London Inhabitants,* pp. xv–xvii, lists the known surviving fragments.

49. For King's involvement, see Hollingsworth, *Historical Demography,* pp. 125–27, and Glass, *London Inhabitants,* pp. xvi–xvii. The title of King's tract, *Natural and Political Observations and Conclusions upon the State and Condition of England,* shows his debt to prior efforts in political arithmetic, for it follows the title of John Graunt's *Natural and Political Observations on the Bills of Mortality* (London, 1662).

50. For the "sin of David," see 2 Sam. 24 and 1 Chron. 21. In 1753 Parliament entertained a bill calling for the complete enumeration and registration of the people of England. In the heated debate one Member of Parliament declared that, while he himself was not superstitious, letters from all over the country informed him that many people did fear that a numbering would lead to a catastrophe. See *Cobbett's Parliamentary History of England, 1066–1803,* vol. 14 (1806), pp. 1330–31.

51. Coles, *An English Dictionary,* s.v. "censor."

52. Quoted in Glass, *London Inhabitants,* p. xv.

53. Hollingsworth, *Historical Demography,* pp. 112–13. David Herlihy, who has put the 1427 *catasto* to modern use by converting it to machine-readable form, describes the format and explains the nonaggregative purpose of the Florentine surveys in "Problems of Record Linkages in Tuscan Fiscal Records of the Fifteenth Century," in E. A. Wrigley, ed., *Identifying People in the Past* (London: E. Arnold, 1973), pp. 41–56.

54. Hollingsworth, *Historical Demography,* pp. 79–81.

55. Jean Bodin, *Six Bookes of a Commonweale,* facsimile reprint of the English translation of 1606, ed. Kenneth D. McRae (Cambridge, Mass.: Harvard University Press, 1962), pp. 637–46.

56. Ibid., p. 641.

57. A. J. Tawney and R. H. Tawney, "An Occupational Census of the Seventeenth Century," *Economic History Review* 5 (1934–35): 25–64.

58. Peter Laslett and John Harrison, "Clayworth and Cogenhoe," in H. E. Bell and R. L. Ollard, eds., *Historical Essays 1600–1750, Presented to David Ogg* (New York: Barnes & Noble, 1963), pp. 157–64, 175.

59. Coles, *An English Dictionary;* Blount, *Glossographia.*

60. C. M. Law, "Local Censuses in the 18th Century," *Population Studies* 23 (1969): 87–97; Robert V. Wells, *The Population of the British Colonies in America before 1776: A Survey of Census Data* (Princeton: Princeton University Press, 1975).

61. E. G. R. Taylor, *The Mathematical Practitioners of Tudor and Stuart England* (Cambridge, Eng.: Institute of Navigation, at the Cambridge University Press, 1954), has catalogued nearly 600 practical mathematicians (teachers and instrument-makers) for the years 1485–1715. Taylor lists about 300 in business in the period 1660–1700; there were a few more, like Petty and William Derham, who were not practitioners, so the total number must rise somewhat above 300.

62. John Graunt, *Natural and Political Observations on the Bills of Mortality* (London, 1662), in Hull, *Economic Writings of Sir William Petty,* vol. 2. There has long been a debate over the authorship of this work, arising from the fact that Petty on occasion claimed the work as his own. Scholars generally agree that Graunt's mathematical work is far too careful to be the product of Petty's disorderly mind.

63. William Derham, *Physico-Theology, or, a Demonstration of the Being and Attributes of God from his Work of Creation,* 6th ed. (London, 1723), pp. 171–76. In another book Derham mused about the heights of mountains in Peru, the Alps, and the well–studied peak of Teneriffe and then applied a long-distance version of triangulation to lunar mountains; see his *Astro-Theology, or, a Demonstration of the Being and Attributes of God, from a Survey of the Heavens,* 5th ed. (London, 1726), pp. 117–21.

64. W. E. Knowles Middleton, in his *A History of the Thermometer and Its Use in Meteorology* (Baltimore: Johns Hopkins University Press, 1966), pp. 48–49, briefly discusses the oddities of formulating temperature as a quantity.

65. Mildred Campbell, " 'Of People either too Few or too Many': The Conflict of Opinion on Population and Its Relation to Emigration," in William A. Aiken and Basil Duke Henning, eds., *Conflict in Stuart England: Essays in Honour of Wallace Notestein* (New York: New York University Press, 1960), pp. 171–201.

66. Max Weber, *The Protestant Ethic and the Spirit of Capitalism,* trans. Talcott Parsons, with a foreword by R. H. Tawney (New York: Scribners', 1958).

67. Christopher Hill, *Intellectual Origins of the English Revolution* (Oxford: Clarendon Press, 1965).

68. Theodore K. Rabb, "Religion and the Rise of Modern Science," *Past and Present* 31 (1965): 376–443; Richard L. Greaves, "Puritanism and Science: The Anatomy of a Controversy," *Journal of the History of Ideas* 30 (1969): 345–68.

69. A coherent picture of the seventeenth-century crisis is presented by T. K. Rabb in his *The Struggle for Stability in Early Modern Europe* (New York: Oxford University Press, 1975).

70. Bodin, *Six Bookes,* p. 644.

Chapter 2 • Colonial Counting

1. The handiest printed sources for promotional literature include the four volumes by Peter Force, *Tracts and other Papers Relating Principally to the Origin, Settlement and Progress of the Colonies in North America* (1836) (reprint ed., Gloucester, Mass.: Peter Smith, 1963), and the multivolume series of *Original*

Narratives of Early American History, ed. J. Franklin Jameson (New York: Scribner's, 1900–1911).

2. Beauchamp Plantagenet, *A Description of the Province of New Albion* (1648), p. 20; Thomas Morton, *New English Canaan* (1632), p. 59; and John Smith, *A Description of New England* (1616), pp. 4, 15—all in Force, *Tracts*, vol. 2.

3. Raymond P. Stearns, *Science in the British Colonies of America* (Urbana: University of Illinois Press, 1970), pp. 71–74; James P. Cassedy, *Demography in Early America* (Cambridge, Mass.: Harvard University Press, 1969), pp. 11–14.

4. Smith, *Description of New England*, pp. 1–10, 12, 21.

5. Anonymous, *A Perfect Description of Virginia* (1649), in Force, *Tracts*, 2:1, 10–11.

6. Plantagenet, *Description of New Albion*, p. 5. For estimates of emigration flows, see Wesley Frank Craven, *White, Red, and Black: The Seventeenth–Century Virginian* (New York: Norton, 1971), pp. 14–16. Craven based his figures on records of headrights granted.

7. Anonymous, *New England's Plantation* (1630), p. 8, in Force, *Tracts*, vol. 1; Morton, *New English Canaan*, and Plantagenet, *Description of New Albion*, p. 20, both in *Tracts*, vol. 2; E[dward] W[illiams], *Virginia: More Especially the South Part Thereof, Richly and Truly Valued* (1650), p. 12, in *Tracts*, vol. 3.

8. Morton, *New English Canaan*, p. 32; *Calendar of State Papers, Colonial Series, 1574–1660*, 1:156 (hereafter cited as *CSPC*).

9. Winthrop to Sir Nathaniel Rich, 22 May 1634: "for the number of our people, we never took any surveigh of them, nor doe we intend it, except enforced throughe urgent occasion (Davids example stickes somewhat with us) but I esteeme them to be in all about 4000: Soules & upwarde"; Massachusetts Historical Society *Proceedings* 20 (1882–83): 43. The "Relation Concerning the Estate of New-England" appears in the *New England Historical and Genealogical Register* 40 (1886): 66–72.

10. "Relation Concerning the Estate of New-England," p. 73. Only three sorts of numbers were mentioned in it: the population, the number of cattle, and the weight of beaver skins trafficked by the Dutch.

11. Richard S. Dunn, *Sugar and Slaves: The Rise of the Planter Class in the English West Indies, 1624–1713* (Chapel Hill: University of North Carolina Press, 1972), p. 75.

12. *Nova Britannia: Offering Most Excellent Fruites by Planting in Virginia* (1609), p. 19, in Force, *Tracts*, vol. 1. For similar ideas, see *The Planter's Plea* (1630), pp. 9–11, in Force, *Tracts*, vol. 2.

13. Robert Gray, *A Good Speed to Virginia* (1609), quoted in Mildred Campbell, " 'Of People either too Few or too Many': The Conflict of Opinion on Population and Its Relation to Emigration," in William A. Aiken and Basil D. Henning, eds., *Conflict in Stuart England: Essays in Honour of Wallace Notestein* (New York: New York University Press, 1960), pp. 169–202. I am especially indebted to this article for a discussion of prequantitative attitudes toward population in Stuart England.

14. Campbell, " 'Of People either too Few or too Many,' " pp. 175 ff. E. A. Wrigley and R. S. Schofield, *The Population History of England, 1541–1871* (London: Edward Arnold, 1981), is the definitive demographic study.

15. Peter Laslett, *The World We Have Lost* (New York: Scribner's, 1965), esp. chap. 5, "Did the Peasants Really Starve?"

16. Governor Thomas Dudley's Letter to the Countess of Lincoln, March, 1631, in Force, *Tracts*, 2:8, 9, 13; and William Bradford, *The History of Plymouth Plantation, 1606–1646*, edited by William T. Davis, in Jameson, ed., *Original Narratives of Early American History*, 4:108.

17. In the 1630s Virginia, Massachusetts, and Connecticut passed laws requiring registration of burials and baptisms, echoing the spirit of the parish registers that were already traditional in England. But continuous registers of vital events do not necessarily entail any concept of magnitudes of fertility or mortality. Such early registers were maintained chiefly as a legal record to establish birth, parentage, and inheritance rights. Bills of mortality were not drawn from them until the eighteenth century. See S. Shapiro, "The Development of Birth Registration and Birth Statistics in the United States," *Population Studies* 4 (1950): 86–111; Robert Gutman, "Birth and Death Registration in Massachusetts: The Colonial Background, 1639–1800," *Milbank Memorial Fund Quarterly* 36 (1958): 58–74. Not only were the registers not kept as a tally sheet for mortality for a long time; in many places they were not kept at all, or only sporadically.

18. See Wesley Frank Craven, *Dissolution of the Virginia Company: The Failure of a Colonial Experiment* (New York: Oxford, 1932), 27–28; and *Dictionary of National Biography*, s.vv. "Ferrar, Nicholas," and "Sandys, Edwin."

19. Karen Ordahl Kupperman, "Apathy and Death in Early Jamestown," *Journal of American History* 66 (1979): 24–40; Carville V. Earle, "Environment, Disease, and Mortality in Early Virginia," in Thad W. Tate and David L. Ammerman, eds., *The Chesapeake in the Seventeenth Century* (New York: Norton, 1979), pp. 96–125; and Edmund S. Morgan, *American Slavery, American Freedom: The Ordeal of Colonial Virginia* (New York: Norton, 1975), chap. 4.

20. Susan Myra Kingsbury, ed., *Records of the Virginia Company of London*, 4 vols. (Washington, D.C.: U.S. Government Printing Office, 1935), 1:77, 356, and 3:115–16, 239–41, 639–43 (hereafter cited as *Rec. of Va. Co.*). Except for the broadsides and a few ship manifests, the company's records of emigrants have not survived. One of the few extant lists illustrates the careful work of Ferrar, for the word "dead" appears beside thirty-two out of the thirty-six names. Evidently a company man in Virginia reported on the size of the human cargo at arrival; see "A Lyst of the Men Nowe Sent for Plantation . . . ," of September, 1619, and letter of John Pory to Sir Edwin Sandys, dated January 14, 1619/20, both in *Rec. of Va. Co.*, 3:197–98, 254.

21. John Rolfe, *A Relation of the State of Virginia* (1617), in Edward D. Neill, *A History of the Virginia Company of London* (1869) (reprint ed., New York: Burt Franklin, 1968), pp. 106–12. Typically, Rolfe's figures for individual settlements in the colony do not add up to 351, despite his assertion that 351 was the exact population; see *Rec. of Va. Co.*, 3:353, 4:158, and William Waller Hening, *The Statutes at Large of the Laws of Virginia*, 13 vols. (New York, R. & W. & G. Bartow, 1814–1823), 1:115.

22. See *Rec. of Va. Co.*, 1:329–30, 334–35; and Craven, *Dissolution*, chap. 5.

23. A nineteenth-century editor of this last account felt compelled to calculate the survivors with the bracketed note "[347 × 11 = 3817]." See John Smith, *The General Historie of Virginia* (1624), in *Works*, ed. Edward Arber (The English Scholar's Library, 1884), pp. 577, 582–83. See also Edward Waterhouse, "A Declaration of the State of the Colony and Affairs in Virginia, With a Relation of the Barbarous Massacre" (1622), in *Rec. of Va. Co.*, 3:565–71; and Karen Ordahl Kupperman, *Settling with the Indians: The Meeting of English and Indian*

Cultures in America, 1580–1640 (Totawa, N.J.: Rowman & Littlefield, 1980), pp. 176–78.

24. *Rec. of Va. Co.*, 4:158.

25. Ibid., 4:158, 347.

26. George Sandys to Samuel Wrote, March 28, 1623, ibid., 4:65 (emphasis in the original).

27. "Notes from Lists Showing Total Number of Emigrants to Virginia," ibid., 3:536–37. This document is dated 1622 by the editor; but since it includes mortality reports from the Dupper's beer incident, it must have been written after April, 1623.

28. See Nathaniel Butler, "The Unmasking of Virginia" (1622), in Neill, *History of the Virginia Company*, pp. 395–402, and *Rec. of Va. Co.*, 4:174–82, 183–87.

29. Ibid., 2:399.

30. Christopher Davison to John Ferrar, April 14, 1623, ibid., 4:115–16, and *CSPC*, 1:43, 57.

31. *Rec. of Va. Co.*, 4:441.

32. Order of the Privy Council, October 24, 1623, *CSPC*, 1:53–54.

33. One commissioner, John Harvey, documented his entry into the colony by stepping off the ship with a petition of complaint against the captain and first mate; see *Rec. of Va. Co.*, 4:495–96.

34. *CSPC*, 1:57. The *Calendar* only abstracts the list; the list itself has been published in J. C. Hotten, *The Original Lists of Persons of Quality* (New York: J. W. Bouton, 1874), but with errors. The original has been put on microfilm as part of the Virginia Colony Records Project.

35. There were, of course, other reasons why the crown was disposed to dissolve the company, including the near bankruptcy of the operation and the machinations of English politicians connected to the various factions. The details are in Craven, *Dissolution*.

36. Irene Hecht, "The Virginia Muster of 1624/25 as a Source for Demographic History," *William and Mary Quarterly* 3d ser. 30 (1973): 65–92. Hecht presents a computer analysis of demographic characteristics of the population. Edmund Morgan has used the census to reach intriguing conclusions about Virginia masters and servants in "The First American Boom: Virginia 1618–1630," *WMQ* 3d ser. 30 (1972): 469–78. Abstracts of the census appear in *CSPC*, 1:72, and in A. C. Quisenberry, "The Virginia Census, 1624–1625," *Virginia Magazine of History and Biography* 7 (1899–1900): 364–67.

37. *Rec. of Va. Co.*, 4:563.

38. *CSPC*, 1:79.

39. John Harvey to Nathaniel Rich, April 24, 1624, in *Rec. of Va. Co.*, 4:476.

40. It is difficult to be exact about numbers, since the census lists are, in places, open to interpretation. Hecht, Morgan, and Craven all come to different conclusions about the actual total number of people counted. For a discussion of the vagaries of the data, see Morgan, *American Slavery, American Freedom*, pp. 395–405.

41. Craven, *Red, White, and Black*, pp. 15–16; *CSPC*, 1:77, 81–82, 84–85, 175, 208.

42. Hening, *Statutes at Large*, 1:166, 191.

43. Ibid., pp. 174–75, 200.

44. *CSPC*, 1:281, 287.

45. Ibid., pp. 175, 201.

46. To find out how much of a problem it was, historians have had to develop rather ingenious techniques; see Russell R. Menard and Lorena S. Walsh, "Death in the Chesapeake: Two Life Tables for Men in Early Colonial Maryland," *Maryland Historical Magazine* 69 (1974): 211–27.

47. Hening, *Statutes at Large*, 1:157, 164, 206, 212; *CSPC*, 1:113.

48. *CSPC*, 1:160, 175.

49. Ibid., p. 266.

50. J. Mills Thornton, "The Thrusting Out of Governor Harvey: A Seventeenth-Century Rebellion," *Virginia Magazine of History and Biography* 76 (1968): 11–26; Bernard Bailyn, "Politics and Social Structure in Virginia," in J. M. Smith, ed., *Seventeenth-Century America* (Chapel Hill: University of North Carolina Press, 1959), pp. 94–98.

51. Robert V. Wells's book on colonial censuses, *The Population of the British Colonies in America before 1776* (Princeton: Princeton University Press, 1975), is an invaluable guide to official records, printed and archival. Wells's principal task was to analyze the best of these censuses for standard demographic measures. He did not delve into the context of each census and only occasionally and fleetingly suggests the motivation behind some of the enumerations. He restricted his interest to province–wide censuses, ignoring censuses of smaller geographical areas.

A second indispensable guide, this one to the West Indies censuses, is Richard S. Dunn, *Sugar and Slaves: The Rise of the Planter Class in the English West Indies, 1624–1713* (Chapel Hill: University of North Carolina Press, 1972). Like Wells, Dunn was more interested in what he could learn about social structure from the few good censuses.

52. The informal survey is abstracted in *CSPC*, 1:492.

53. Ibid., pp. 492–93.

54. For 1661, see *CSPC*, 5:65; for 1662, see Dunn, *Sugar and Slaves*, p. 155; for 1665, see Wells, *Population of the British Colonies*, p. 194; for 1670, see *CSPC*, 7:99–104; for 1671, see *CSPC*, 7:304 (list mentioned but not included); for 1673, see *CPSC*, 7:476; for 1680, see *CSPC*, 10:537–43.

55. Its entry in *CSPC* indicates nothing about its origin, and historian Robert Wells, who has studied the original in the Colonial Office, does not give further details about the circumstances surrounding the document. No official royal governor was as yet established in Jamaica, so it is hard to determine responsibility for the document; see *CSPC*, 5:65, and Wells, *Population of the British Colonies*, p. 194.

56. Instructions to Lord Windsor, *CSPC*, 5:81.

57. Ibid., pp. 117–18.

58. Dunn, *Sugar and Slaves*, p. 155.

59. For suggestion of a 1665 census, see Wells, *Population of the British Colonies*, p. 194. The 1670 survey refers to a list "made two years since" (*CSPC*, 7:104). Dunn (*Sugar and Slaves*, p. 155) says that a census of 1662 appears in *Journals of the House of Assembly of Jamaica* 1 (1811–29): 20.

60. *CSPC*, 7:98–104.

61. Ibid., p. 104.

62. Ibid., pp. 106–7 (September 28, 1670).

63. Thomas Modyford to the Earl of Arlington, August 20, 1670 (ibid., p. 83).

64. Charles Andrews, *The Colonial Period of American History*, 4 vols. (New Haven: Yale University Press, 1934–38), 4:56–58.

65. Arlington to Modyford, June 12, 1670 (*CSPC*, 7:69).

66. Modyford to Arlington, August 20, 1670 (ibid., p. 83).

67. September 23, 1670 (ibid., p. 98).

68. Ibid., pp. xxvi–xxvii.

69. Ibid., pp. 77–78.

70. Leonard Woods Labaree, ed., *Royal Instructions to British Colonial Governors, 1670–1776,* 2 vols. (New York: Appleton-Century, 1935), 2:746–47.

71. "The Governor of Jamaica's answers to the inquiries of his Majesty's Commissioners," *CSPC,* 7:302–7.

72. Ibid., p. 476. The count itself was not preserved with the letter in the colonial office.

73. Dunn, *Sugar and Slaves,* p. 155.

74. Andrews, *Colonial Period,* 4:58.

75. *CSPC,* 10:468–69.

76. See ibid., pp. 537–43, for abstracts. The manuscript census is at the Public Record Office and has been consulted by Dunn and Wells, who perform interesting and very different analyses of it.

77. The survey listed the names of the militia leader and the *Custos Rotulorum* for each district, and in five of seven cases the names are the same. Such an overlap makes it hard to claim that this survey differed significantly from the 1673 census in terms of the method of enumeration; in the earlier year the militia leaders had conducted it.

78. Wells's phrase, in *Population of the British Colonies,* p. 202.

79. Dunn, *Sugar and Slaves,* p. 174, gives a sample abstract.

80. Dunn and Wells consider these to have been censuses; see Dunn, *Sugar and Slaves,* p. 87, and Wells, *Population of the British Colonies,* pp. 236–37.

81. *CSPC,* 7:495–97.

82. Ibid., p. 495.

83. Ibid., 9:348–49.

84. Ibid., pp. 422–23.

85. Ibid., 10:387–88 and 401–2, for complaints from the Lords to Atkins about his inability to comply.

86. Ibid., pp. 742–43.

87. Ibid., pp. 501–15.

88. Ibid., pp. 504–5.

89. Ibid., pp. 566–67.

90. Ibid., pp. 504, 567, 584.

91. All ably analyzed by Richard Dunn in *Sugar and Slaves,* chap. 3 (originally published as "The Barbados Census of 1680," *William and Mary Quarterly* 3d ser. 26 (1969): 3–30).

92. *CSPC,* 11:70–72, 75, 119, 151, 205.

93. Quoted in Dunn, *Sugar and Slaves,* p. 89, note.

94. *CSPC,* 10:153. For an abstract of returns, see ibid., pp. 262–68. The original is in the Colonial Office, and the data are analyzed by Dunn in *Sugar and Slaves,* pp. 126–31. For the 1707 census, see Wells, *Population of the British Colonies,* p. 8.

95. *CSPC,* 10:153, 156, 417, 643, and 9:259, 275–77, 508–9.

96. Andrews, *Colonial Period,* 4:120.

97. G. N. Clark, *Guide to English Commercial Statistics, 1696–1782* (London: Royal Historical Society, 1938), p. xvi. None of the Naval Lists from before 1689

survives in the Public Record Office, according to Andrews, *Colonial Period,* 4:189, note.

98. Andrews, *Colonial Period,* 4:189, note.

99. Peter Laslett, "John Locke and the Origins of the Board of Trade, 1695–1698," *William and Mary Quarterly* 3d ser. 14 (1957): 370–95; Clark, *Guide to English Commercial Statistics,* pp. 1–15; and Michael G. Hall, "The House of Lords, Edward Randolph, and the Navigation Act of 1696," *William and Mary Quarterly* 3d ser. 14 (1957): 494–515.

100. Laslett, "John Locke," pp. 370–71. John Locke, Charles Montagu, and John Somers were the three. See chap. 1, above.

101. John J. McCusker, "The Current Value of English Exports, 1697–1800," *William and Mary Quarterly* 3d ser. 28 (1971): 609.

102. All these censuses have been noted by Wells in *Population of the British Colonies.*

103. The census-taking mentality was not totally absent in these provinces. Occasional local censuses, such as the Bristol census of 1689, show that New England residents shared the new interest in enumerating and enrolling the population. The original purpose of the Bristol census is now quite lost; historian John Demos found the census itself in a transcribed version in the *New England Historical and Genealogical Register* 34 (1880): 404–5, with no clue as to its authorship or motivation. Demos's particular use of it is, of course, a product of the new interest in the 1960s in quantified social history; see his "Families in Colonial Bristol, Rhode Island: An Exercise in Historical Demography," *William and Mary Quarterly* 3d ser. 25 (1968): 40–57.

The *New England Historical and Genealogical Register* often printed raw data like tax lists and registers, in keeping with the nineteenth-century fondness for "positive" knowledge. In 1851 (vol. 5, pp. 171–74), the editors presented a report titled "Middlesex Statistics, 1680," consisting of figures collected in six towns in Middlesex County, Massachusetts, and returned to the county court of Charlestown. The figures include counts of taxable males; families; aged, poor, and widows; schools and scholars; tithingmen; single persons and other "inmates"; and a report of the minister's salary. There is no indication of why the county court wanted this information.

The *Register* is also the only source for a 1675 document titled "Account of New England," which estimated total population, families, and militia and mentioned other quantities based on guesswork: 5 ironworks, 15 merchants worth £50,000, 500 persons worth £3,000 each (a cynical "I doubt it" appears in the margin here), 35 rivers and harbors, and so on. The desire to have quantified accounts of New England clearly existed in the late seventeenth century; the motivation can only be guessed at.

104. Robert G. Pope, *The Half–Way Covenant: Church Membership in Puritan New England* (Princeton: Princeton University Press, 1969).

105. Edgar Knight, ed., *A Documentary History of Education in the South before 1860,* 5 vols. (Chapel Hill: University of North Carolina Press, 1949), 1:74.

106. David Humphreys, *An Historical Account of the Incorporated Society for the Propagation of the Gospel in Foreign Parts* (London, 1730), p. 71.

Chapter 3 • Patterns and Providence

1. "On the Usefulness of the Mathematicks," *Pennsylvania Gazette,* October 23, 1735.

2. *Benjamin Franklin: The Autobiography and Other Writings,* ed. L. Jesse Lemisch (New York: New American Library, 1961), p. 30.

3. For discussions of the rise of the capitalist mentality in eighteenth-century agriculture, see James Henretta, "Families and Farms: *Mentalité* in Pre-Industrial America," *William and Mary Quarterly* 3d ser. 35 (1978): 3–32; and Joyce Appleby, "Commercial Farming and the 'Agrarian Myth' in the Early Republic," *Journal of American History* 68 (1982): 833–49.

4. W. T. Baxter, "Accounting in Colonial America," in B. S. Yamey and A. C. Littleton, eds., *Studies in the History of Accounting* (London: Sweet & Maxwell, 1956), pp. 272–87; Roy J. Sampson, "American Accounting Education, Textbooks and Public Practice Prior to 1900," *Business History Review* 34 (1960): 459–66.

5. Nathaniel Bowen, *The New-England Diary, or Almanack for 1736* (Boston, 1735); Benjamin Franklin, *Poor Richard Improved, for 1750* (Philadelphia, 1749); *The New York Gazette,* July 12, 1731; *The Pennsylvania Gazette,* August 5, 1731. The Royal Society's *Philosophical Transactions,* in which quite a number of demographic articles were published, was also read by the scientific community in the colonies.

6. Americans were not alone in this view of demography as an expression of the divine order. Both William Derham and John Arbuthnot in England were convinced they had uncovered the fixed laws of God, as was J. P. Süssmilch, a German clergyman whose demographic book, *Die gottliche Ordnung,* appeared in 1741.

7. Silvio A. Bedini, *Thinkers and Tinkers: Early American Men of Science* (New York: Scribner's, 1975), pp. 63–64, 150–62, 272–73; Bedini, *Early American Scientific Instruments and Their Makers,* United States National Museum *Bulletin* no. 231 (Washington, D.C., 1964); and E. G. R. Taylor, *The Mathematical Practitioners of Tudor and Stuart England* (Cambridge, Eng.: At the University Press, 1954).

8. Bedini, *Thinkers and Tinkers,* pp. 157–58, 160.

9. Marian Barber Stowell, *Early American Almanacs: The Colonial Weekday Bible* (New York: Burt Franklin, 1977); Charles L. Nichols, *Notes on the Almanacs of Massachusetts* (Worcester, Mass.: American Antiquarian Society, 1912).

10. Brooke Hindle, *The Pursuit of Science in Revolutionary America* (Chapel Hill: University of North Carolina Press, 1956), remains the classic work on these scientists and their achievements.

11. An excellent guide to colonial bills of mortality appears in James H. Cassedy, *Demography in Early America* (Cambridge, Mass.: Harvard University Press, 1969), pp. 117–47. For vital registration laws, see Robert Gutman, "Birth and Death Registration in Massachusetts," *Milbank Memorial Fund Quarterly* 36 (1958): 58–74; Robert Kuczynski, "The Registration Laws in the Colonies of Massachusetts Bay and New Plymouth," *Journal of the American Statistical Association* 7 (1900): 65–73.

12. *Boston News-Letter,* July 3, 1704.

13. A convenient summary discussion of the origins and uses of the London bills is included in T. H. Hollingsworth, *Historical Demography* (Ithaca: Cornell University Press, 1969), p. 145.

14. Thomas Prince, "An Account of the Burials in Boston, in New England, from the Year 1701 to 1752, and of the Christenings from 1731 to 1752," *Gentleman's Magazine* 23 (1753): 413–15; *Pennsylvania Gazette*, August 19–22, 1731; "An Account of Burials and Baptisms in Boston, from the Year 1701 to 1774," Massachusetts Historical Society, *Collections* 1st ser. 4 (1795): 213–16.

15. *Boston News-Letter*, July 3, 1704. A mortality of 1 in 50 translates to a crude death rate of 20 per 1,000 population, which would indeed be a very healthy rate for any place in the eighteenth century. John Blake has calculated death rates for Boston using these bills and population estimates for the city; he puts the death rate at 31 for the year 1704, and figures a five–year average death rate of 36 for the years 1701–5. (John Blake, *Public Health in the Town of Boston, 1630–1822* [Cambridge, Mass.: Harvard University Press, 1959], pp. 246–50).

16. *Boston News-Letter*, March 10, 1706/7.

17. Ibid., June 10, 1706.

18. *Boston Gazette*, March 13, 1721/22.

19. William Petty, "Of Lands & Hands," Statistical Paper no. 58, in Lord Lansdowne, ed., *The Petty Papers*, 2 vols. (London: Constable, 1927), 2:195.

20. David E. Stannard, in *The Puritan Way of Death* (New York: Oxford University Press, 1977), discusses the Puritan preoccupation with death as an important tension in Puritan culture.

21. *The Spectator*, January 31, 1712, in *The Spectator [by] Addison & Steel, and Others*, ed. Gregory Smith, 4 vols. (New York: Dutton, 1956–61), 2:362.

22. Edward Johnson, *Wonder-Working Providence of Sion's Saviour in New England, 1628–1651*, in J. Franklin Jameson, ed., *Original Narratives of Early American History* (New York: Scribner's, 1910), pp. 254–56.

23. John Brown, *The Number of Deaths in Haverhill, And Also Some Comfortable Instances Thereof Among the Children, under the Late Distemper in the Throat, with an Address to the Bereaved*, 2d ed. (Boston, 1738). The tables of dead appear on pages numbered 1 to 3; but with the prose accounts of deathbed scenes, the pagination begins again, with pages 1–69. Possibly the tables were added later, after the body of the work had gone to press. The first edition of 1736 has not survived.

24. I can find no evidence that this projected publication ever materialized. The standard account of the epidemic is Ernest Caulfield's "A History of the Terrible Epidemic, Vulgarly Called the Throat Distemper, as it Occurred in His Majesty's New England Colonies between 1735 and 1740," *Yale Journal of Biology and Medicine* 11 (1938–39): 219–72, 277–335.

25. Jabez Fitch, *An Account of the Numbers that have died of the Distemper in the Throat, within the Province of New-Hampshire, with some Reflections thereon* (Boston, 1736), p. 1. Fitch's pamphlet was dated July 26, 1736, the same year as the first edition of Brown's pamphlet on Haverhill. Their publishers were not the same, so it seems unlikely that Fitch's pamphlet was the product of Brown's request for more data.

26. Joseph Emerson, *A Word to those that are Afflicted* (Boston, 1738), p. 5. A "besom" is a broom made of twigs.

27. Jabez Fitch, *Two Sermons on Occasion of the fatal Distemper which prevailed in sundry Towns within the Province of New Hampshire* (Boston, 1736), p. 1.

28. Fitch, *An Account of the Numbers,* p. 7.

29. David Stannard, in "Death and the Puritan Child," *American Quarterly* 26 (1974): 456–76, discusses the literary evidence that Puritans taught their children to be obsessed with death, and he speculates on the possible effects that this had on personality development.

30. Fitch, *An Account of the Numbers,* pp. 9–11.

31. Maris A. Vinovskis, in "Angels' Heads and Weeping Willows: Death in Early America," American Antiquarian Society *Proceedings* 86 (1976): 273–302, takes up the question why the great improvement in mortality rates in colonial America was not perceived by the Puritans, who continued to be obsessed with death even when death was in fact no longer so imminent. His answer is that the experience of death, in small towns and large families, was much closer then than it is today, even though adult mortality today is only fractionally improved over the colonists'.

For changing attitudes toward children in the colonies, see John F. Walzer, "A Period of Ambivalence: Eighteenth-Century American Childhood," in Lloyd deMause, ed., *The History of Childhood* (New York: Harper Torchbooks, 1974), pp. 351–82.

32. Cotton Mather, *Seasonable Thoughts Upon Mortality* (Boston, 1712), pp. 2, 15. Another minister who used political arithmetic in his sermons was Thomas Prince; see his *A Sermon Occasioned by the Death of the Honourable Mary Belcher* (Boston, 1736).

33. Sermons delivered during funerals of young people referred to early deaths but did not convey the sense that the deaths were unnecessary or preventable. For example, the Reverend Thomas Prince mourned the death of a youth in his twenties, who died an "early death" in the "Flower of Life," a youth who was so "Hopeful" to his parents that it was hard not to think that he was being prepared for some great work on earth. But God took him away to an "Early Death"; "How unsearchable are his Judgments!" The youth was "like a blazing meteor"; his life demonstrated God's power to create spectacular things and then make them vanish. See Thomas Prince, *A Sermon Occasioned by the Death of Young Mr. Daniel Oliver* (Boston, 1727), pp. 2, 3, 11, 12.

34. *New York Gazette,* July 12, 1731, and the *Pennsylvania Gazette,* August 5, 1731; the article was taken from the *Political State* (London), February and March, 1730/31.

35. Bowen, *The New-England Diary, or Almanack for 1736.*

36. *New York Gazette,* July 12, 1731.

37. See Otho T. Beall, Jr., and Richard H. Shryock, *Cotton Mather, First Significant Figure in American Medicine* (Baltimore: Johns Hopkins University Press, 1954); Raymond P. Stearns, *Science in the British Colonies* (Urbana: University of Illinois Press, 1970), pp. 417–23; Blake, *Public Health in the Town of Boston,* chaps. 4, 5, 6; and Ola Elizabeth Winslow, *A Destroying Angel: The Conquest of Smallpox in Colonial Boston* (Boston: Houghton, Mifflin, 1974). In an opposing view, Robert Middlekauff argues that Mather was not a significant innovator in medicine and that only luck saved him from being the agent of a horrendous calamity, an epidemical combustion of the disease, as the result of

his inoculations. See Middlekauff's *The Mathers: Three Generations of Puritan Intellectuals, 1596–1728* (New York: Oxford University Press, 1971), pp. 354–59.

38. Stearns, *Science in the British Colonies,* p. 679.

39. Perry Miller's chapter on smallpox in *The New England Mind, from Colony to Province* (Cambridge, Mass.: Harvard University Press, 1953), pp. 345–66, clarifies this distinction between the religious and medical significance of inoculation but makes no reference to the implications of the power of empirical facts.

40. According to the *Boston Gazette* of July 27, 1721, only six ministers were publicly associated with inoculation: Cotton Mather, Increase Mather, Benjamin Colman, Thomas Prince, John Webb, and William Cooper. Their medical opponent, Douglass, pointed out that this was only six out of the sixteen ministers in Boston; see William Douglass, *The Abuses and Scandals of some late Pamphlets in Favour of Inoculation of the Smallpox* (Boston, 1722), p. i.

41. Samuel Grainger, *The Imposition of Inoculation as a Duty Religiously Considered* (Boston, 1721/22).

42. *Boston News-Letter,* issues of May 15, 22, and 29, 1721. The thoroughness of the count was attested to by the force deployed: the justices, selectmen, overseers of the poor, and town constables all "made a strict search and enquiry of the Inhabitants at their respective Houses, touching the Smallpox."

43. *The Diary of Cotton Mather,* 2 vols. (New York: Frederick Ungar, 1957), 2:621, 624. On May 26 Mather noted his intention to circulate the letter, and on June 6 he did so. Mather's source was Emanuel Timonius, "An Account, or History, of the Procuring the Small Pox by Incision, or Inoculation; as it has for some time been practised at Constantinople," Royal Society, *Philosophical Transactions* 29 (1714): 72–76; and Jacobus Pylarinus, ibid. 29 (1716): 393.

44. Zabdiel Boylston, *An Historical Account of the Small Pox Inoculation in New England* (Boston, 1730).

45. *Diary of Cotton Mather,* 2:628, entry for June 30, 1721; *Boston Gazette,* July 10, 1721; Boylston, *Historical Account,* pp. 51–54.

46. "W. Philanthropos," *Boston News-Letter,* July 23, 1721.

47. *Diary of Cotton Mather,* 2:632, entries for July 16 and 18, 1721.

48. Boylston, *Some Account of What is Said of Inoculation for Transplanting the Small Pox* (Boston, 1721). This pamphlet is attributed to Mather by Blake and others. It was probably written by Mather in June or July, 1721, and published under Boylston's name in August. In his diary for those months Mather discussed a tract he had written on this topic. Perry Miller, without citing authority or reason, says this pamphlet was published in February, 1722. Since the author did not concede that inoculation could cause death, and since both Boylston and Mather agreed by 1722 that it could, I put the date of this piece earlier, before the first acknowledged death.

49. Grainger, *The Imposition of Inoculation,* p. 7. For the authorship of this pamphlet and a brief biography of Grainger, see the long introduction by George L. Kittredge to the reprinted versions of Increase Mather's *Several Reasons Proving that Inoculating or Transplanting the Small Pox is a Lawful Practice,* and Cotton Mather's *Sentiments on the Small Pox Inoculated,* both originally published in 1721 (Cleveland: Printed for private distribution, 1921), pp. 24–26.

50. Ibid., pp. 14, 25.

51. See, for example, the letter of the six ministers, published in the *Boston Gazette,* July 31, 1721, and Boylston's *Some Account of What is Said.*

52. William Cooper, *A Letter to a Friend in the Country, Attempting a Solution of the Scruples and Objections of a Conscientious or Religious Nature, Commonly made against the New Way of receiving the Small Pox* (Boston, 1721; dated November 10), p. 10.

53. Boylston, *An Historical Account*, pp. 51–54.

54. *Boston News-Letter*, May 22 and 29, June 5, July 31, September 25, October 9, 1721, and February 24, 1722; see also the *Boston Gazette*, October 6, 1721. The *News-Letter* misprinted the death toll as 233 but gave subtotals that added up to 203; the *Gazette* printed 203, correctly.

55. William Douglass, *Inoculation of the Small-Pox as Practiced in Boston* (Boston, 1722), p. 20; Douglass, *Abuses and Scandals*, p. 11; Benjamin Colman, *Some Observations on the New Method of Receiving the Small-Pox* (Boston, 1721), p. 3. Colman, a proponent of inoculation, innocently boasted that inoculated patients had such a slight case that their friends visited them and "stood smiling about them."

56. Douglass, *Abuses and Scandals*, pp. 6–7.

57. *Boston Gazette*, October 23, 1721.

58. Boylston's *Historical Account* gives a case-by-case summary from which one can reconstruct the daily fluctuations in inoculations.

59. Douglass was never more specific than "several" in his pamphlets of 1722; see, for example, his *Inoculation of the Small-Pox*, pp. 5, 11. See also Boylston, *Historical Account*, p. 34.

60. Boylston, *Historical Account*, pp. 32–32, 50.

61. Boylston's phrase, one in "six or seven," was a circumlocution necessitated by the eighteenth-century preference for expressing risks in the form "1 out of x chances." If the fraction reduced to 2 out of x, and x was not an even number, as in the case of 2 out of 13, then the inexact phrase "1 in 6 or 7" gave a close enough answer. Today we prefer to convert the denominator to 100, so this risk would be expressed as 15.4 percent; that is, 15.4 out of every 100 who caught smallpox died, compared to 1.1 percent of the inoculated patients.

62. Mather did not keep complete quantitative records of the progress of inoculation or of the disease. At the height of the epidemic, in October and November, he did note in the margins of his diary the numbers of people asking for special prayers for the sick among his congregation alone. These numbers indicated the measure of his duty to pray, not a measure of the disease. In England, James Jurin used Mather's data in an essay in the Royal Society's *Philosophical Transactions* 32 (1722): 213–25.

63. Douglass, *A Dissertation Concerning Inoculation of the Small-Pox* (Boston, 1730), pp. 14–15.

64. Ibid., p. 23.

65. The two doctors whose records survive are Boylston, *New-England Weekly Journal*, April 20, 1730, and Nathanael Williams, *The Method of Practice in the Small-Pox, with Observations in the Way of Inoculation* (Boston, 1752), both noted in Blake, *Public Health in the Town of Boston*, p. 77. More than two decades after the epidemic William Douglass estimated that a total of 400 had been inoculated in 1730; see his *Summary, Historical and Political, of the First Planting, Progressive Improvements, and Present State of the British Settlements in North-America*, 2 vols. (London, 1755), 2:397.

66. Prince, "An Account of the Burials in Boston," pp. 413–15 (see n. 14, above).

67. Ibid.

68. Lauchlin Macleane, *An Essay on the Expediency of Inoculation* (Philadelphia, 1756), pp. 13, 15, 20–21.

69. Blake *(Public Health in the Town of Boston*, pp. 243–46) conveniently tabulates the statistics of smallpox for eighteenth-century Boston. The 1764 figures were collected by the selectmen.

70. "A Description of Boston," Massachusetts Historical Society *Collections* 1st ser. 3 (1794): 291–92.

71. Vinovskis ("Angels' Heads and Weeping Willows," pp. 273–79) evaluates the research of Philip Greven, John Demos, John Blake, and others on the mortality picture for colonial New England and agrees with them that life-expectancy was astonishingly high in the seventeenth and eighteenth centuries. A recent reevaluation of the evidence by David Hackett Fischer suggests a more moderate picture but grants that life-expectancy was still far greater than anywhere else in the English world; see Fischer, *Growing Old in America* (New York: Oxford University Press, 1977), pp. 27–28, 225–26.

72. Vinovskis, "Angels' Heads and Weeping Willows."

73. James H. Cassedy, "Meteorology and Medicine in Colonial America: Beginnings of the Experimental Approach," *Journal of the History of Medicine* 24 (1969): 193–204. Cassedy discusses American physicians who monitored the weather in order to seek connections with diseases. A fuller list than Cassedy's (but one still not exhaustive) of pre-Revolutionary weather-charters would include Cadwallader Colden of New York and Thomas Robie of Harvard in the 1710s; William Douglass of Boston and Isaac Greenwood of Harvard in the 1720s; John Lining of Charleston in the 1730s; Thomas Clap of Yale and John Winthrop IV of Harvard in the 1740s; Lionel Chalmers of South Carolina, Richard Brooke of Maryland, and Henry Ellis of Georgia in the 1750s; George Milligen of South Carolina, J. Lorimer of Florida, and Ezra Stiles and James Moffat of Newport, Rhode Island, in the 1760s. In the 1750s and 1760s several American periodicals began to print tables of monthly weather readings: the *New American Magazine,* the *New York Weekly Mercury,* the *Maryland Gazette,* and the *Pennsylvania Chronicle* (noted in Hindle, *Pursuit of Science,* p. 183 [see n. 10, above]). After the Revolution, in the 1780s, quantitative weather records were commonplace in the press.

74. "Extracts of Two Letters from Dr. John Lining, Physician at Charles Town in South Carolina, to James Jurin, M.D.F.R.S., giving an Account of Statical Experiments made several times in a Day upon himself, for one whole year, accompanied with Meteorological Observations," Royal Society, *Philosophical Transactions* 42 (1742–43): 491–509; see also further comments, ibid. 43 (1744–45): 318–30. "Statics" meant the art of weighing; around 1800 it was sometimes confused with the new word "statistics," which means "affairs of state," from Latin *status,* "state," plus *-isticus, -*istic.

75. Ibid., 43 (1744-45): 319.

76. Edmund S. Morgan, *The Gentle Puritan: A Life of Ezra Stiles, 1727–1795* (New Haven: Yale University Press, 1962), pp. 117, 123–24, 126, 139.

77. *The Literary Diary of Ezra Stiles,* ed. Franklin Bowditch Dexter, 3 vols. (New York: Scribner's, 1901), 1:8–9.

78. Morgan, *Gentle Puritan,* pp. 135, 140–41; Cassedy, *Demography in Early America,* pp. 111–16.

79. Garry Wills develops at length the view of Jefferson as quantifier in *Inventing America: Jefferson's Declaration of Independence* (Garden City, N.Y.: Doubleday, 1978), pp. 93–164.

80. Herbert L. Ganter, "William Small, Jefferson's Beloved Teacher," *William and Mary Quarterly* 3d ser. 4 (1947): 505–9; Thomas Jefferson, "Second State of the Reports of Weights and Measures," April–May 1790, in Julian P. Boyd, ed., *The Papers of Thomas Jefferson,* vol. 16 (Princeton: Princeton University Press, 1961), p. 631; William Pattison, "Reflections on the American Rectangular Land Survey System," and Hildegard Binder Johnson, "The United States Land Survey as a Principle of Order," both in Ralph E. Ehrenberg, ed., *Patterns and Process: Research in Historical Geography* (Washington, D.C.: Howard University Press, 1975), pp. 114–38; Hildegard Binder Johnson, *Order upon the Land: The United States Rectangular Land Survey and the Upper Mississippi Country* (New York: Oxford University Press, 1976).

81. Quoted in Wills, *Inventing America,* p. 119, from Jefferson's *Garden Book,* entry for May 23, 1773 (page 44).

82. Dumas Malone's comment on this incident *(Jefferson the Virginian* [Boston: Little, Brown, 1948], p. 161) is that Jefferson "did not wear his heart upon his sleeve" and turned "for relief to figures."

83. Ben Franklin to Catherine Ray, October 16, 1755, in Lemisch, ed., *Benjamin Franklin: Autobiography,* pp. 285–86.

84. Alfred O. Aldridge, "Franklin as Demographer," *Journal of Economic History* 9 (1949): 29–44. Not until the 1790s did someone try to flesh out Franklin's guess with data; see William Barton, *Observations on the Progress of Population and the Probabilities of the Duration of Human Life, in the United States of America* (Philadelphia, 1791).

85. Lemisch, ed., *Benjamin Franklin: Autobiography,* p. 72.

86. John Johnson, *A Mathematical Question, Propounded by the Viceregent of the World, Answered by the King of Glory* (Boston, 1762; Exeter, 1789; Hartford, 1790; Boston, 1794; Windsor, Vt., 1794; Amherst, N.H., 1797), pp. 1–11, 63–75.

Chapter 4 • Republican Arithmetic

1. *The Portfolio* 1 (1801): 110. "Oliver Oldschool" was the pen name of journalist Joseph Dennie, a one-time New Hampshire lawyer who found county-level courts too boring for his tastes. He attended Harvard in the late 1780s, at a time when several Harvard students complained about the practice of appointing mathematics tutors who were better classicists than mathematicians. Perhaps Dennie suffered through arithmetic under a tutor who would have preferred to teach Greek. See the *National Cyclopaedia of American Biography,* s.v. "Dennie, Joseph," and Cajori's *The Teaching and History of Mathematics in the United States* (Washington, D.C.: Bureau of Education Circular, 1890), p. 57.

2. The history of the teaching of elementary mathematics is still a quite unworked field. Cajori's *Teaching and History of Mathematics* and his later work, *A History of Elementary Mathematics* (New York: Macmillan, 1896), remain the most valuable works on the subject, but they are flawed by inattention to detail; footnotes are scanty and in several cases the sources do not contain the information attributed to them. Augustus de Morgan's well-annotated bibliography, *Arithmetical Books from the Invention of Printing to the Present Time* (London:

Taylor & Walton, 1847), is very helpful for marking out trends, as is Louis C. Karpinski's *Bibliography of Mathematical Works Printed in America through 1850* (Ann Arbor: University of Michigan Press, 1940). David Eugene Smith, *A History of Mathematics,* 2 vols. (Boston: Ginn, 1923), is large in scope but very thin in detail; Smith's *History of Mathematics in America before 1900,* coauthored with Jekuthiel Ginsburg (Chicago: Open Court, 1934), skims the surface and has no footnotes. Clifton Johnson, *Old Time Schools and School Books* (New York: Macmillan, 1917), and George Emery Littlefield, *Early Schools and Schoolbooks of New England* (New York: Russell & Russell, 1905), contain useful comments on the major textbooks of arithmetic but limit themselves to a narrow institutional definition of education. Florence Yeldham, *The Teaching of Arithmetic through Four Hundred Years, 1535–1935* (London: Harrap, 1936), omits the whole genre of commercial texts.

A more recent book, *A History of Mathematics Education in the United States and Canada,* Thirty-second Yearbook of the National Council of Teachers of Mathematics, (Washington, D.C., 1970), leans heavily on Cajori, with an acknowledgement of the debt. Lawrence Cremin, in both his *American Education: The Colonial Experience, 1607–1783,* and his *American Education: The National Experience* (New York: Harper & Row, 1970, 1978), makes only sporadic and limited reference to arithmetic teaching. Robert Middlekauff's *Ancients and Axioms* (New Haven: Yale University Press, 1963) contains a very useful chapter on the mathematics taught in secondary schools in the colonies. Daniel Calhoun, in his *The Intelligence of a People* (Princeton: Princeton University Press, 1973), does the best job of uncovering what children in the nineteenth century were taught in the way of verbal and quantitative skills.

3. Quoted in David Tyack, ed., *Turning Points in American Education History* (Waltham, Mass.: Blaisdell, 1967), p. 21.

4. John Arbuthnot, "An Essay on the Usefulness of Mathematical Learning," in *The Life and Works of John Arbuthnot,* ed. George Atherton Aitken (Oxford: Clarendon Press, 1892), p. 421.

5. A. S., Jr., letter to editor, *Connecticut Common School Journal and Annals of Education* 2 (1839): 93–94.

6. Edward Cocker's *Arithmetick* (London, 1677) and James Hodder's *Arithmetick* (London, 1661) were imported in large numbers and were reprinted in American editions in the eighteenth century; see Cremin, *American Education,* pp. 501–2.

7. "Extracts from Confessions of a School Master," *Connecticut Common School Journal and Annals of Education* 2 (1839): 77.

8. "History of a Common School, From 1801 to 1831," *American Annals of Instruction* 2 (1831): 472.

9. Isaac Greenwood, *Arithmetick Vulgar and Decimal, with the Application thereof, to a Variety of Cases in Trade, and Commerce* (Boston, 1729), pp. ii, iv.

10. Middlekauff, *Ancients and Axioms,* p. 13.

11. Benjamin Franklin, "Proposals Relating to the Education of Youth in Pennsylvania," in *Benjamin Franklin: The Autobiography and Other Writings,* ed. L. Jesse Lemisch (New York: New American Library, 1961), p. 213.

12. "Daniel Webster—Autobiography (1829)," *American Journal of Education* 27 (1877): 282–83.

13. "Memoirs of Caleb Bingham," *Barnard's Journal of Education* 5 (1855): 336.

14. Harvard University has some five dozen manuscript copybooks made by New England students between 1739 and 1850; Bradford College in Bradford, Massachusetts, has an additional three.

15. The problems in the text are taken from the copybooks of Samuel Whitteman, Cambridge, Massachusetts, 1776, Theophilus Manning, 1797, and Lydia Thayer, undated; all at the Widener Library, Harvard; and an anonymous, undated copybook at Bradford, from the early 1800s.

16. Cajori, *Teaching and History of Mathematics,* pp. 18–35, 55–74; Middlekauff, *Ancients and Axioms,* pp. 92–93; Leonard Tucker, "President Thomas Clap of Yale College: Another 'Founding Father' of American Science," *Isis* 52 (1961): 55–77.

17. *Boston Gazette,* March 21, 1719/20. This was the same Samuel Grainger whose antiinoculation pamphlet argued that numerical proofs of the success of smallpox inoculation were of no consequence; see chapter 3, above.

18. Cajori, *Teaching and History of Mathematics,* p. 24; Smith and Ginsburg, *History of Mathematics in America,* pp. 33–34.

19. These notices (plus forty-five more) are printed in full in Edgar W. Knight, ed., *A Documentary History of Education in the South before 1860,* 5 vols. (Chapel Hill: University of North Carolina Press, 1949), 1:653. Perhaps this George Brownell of South Carolina was the same Brownell who had met with failure in trying to teach arithmetic to the nine-year-old Benjamin Franklin in Boston in 1715, some thirty years earlier. Franklin recalled that his father "sent me to a school for writing and arithmetic kept by a then famous man, Mr. Geo. Brownell. He was a skillful master, and successful in his profession, employing the mildest and most encouraging methods. Under him I learned to write a good hand pretty soon, but I failed in the arithmetic and made no progress in it" *(Benjamin Franklin: Autobiography,* p. 23).

20. *Virginia Gazette,* May 2, 1771, quoted in Knight, *Documentary History,* 1:658.

21. Knight, *Documentary History,* 1:34–51, lists laws for southern colonies. James Axtell, *The School upon a Hill: Education and Society in Colonial New England* (New York: Norton, 1974), pp. 114–15, quotes a typical apprenticeship contract of the eighteenth century that also includes this phrase.

22. This assumption grows out of the broader view of education that has been taken by historians since the publication of Bernard Bailyn's *Education in the Forming of American Society* (Chapel Hill: University of North Carolina Press, 1960), which suggested that institutional arrangements are only part of the story of how a culture transmits its essentials from generation to generation.

23. *Virginia Gazette,* October 15, 1767, in Knight, *Documentary History,* 1:657.

24. See Brooke Hindle, *David Rittenhouse* (Princeton: Princeton University Press, 1964), pp. 14–15; Cajori, *Teaching and History of Mathematics,* pp. 37–43.

25. Franklin, *Autobiography,* p. 30.

26. Daniel Fenning, *The Ready Reckoner, or Trader's Useful Assistant* (Reading, Pa., 1789), preface.

27. Ibid., editions from Germantown (1774), Reading (1798), and Newburyport (1794).

28. Thomas Prince, *The Vade Mecum for America: or a Companion for Traders and Travellers* (Boston, 1731), preface.

29. Ibid., part VII.

30. Theodore Hornberger, "The Science of Thomas Prince," *New England Quarterly* 9 (1936): 20–42; James Cassedy, *Demography in Early America* (Cambridge, Mass.: Harvard University Press, 1969), pp. 108–9. For Prince on smallpox statistics, see chapter 3, above.

31. Prince's impulse was echoed a half-century later by Ezra Stiles, who during his presidency at Yale put students to work counting New Haven houses and measuring the streets; but Stiles consigned the information to his diary instead of trying to sell it to the public. See Edmund S. Morgan, *Gentle Puritan: A Life of Ezra Stiles, 1727–1795* (New Haven: Yale University Press, 1962), pp. 379, 442.

32. Thomas Jefferson, "Autobiography," in *Life and Selected Writings,* ed. Adrienne Koch and William Peden (New York: Modern Library, 1944), pp. 55–56.

33. Jefferson, "Second State of the Report of Weights and Measures," April–May 1790, in Julian P. Boyd, ed., *The Papers of Thomas Jefferson,* vol. 16 (Princeton: Princeton University Press, 1961), p. 631. Jefferson here was speaking of the advantages of a decimal system for both currency and weights and measures; the coins did not appear for two more years, the measuring system is only now slowly arriving.

34. Samuel A. Ruddock, *Valuable Tables for Rendering the Value of Federal Money Easy and Intelligible* (Worcester, Mass., 1795).

35. *Letter Addressed to the Legislators of the Several States . . . Recommending an Uniform Continental Currency* (New York, 1797), preface.

36. Josiah Burroughs, *The Assistant, or a Treatise* (Newburyport, Mass., 1796), preface.

37. Erastus Root, *An Introduction to Arithmetic* (Norwich, Conn., 1795). Root later became a prominent Whig politician.

38. Ibid., p. vi.

39. *Life and Selected Writings of Thomas Jefferson,* pp. 262–63.

40. Benjamin Rush, "A Plan for the Establishment of Public Schools and the Diffusion of Knowledge in Pennsylvania" (1786), in Frederick Rudolph, ed., *Essays on Education in the Early Republic* (Cambridge, Mass.: Harvard University Press, 1965), p. 5.

41. Noah Webster, "On the Education of Youth in America" (1790), ibid., p. 51.

42. Samuel Harrison Smith, "Remarks on Education" (1797) and Samuel Knox, "An Essay on the Best System of Liberal Education" (1799), ibid., pp. 194, 210, 327, 330.

43. Stanley K. Schultz, *The Culture Factory: Boston Public Schools, 1789–1860* (New York: Oxford University Press, 1973), pp. 18–19.

44. *Connecticut Common School Journal* 2 (1839): 93.

45. Benjamin Latrobe to Ferdinand Fairfax, May 28, 1798, in Knight, *Documentary History,* 2:520–21.

46. For example, John Arbuthnot linked the want of mathematical training in English universities in 1701 to an aversion to close reasoning and attention to detail; see his "An Essay on the Usefulness of Mathematical Learning," p. 409.

47. George Washington to Nicolas Pike, June 20, 1788, quoted in Littlefield, *Early Schools and School Books,* p. 181 (see n. 2, above).

48. A quantitative approach to problem-solving must have appealed to Washington on that particular day, June 20, 1788; nine states had just ratified the new Constitution, and a heated battle was in progress in the Virginia legislature. Five days later a close vote, 89 to 79, assured the existence of the new government

and practically assured that Washington would be the first president of the United States.

49. Jefferson to Colonel William Duane, October, 1812, quoted in Cajori, *Teaching and History of Mathematics*, p. 35.

50. *North American Review* 13 (1821): 364, in a review of four mathematics texts.

51. David Cook, Jr., *Cook's American Arithmetic, Being a System of Decimal Arithmetic* (New Haven, 1800), p. 5.

52. Titus Bennett, *A New System of Practical Arithmetic* (Philadelphia, 1807). Other texts inspired by decimal money include: Joseph Chaplin, *The Trader's Best Companion* (Newburyport, Mass., 1795); *The American Tutor's Assistant; Or, A Compendious System of Practical Arithmetic* (Philadelphia, 1797); Daniel Adams, *The Scholar's Arithmetic, or Federal Accountant* (Leominster, Mass., 1801); Caleb Alexander, *New and Complete System of Arithmetic* (Albany, N.Y., 1802); Osgood Carleton, *Carleton's Compendium of Practical Arithmetic, Applied to the Federal and other Currencies* (Boston, 1810); Jacob Willetts, *The Scholar's Arithmetic* (Poughkeepsie, N.Y., 1817); Nathan Daboll, *Daboll's School-Master's Assistant, Improved and Enlarged* (Norwich, Conn., 1818); Stephen Pike, *The Teacher's Assistant, or a System of Practical Arithmetic* (Philadelphia, 1817); Samuel Temple, *A Concise Introduction to Practical Arithmetic, in which all the Rules that Occur in Common Business are applied to the Federal Currency* (Boston, 1818); Michael Walsh, *A New System of Mercantile Arithmetic adapted to the Commerce of the United States* (Salem, Mass., 1818); Oliver Welch, *The American Arithmetic, Adapted to the Currency of the United States* (Exeter, N.H., 1820); John Lyman Newall, *The New American Arithmetic, in the Coin of the United States* (Hartford, Conn., 1822).

53. *The Columbian Arithmetician, or New System of Theoretical and Practical Arithmetic, By an American* (Haverhill, Mass., 1811), p. 8.

54. Examples of school prize cards are in the May-Goddard papers, file 11, Schlesinger Library, Radcliffe College; a multiplication circle game is explained in [Catharine Esther Beecher], *The Lyceum Arithmetic in Three Parts* (Boston, 1835), p. v; Charles Davies advocated instant recognition in *The Arithmetical Table-Book; or The Method of Teaching the Combinations of Figures by Sight* (New York, 1848; 2d ed., 1851). Other texts that simplified arithmetic and addressed a young audience include: John J. White, *Arithmetic Simplified* (Hartford, 1819); Leonard Peirce, *Conversations on Arithmetic, with Demonstrations to each Rule, in Easy and Familiar Language* (Boston, 1823); Victor Value, *Arithmetic, Theoretical and Practical* (Philadelphia, 1823); James Robinson, Jr., *Elements of Arithmetick, By Question and Answer, Designed for the Use of the Younger Classes in Publick and Private Schools* (Boston, 1824); Noble Heath, *Elements of Arithmetic for the Use of Schools* (New York, 1826); Frederick Emerson, *Primary Lessons in Arithmetick* (Boston, 1827); Zadock Thompson, *The Youth's Assistant in Practical Arithmetick* (Woodstock, Vt., 1825); Seth Davis, *The Pupil's Arithmetick* (Boston, 1826); Catharine E. Beecher, *Arithmetic Simplified* (Hartford, 1833); *Peter Parley's Method of Teaching Arithmetic to Children* (Boston, 1833).

55. Samuel Goodrich, *The Child's Arithmetic* (Hartford, Conn., 1818), pp. iii–iv.

56. *North American Review* 14 (1822): 381–82.

57. Other books stressing mental calculation include: William B. Fowle, *The Child's Arithmetick, or the Elements of Calculation, in the Spirit of Pestalozzi's*

Method, for the Use of Children Between the Ages of Three and Seven Years (Boston, 1827); E. Davis, *The Franklin Intellectual Arithmetic for the Use of Schools* (Springfield, Mass., 1833); and H. L. Barnum, *Barnum's Intellectual Arithmetic for Young Children* (Boston, 1833).

58. Colburn, *Arithmetic upon the Inductive Method of Instruction* (Boston, 1826), pp. 4–5.

59. "Improvement in Arithmetical Instruction," *American Journal of Education* 2 (1827): 30–37.

60. S. J. May, "Errors in Common Education," *American Journal of Education* 4 (1829): 213–25, quotation on p. 221.

61. Colburn, *Introduction to Algebra upon the Inductive Method of Instruction* (Boston, 1825), p. 5.

62. Colburn, *Arithmetic upon the Inductive Method*, p. 6–7.

63. Gerald Lee Gutek, *Pestalozzi and Education* (New York: Random House, 1968), presents a good summary of Pestalozzi's theory.

64. Robert H. Bremner, ed., *Children and Youth in America: A Documentary History*, 2 vols. (Cambridge, Mass.: Harvard University Press, 1970), presents much evidence to support the theory that the 1820s marked an important turning point in the history of childhood.

65. Colburn, *Arithmetic upon the Inductive Method*, p. 5.

66. David Rothman, "Documents in Search of a Historian: Toward a History of Childhood and Youth in America," *Journal of Interdisciplinary History* 2 (1971): 367–77, argues that the appearance of schools and orphanages was related not to a solicitude for children but to a concern for social control and discipline.

67. *Connecticut Journal of Education* 2 (1839): 234.

68. *American Journal of Education* 3 (1828): 693; *Connecticut Common School Journal* 2 (1839): 31.

69. The Reverend Theodore Edson, "Warren Colburn," *American Journal of Education* 2 (1856): 294–316. Edson probably exaggerated the sales of Colburn's texts. The *Connecticut Common School Journal* yearly presented quantitative assessments of education in that state, including statistics on the texts in use; in 1838 and 1839 Colburn had not overtaken Daboll's *Schoolmaster's Assistant*, a traditional text first published in 1800; see *Connecticut Common School Journal* 1 (1838): 192; 2 (1839): 224.

70. *American Annals of Education* 4 (1834): 148. In another issue of this journal Colburn's inductive method was criticized in words that would have sounded familiar in the 1970s to Americans who followed the controversy over the "new math": "We imagine its friends, in forming this favorable opinion, considered more its intrinsic scientific beauty than its actual adaptedness to the purposes of instruction. There is now an evident tendency to return to the old mode [of taking some rules on trust and then practicing until they are understood]" *(American Annals of Education* 9 [1839]: 265).

Other inductive texts, in addition to Colburn's, included: Daniel Adams, *Adams' New Arithmetic, in which the Principles of Operating by Numbers are Analytically Explained and Synthetically Applied* (Keene, N.H., 1828); Frederick Barnard, *A Treatise on Arithmetic, designed particularly as a Text Book for Classes in which the Principles of the Science are Inductively Developed* (Hartford, Conn., 1830); James Robinson, *Elementary Lessons in Intellectual Arithmetic, illustrated upon Analytic and Inductive Principles* (Boston, 1831); William Ruger, *A New System of Arithmetick; in which the Rules are Familiarly Demonstrated and the Principles of the Science clearly and fully Explained* (Watertown, N.J., 1832); Richard W. Green, *An Arithmetical Guide, in Which the Principles of Numbers are Inductively Explained* (Philadelphia, 1836); Benjamin Greenleaf, *A Mental Arithmetic upon the Inductive Plan* (Boston, 1857); Edward Brooks, *The Normal Mental Arithmetic: A Thorough and Complete Course by Analysis and Induction* (Philadelphia, 1858); Daniel Fish, ed., *Robinson's Progressive Intellectual Arithmetic On the Inductive Plan* (New York, 1858). Opponents of the inductive method included B. Bridge, *The Southern and Western Calculator* (Philadelphia, 1831); L. Olney, *A Practical System of Arithmetic for the Use of Schools* (Hartford, Conn., 1836); and James D. Dodd, "An Essay on Mathematical Textbooks and the Prevailing System of Mathematical Education," paper read before the Teacher's Association of New York City, November 5, 1859.

71. Current education research finds that sex differences in mathematical ability do not appear until after the fifth grade or later, which strongly suggests that what inhibits girls is not nature but cultural attitudes about sex roles. See Lynn Fox, Linda Brody, and Dianne Tobin, eds., *Women and the Mathematical Mystique* (Baltimore: Johns Hopkins University Press, 1980); John Ernest, "Mathematics and Sex," *American Mathematical Monthly* 83 (1976): 595–614; and Elizabeth Fennema, "Mathematical Learning and the Sexes, a Review," *Journal for Research in Mathematics Education* 5 (1974): 126–39.

72. Arbuthnot, "Essay on the Usefulness of Mathematical Learning," pp. 411–12.

73. Josiah Child, *A New Discourse of Trade* (1693), in *Selected Works, 1668–1697* (Farnborough, Eng.: Gregg Press, 1968), pp. 4–5.

74. Alice Messing, "From Tradition to Prescription: Cookbooks for the New World," and Rachel Maines, "Designer and Artisan in the Textile Arts," papers delivered at the Annual Meeting of the Society for the History of Technology, October 14, 1981, Milwaukee, Wisconsin.

75. *Benjamin Franklin: Autobiography,* p. 109. Further evidence for this assertion about the low level of female numeracy in colonial America is drawn from scattered sources. One historian of colonial education located several girls' arithmetic copybooks that showed a progression identical to boys' books through the first four rules but no further. He concluded that colonial girls never studied geometry or algebra (see Middlekauff, *Ancients and Axioms,* pp. 104–5). The Harvard collection of copybooks contains six by colonial girls, and none goes beyond problems in simple interest. Philip Fithian, a young Princeton graduate, was tutor in a rich Virginia household in 1773–74 and had charge of the education of three boys and four girls. The boys, all adolescents, studied arithmetic though the Rule of Three; only the oldest girl, aged fifteen, joined them; she began with ciphering and progressed through division in less than a year (see the "Journal of Philip Fithian," in Knight, *Documentary History,* 1:578, 582, 592, 604). William Woodbridge, editor of the *American Annals of Education,* remarked that in Connecticut schools of the 1770s girls were taught spelling, reading, writing, but "rarely even the first rules of arithmetic. . . . I have known boys that could do something in the four first rules of arithmetic. Girls were never taught it" ("Female Education Prior to 1800," *Barnard's Journal of Education* 27 [1877]: 273–76).

76. Linda Kerber, "Daughters of Columbia: Educating Women for the Republic, 1787–1805," in *The Hofstadter Aegis: A Memorial,* ed. Stanley Elkins and Eric McKitrick (New York: Knopf, 1974), pp. 36–59. See also Linda Kerber, *Women of the Republic: Intellect and Ideology in Revolutionary America* (Chapel Hill:

University of North Carolina Press, 1980), and Mary Beth Norton, *Liberty's Daughters: The Revolutionary Experience of American Women, 1750–1800* (Boston: Little, Brown, 1980).

77. Rush, "A Plan for the Establishment of Public Schools," p. 29; echoed in Noah Webster, "On the Education of Youth," both in Rudolph, ed., *Essays on Education,* p. 70 (see n. 40, above).

78. John Burton, *Lectures on Female Education and Manners* (1793) (reprint ed., New York: Source Books Press, 1970), pp. 113–15.

79. *The Rise and Progress of the Young Ladies' Academy of Philadelphia* (Philadelphia, 1794), p. 32; [Hannah W. Foster], *The Boarding School, or, Lessons of a Preceptress to her Pupils* (Boston, 1798), pp. 35–38.

80. Mary Beth Norton, "Eighteenth-Century American Women in Peace and War: The Case of the Loyalists," *William and Mary Quarterly* 3d ser. 33 (1976): 386–409.

81. Norton holds to the second view in her article (cited in n. 80). Knowledge of family finances and control over them are of course two very different things, and there is no reason to suppose that turning household accounts and responsibility for bills into women's work altered the distribution of power within the family. Recent studies suggest that husbands are more likely to let wives handle bill-paying when the family income falls below expectations; in that way the husband spares himself the embarrassment of confronting his failure to provide adequately, and a painful task becomes women's work. See Lillian Breslow Rubin, *Worlds of Pain: Life in the Working-Class Family* (New York: Basic Books, 1977), pp. 106–12.

82. John Bennett, *Strictures on Female Education* (Worcester, Mass., 1795) (reprint ed., New York: Source Book Press, 1971), p. 21.

83. Ibid., pp. 80–84.

84. For the classic statement of this view, see Barbara Welter, "The Cult of True Womanhood, 1820–1860," *American Quarterly* 18 (1966): 151–174. A fine recent work is Nancy Cott's *The Bonds of Womanhood* (New Haven: Yale University Press, 1977), which links prescriptive formulations of womanhood to the realities of New England women's lives.

85. Quoted without attribution in Harriet Webster Marr, *The Old New England Academies Founded before 1826* (New York: Comet, 1959), p. 104.

86. *The Portfolio* 17 (1824): 456. This was a revived *Portfolio* in Philadelphia, resuming more than a decade after Oliver Oldschool's death.

87. Ibid., p. 456.

88. Alma Lutz, *Emma Willard: Pioneer Educator of American Women* (Boston: Beacon Press, 1964), pp. 35–36, 91; Marr, *Old New England Academies,* p. 203; and E. Douglas Branch, *The Sentimental Years, 1836–1860* (New York: Hill & Wang, 1965), p. 208.

89. Almira H. Lincoln Phelps, *The Female Student, or, Lectures to Young Ladies on Female Education,* 2d ed. (New York, 1836), pp. 222, 303–23.

90. [Catharine Beecher?], "Hartford Female Seminary," *American Annals of Education* 2 (1832): 65.

91. Catharine Beecher, *Educational Reminiscences and Suggestions* (New York, 1874), pp. 15–16, 28–29.

92. Ibid., pp. 34–35, 37, 43–44; and Catharine Beecher, *Suggestions Respecting Improvements in Education* (Hartford, 1829), pp. 25–29, 36–37.

93. Catharine Beecher, "First School Closing Address," October 18, 1823, Beecher Collection, folder 314, Schlesinger Library, Radcliffe College.

94. See Mae Elizabeth Harveson, *Catharine Esther Beecher, Pioneer Educator* (Philadelphia: Science Press, 1932), pp. 85–86; the quotation in the text is from a letter of Catharine Beecher to Mary Lyon, dated October 15, 1834. See also Kathryn Kish Sklar, *Catharine Beecher: A Study in American Domesticity* (New Haven: Yale University Press, 1973), p. 301. The anonymous text is *The Lyceum Arithmetic in Three Parts* (cited in n. 54, above).

95. Phelps, *The Female Student*, p. 46; Woodbridge, "Female Education Prior to 1800," p. 276 (see n. 75, above).

96. Andrew Wylie, "Female Influences and Education," *American Annals of Education* 8 (1838): 386.

97. Woodbridge, "Female Education Prior to 1800," p. 276.

98. John Brown, "Female Instruction Should Be Thorough," *American Annals of Education* 8 (1838): 386.

99. "Account of a Female School," *American Annals of Education* 2 (1832): 215.

100. Phelps, *The Female Student,* p. 322.

101. Joseph Emerson, "Female Education: A Discourse, Delivered at the Dedication of the Seminary Hall in Saugus, January 15, 1822" (Boston, 1822), p. 21.

102. Richard Bernard and Maris Vinovskis, "The Female School Teacher in Ante-Bellum Massachusetts," *Journal of Social History* 10 (1977): 332–45.

103. See Margaret Rossiter, " 'Women's Work' in Science, 1880–1910," *Isis* 71 (1980): 381–98.

Chapter 5 · Statistics and the State

1. Noah Webster, *A Compendious Dictionary of the English Language* (New Haven, Conn., 1806), and John Walker, *A Critical Pronouncing Dictionary and Expositor of the English Language* (Philadelphia, 1803), s.v. "Statisticks." The earlier English edition of Walker's work (London, 1791) did not contain the word. Americans universally gave credit to Sir John Sinclair of Scotland for coining the word "statisticks," after a German word for the study of the state, but there were a few before Sinclair who used the word in the 1770s and 1780s in England. Sinclair himself claimed that he had invented the word; see his *Statistical Account of Scotland,* 20 vols. (Edinburgh, 1791–99), 20:lxv–lxvi. For the German and English development of statistics see M. J. Cullen, *The Statistical Movement in Early Victorian Britain: The Foundations of Empirical Social Research* (New York: Barnes & Noble, 1975), pp. 9–11; Paul F. Lazarsfeld, "Notes on the History of Quantification in Sociology—Trends, Sources and Problems," *Isis* 52 (1961): 277–333; and Anthony Oberschall, ed., *The Establishment of Empirical Sociology: Studies in Continuity, Discontinuity, and Institutionalization* (New York: Harper & Row, 1972).

2. William Douglass, *A Summary, Historical and Political, of the First Planting, Progressive Improvements, and Present State of the British Settlements in North-America* (London, 1771); *Peter Kalm's Travels in North America,* ed. and trans. Adolph B. Benson, 2 vols. (New York: Wilson-Erickson, 1937); Thomas Jefferson, *Notes on the State of Virginia,* ed. William Peden (Chapel Hill: University of North Carolina Press, 1955). For a discussion of the traditional literary form of

geographical description and travel in America, see Kathryn and Philip Whitford, "Timothy Dwight's Place in Eighteenth-Century American Science," American Philosophical Society, *Proceedings* 114 (1970): 60–71.

3. Works representative of the genre include Jeremy Belknap, *The History of New-Hampshire,* 3 vols. (Philadelphia, 1784–92); Samuel Williams, *The Natural and Civil History of Vermont* (Walpole, N.H., 1794); W[illiam] Winterbotham, *A Geographical, Commercial, and Philosophical View of the Present Situation of the United States* (New York, 1795); Benjamin Davies, *Some Account of the City of Philadelphia* (Philadelphia, 1794); James Sullivan, *The History of the District of Maine* (Boston, 1795); David Ramsay, *A Sketch of the Soil, Climate, Weather, and Diseases of South Carolina* (Charleston, S.C., 1796); [Charles Williamson], *A Description of the Genesee Country, Its Rapidly Progressive Population and Improvements* (Albany, N.Y., 1798); [John Peck], *Facts and Calculations Respecting the Population and Territory of the United States* [Boston, 1799]; *A Topographical and Statistical Account of the Province of Louisiana* (Baltimore, 1803); [Samuel L. Mitchell], *The Picture of New York* (New York, 1807); Joseph Scott, *A Geographical Description of the States of Maryland and Delaware* (Philadelphia, 1807); James Dean, *An Alphabetical Atlas, or Gazetteer of Vermont* (Montpelier, Vt., 1808); David Ramsay, *The History of South Carolina* (Charleston, S.C., 1809); Timothy Dwight, *A Statistical Account of the City of New-Haven,* vol. 1 of the *Memoirs* of the Connecticut Academy of Arts and Sciences (New Haven, Conn., 1811); James Morris, *A Statistical Account of Several Towns in the County of Litchfield,* vol. 1 (1811) of the same *Memoirs;* Sterling Goodenow, *A Brief Topographical and Statistical Manual of the State of New-York* (New York, 1811); James Mease, *The Picture of Philadelphia* (Philadelphia, 1811); Jervis Cutler, *A Topographical Description of the State of Ohio, Indiana Territory, and Louisiana* (Boston, 1812); Horatio Gates Spafford, *A Gazetteer of the State of New-York* (Albany, N.Y., 1813); Rodolphus Dickinson, *A Geographical and Statistical View of Massachusetts Proper* (Greenfield, Mass., 1813); Daniel Drake, *Natural and Statistical View, or Picture of Cincinnati and the Miami Country* (Cincinnati, 1815); Moses Greenleaf, *A Statistical View of the District of Maine* (Boston, 1816); Samuel R. Brown, *The Western Gazetteer* (Auburn, N.Y., 1817); D[avid] B[ailie] Warden, *A Statistical, Political, and Historical Account of the United States of North America* (Edinburgh and Philadelphia, 1819); David D. Field, *A Statistical Account of the County of Middlesex in Connecticut* (Middletown, Conn., 1819); John Preston, *A Statistical Report of the County of Albany, for the Year 1820* (Albany, N.Y., 1823); Timothy Dwight, *Travels in New-England and New-York,* 4 vols. (New Haven, Conn., 1821); Frederick Hall, *A Statistical Account of the Town of Middlebury, in the State of Vermont* (Boston, 1821); John Melish, *A Statistical View of the United States* (New York, 1825); *A General Outline of the United States of North America, Her Resources and Prospects, with a Statistical Comparison* (Philadelphia, 1825); and Robert Mills, *Statistics of South Carolina* (Charleston, S.C., 1826).

4. Samuel Williams, *The Natural and Civil History of Vermont . . . In Two Volumes,* 2d ed. (Burlington, Vt., 1809), 1:12–13. Williams was more mathematical than most of his contemporaries; in addition to the series of Vermont almanacs in the 1790s, he prepared an edition of Nicholas Pike's *New and Complete System of Arithmetick* (Newburyport, Mass., 1788).

5. Belknap, *History of New-Hampshire,* 2:373–75; 3:3.

6. Ramsay, *History of South Carolina,* 1:vii–xii, 2:539–68.

7. Mills, *Statistics of South Carolina*.

8. Mease, *Picture of Philadelphia*, pp. ix, 25, 357; Dickinson, *Geographical and Statistical View*, p. 2; Warden, *Statistical, Political, and Historical Account*, p. i.

9. *Literary Magazine and American Register* 1 (1804): 388–92.

10. Gordon S. Wood, in his discussion of this topic, says that the Federalists assumed that men of uncommon talent would rise to the top in government and by their gifts correctly intuit the common good, but he does not discuss the importance of statistics to this new natural aristocracy; see his *The Creation of the American Republic, 1776–1787* (Chapel Hill: University of North Carolina Press, 1969), pp. 499–518, 605–15.

11. Noah Webster, *The Revolution in France, Considered in Respect to Its Progress and Effects by an American* (New York, 1794), p. 43.

12. Timothy Dwight, *The True Means of Establishing Public Happiness* (New Haven, Conn., 1795), p. 23. Benjamin Silliman's funeral eulogy of Dwight in 1817 called special attention to his delight in "statisticks" and his abhorrence of "mere speculation"; see *A Sketch of the Life and Character of President Dwight, Delivered as an Eulogium* (New Haven, Conn., 1817), pp. 33–34.

13. Dwight, *Travels*, 1:12.

14. This circular was reprinted in the *Memoirs* of the Connecticut Academy of Arts and Sciences, vol. 1 (1811), pt. ii, pp. vi–xi.

15. The other was James Morris's *Statistical Account of . . . Towns in . . . Litchfield*.

16. Dwight, *Statistical Account*, p. 1.

17. John Cummings, "Statistical Work of the Federal Government of the United States," in John Koren, ed., *The History of Statistics: Their Development and Progress in Many Countries* (New York: Macmillan, 1918), pp. 571–689.

18. Jacob E. Cooke, *Tench Coxe and the Early Republic* (Chapel Hill: University of North Carolina Press, 1978), p. 213. Many of Coxe's essays were drawn together in *A View of the United States of America* (Philadelphia, 1794), which Cooke likens to a statistical abstract in its ability to kill a reader's interest.

19. Coxe, *A View of the United States of America*, pp. 260, 312–13.

20. Sometimes Coxe simply declared his statements to be the truth, offering no supporting evidence. At one such point, in a copy of his essay *Reflexions on the State of the Union* (Philadelphia, 1792), bearing South Carolina Senator Pierce Butler's autograph, a hostile eighteenth-century hand noted in the margin that "the position is not supported by Argum[en]t nor founded in facts," and, on the next page, the remark "Declamation—not argument" blasted Coxe's prediction that the South would languish without domestic iron manufacture (see pp. 5 and 6 in the American Antiquarian Society's copy). It does not appear that the marginal notes and Butler's name are in the same handwriting, and, since Butler and Coxe were longtime friends, it seems especially unlikely that the marginal notes were Butler's.

21. By 1810 Coxe was considerably more sensitive to the necessity for accurate statistics on the economy. He assembled the results of the 1810 maufacturing census and discussed their imperfections with sophistication; see his *A Statement of the Arts and Manufactures of the United States of America for the Year 1810* (Philadelphia, 1814), p. xxv.

22. The best recent account of the development of the United States census is Robert C. Davis, "The Beginnings of American Social Research," in George H.

Daniels, ed., *Nineteenth-Century American Science: A Reappraisal* (Evanston, Ill.: Northwestern University Press, 1972), pp. 154–56. Edward Clark Lunt includes a good history in his "Key to the Publications of the United States Census, 1790–1887," American Statistical Association *Publications* n.s. 1 (1888): 63–125.

23. The debates were printed in the *Congressional Register* (New York, 1790), vol. 3, no. 4, a publication of brief duration based on the shorthand notes of Thomas Lloyd. The dates of the key discussions were January 25 and February 2, 1790 (ibid., pp. 167–68, 205–8.)

24. Ibid., p. 206. No congressman raised against the census the traditional religious objection, based on the sin of David, who brought a plague upon Israel by "numbering" the people (2 Sam. 24:1–25, 1 Chron. 21:1–30). On three occasions colonial governors blamed the biblical prohibition for their inability to administer a census, but it is not clear to what extent they were accurately reflecting a popular concern. For two instances, see letters to the Lords of Trade from the New York governor of 1712 and the New Jersey governor of 1726 in an 1870 congressional report on the history of the census, U.S. Congress, *House Reports,* 41st Cong., 2d sess., Report 3 (January 18), p. 29. In 1763 the Lords of Trade singled out Massachusetts for a special census and encountered great reluctance on the part of both houses of the assembly. Thomas Hutchinson thought that "religious scruples," specifically the sin of David, lay behind the objections, but the assembly's record of debates fails to mention sin at all. See Hutchinson, *History of the Colony and Province of Massachusetts-Bay,* ed. Lawrence Shaw Mayo, 3 vols. (Cambridge, Mass.: Harvard University Press, 1936), 3:75; *Journals of the Honourable House of Representatives . . . of Massachusetts-Bay in New-England, 1763–1764* (Boston: Massachusetts Historical Society, 1970), vol. 40, pp. 44, 48, 99, 103, 260, 266; Josiah H. Benton, Jr., *Early Census Making in Massachusetts, 1643–1765* (Boston: C. E. Goodspeed, 1905), pp. 31–65.

25. *Journal of the Second Session of the Senate of the United States of America* (New York, 1790), pp. 25–28, and passim.

26. See Edgar S. Maclay, ed., *The Journal of William Maclay: United States Senator from Pennsylvania, 1789–1791* (New York: D. Appleton, 1890), pp. 194–95, 197–98; the quotation in the text is from p. 195. The trivial detail debated on February 9 was whether a commissioner or a federal marshal should be in charge of the census in each district.

27. Madison to Jefferson, February 14, 1790, in *Letters and Other Writings of James Madison,* ed. Philip R. Fendall, 4 vols. (Philadelphia: Lippincott, 1865), 1:507. For Jefferson's letter to Madison of September 6, 1789, see Julian P. Boyd et al., eds., *The Papers of Thomas Jefferson,* vol. 15 (Princeton: Princeton University Press, 1958), pp. 392–98.

28. Scholars of a later, more quantitative era have been generally uncritical of Jefferson's ideas uniting political theory with demographic calculations, but Garry Wills exposes the logical fallacies in Jefferson's calculations in *Inventing America: Jefferson's Declaration of Independence* (Garden City, N.Y.: Doubleday, 1978), pp. 123–28. Wills pictures Jefferson as an inveterate calculator, swept away by the possibilities of making politics a quantitative science.

29. *Memorial of the Connecticut Academy of Arts and Sciences* and *The Memorial of the American Philosophical Society* (Philadelphia, 1800), both prepared for the use of the Senate (6th Cong., 1st sess., 1799–1800). Both were later reprinted in U.S. Congress, *House Reports,* 41st Cong., 2d sess., Report 3 (January 18,

1870), pp. 35–36. Dwight's remarks, quoted in the text, are from the Philosophical Society's *Memorial,* p. 3.

30. *Congressional Register,* 3:167–68, 207. Two Boston papers, the *Boston Gazette* of February 8, 1790, and the *Herald of Freedom and the Federal Advertiser* of February 5 and 9, 1790, printed the speeches of Madison, Alexander White, Roger Sherman, Fisher Ames, and Theodore Sedgwick.

31. *Herald of Freedom and the Federal Advertiser,* February 9, 1790; *Congressional Register,* 3:206.

32. For a discussion of the effect of post-Revolutionary economic changes on the conception of the common good, see J. E. Crowley, *This Sheba, Self: The Conceptualization of Economic Life in Eighteenth-Century America* (Baltimore: Johns Hopkins University Press, 1974), pp. 151–57.

33. *North American Review and Miscellaneous Journal* 3 (1816): 364, 367–68.

34. *Niles' Weekly Register* 14 (1818): 142.

35. Ibid. 1 (1811): 16.

36. *A General Outline of the United States of North America, Her Resources and Prospects, with a Statistical Comparison* (Philadelphia, 1825); critically reviewed in the *North American Review* 20 (1825): 446–48.

37. Elijah Middlebrook, *An Agricultural and Economical Almanack for 1817* (New Haven, Conn., 1816), preface. One quick way to monitor changing trends in almanacs is to read through a chronological checklist that outlines the contents of a series of these annual books. In the bibliography compiled by James A. Bear, Jr., and Mary Caperton Bear, *A Checklist of Virginia Almanacs, 1732–1850* (Charlottesville, Va.: Bibliographical Society of the University of Virginia, 1962), one learns that Virginia almanacs from 1812, 1814, 1815, 1817, and 1818 included population tables, whereas earlier none had done so. One of the earliest examples of election statistics printed in almanacs is in Andrew Beers, *Beers' Calendar, or, Southwick's Almanack, for the Year of Our Lord 1817* (Albany, N.Y., 1816), pp. 21–23.

38. "A Statistical View of the United States of America," *Literary Magazine and American Register* 2 (1804): 179–80.

39. *A Geographical, Statistical and Political Amusement* (Philadelphia, 1806).

40. Samuel Blodget, Jr., *Economica: A Statistical Manual for the United States of America* (Washington, D.C., 1806), p. 8.

41. Ibid., p. 80.

42. *North American Review* 3 (1816): 349; Adam Seybert, *Statistical Annals* (Philadelphia, 1818), p. v.

43. Timothy Pitkin, *A Statistical View of the Commerce of the United States of America in Connection with Agriculture and Manufactures* (Hartford, Conn., 1816), p. iii.

44. *North American Review* 3 (1816): 345–54.

45. Ibid. 9 (1819): 223; see also *Dictionary of American Biography,* s.v. "Seybert, Adam."

46. Seybert, *Statistical Annals,* p. 1.

47. *Edinburgh Review* 33 (1820): 69–80.

48. *North American Review* 9 (1819): 217–39.

49. Philadelphia Society for Alleviating the Miseries of Public Prisons, *A Statistical View of the Operation of the Penal Code of Pennsylvania* (Philadelphia, 1817), p. 6.

50. Jesse Appleton, *An Address delivered before the Massachusetts Society for the Suppression of Intemperance* (Boston, 1816), pp. 1–7. For the nonstatistical, moral-suasion temperance argument, see John T. Kirkland, *A Sermon Delivered before the Massachusetts Society for the Suppression of Intemperance* (Boston, 1814).

51. Richard Barbour, *Barbour's Temperance Table* (Boston, 1831).

52. *The Temperance Almanac for 1834* (Albany, N.Y.: New York State Temperance Society, 1833), p. 25.

53. A view accepted by most historians. See W. J. Rorabaugh, *The Alcoholic Republic: An American Tradition* (New York: Oxford University Press, 1979).

54. Stanley K. Schultz, *The Culture Factory: Boston Public Schools, 1798–1860* (New York: Oxford University Press, 1973), p. 32. Details of the survey are in Joseph M. Wightman, *Annals of the Boston Primary School Committee, From its first Establishment in 1818 to its Dissolution in 1855* (Boston: G. C. Rand & Avery, 1860), pp. 20–28.

55. David J. Rothman, *Discovery of the Asylum: Social Order and Disorder in the New Republic* (Boston: Little, Brown, 1971), pp. 157–61, 307.

56. Boston Society for the Moral and Religious Instruction of the Poor, *Annual Report* (Boston, 1817), and *Second Annual Report* (Boston, 1818), p. 10.

Chapter 6 • The Census of 1840

1. Thomas Hamilton, *Men and Manners in America* (1833) (reprint ed., New York: A. M. Kelley, 1968), pp. 115, 157, 222, 337.

2. The classic work on the history of statistics, *Contributions to the History of Statistics* (London: P. S. King & Son, 1932), by Harald L. Westergaard, includes no Americans among the contributors to statistical theory.

3. W. T. Baxter reports that between 1820 and 1840 modern bookkeeping practices were universally adopted in America; see his "Accounting in Colonial America" in B. S. Yamey and A. C. Littleton, eds., *Studies in the History of Accounting* (London: Sweet & Maxwell, 1956), pp. 286–87.

4. William P. Dewees, *A Treatise on the Physical and Medical Treatment of Children* (Philadelphia, 1825), pp. 22–23. Dewees also calculated the average daily gain in weight a pregnant woman could expect (fetus, placenta, and liquids divided by 280 days of a full-term pregnancy, or three-fourths of an ounce of weight per day) as proof that a mother-to-be should not increase her daily intake of food by more than three-fourths of an ounce a day and should not worry about nausea and vomiting, which were nature's way of expelling unnecessary food.

5. "Statistics," *Parley's Magazine* 2 (1835): 169.

6. For pauperism surveys, see Josiah Quincy, *Report of the Committee on Pauperism of the Commonwealth of Massachusetts* (1821). David J. Rothman, *Discovery of the Asylum* (Boston: Little, Brown, 1971), mentions many others. M. Y. Beach's *Wealth and Wealthy Citizens of New York* was an annual publication in New York from 1842 to 1855. Temperance almanacs of the 1830s printed "Temperance Statistics," and in 1831 John McDowell of New York conducted a quick census of prostitutes for volume 1 of his periodical, *McDowell's Journal*. New York and Massachusetts collected detailed educational statistics starting in the 1820s, and by the 1840s common-school teachers were typically required to keep strict attendance records to submit to their states; see Maris A. Vinovskis,

"Trends in Massachusetts Education, 1826–1860," *History of Education Quarterly* 12 (1972): 501–29, for an evaluation of the reliability of the Massachusetts records. Lunatics were the special survey subject of Dr. Edward Jarvis, an early member of the American Statistical Association, and his *Journal of Insanity* in the 1840s published his findings, as well as reports from asylum superintendents; the latter were, like his own findings, highly statistical. Election statistics became a staple of almanacs after 1838, when the New York *Tribune* began to publish the *Whig Almanac and Politician's Register.*

7. Richard D. Brown, *Modernization: The Transformation of American Life, 1600–1865* (New York: Hill & Wang, 1976), p. 134, talks of the influence of the Connecticut clock industry.

8. The history of this census has been discussed by William Stanton, *The Leopard's Spots: Scientific Attitudes toward Race in America, 1815–1859* (Chicago: University of Chicago Press, 1960), pp. 58–81; Albert Deutsch, "The First U.S. Census of the Insane (1840) and Its Use as Pro-Slavery Propaganda," *Bulletin of the History of Medicine* 15 (1944): 469–82; and Gerald Grob, *Edward Jarvis and the Medical World of Nineteenth-Century America* (Knoxville: University of Tennessee Press, 1978), pp. 70–75. None of these works attempts to get to the bottom of the mystery of the census.

9. The 1850 census instead gets the credit for being a landmark census, the first modern census run according to rational principles and conducted by efficient experts.

10. Joseph E. Worcester, *The American Almanac and Repository of Useful Knowledge* 1 (1830): 139.

11. Ibid. 9 (1838): i–ii.

12. Secretary of State John Forsyth to Senator Felix Grundy, July 10, 1840, in "Errors in the Sixth Census," 28th Cong., 2d sess., 1845, House Document 116, p. 21.

13. Leiber's memorial was reprinted in "The Approaching Census," *United States Magazine and Democratic Review* 5 (1839): 79–80.

14. Archibald Russell, *The Principles of Statistical Inquiry* (New York, 1839), p. 7 and passim.

15. Ibid., pp. 3–4.

16. Archibald Russell was the only prominent statistical expert whose name did not appear on the list of founding members; see American Statistical Association, *Constitution and By-Laws of the American Statistical Association, With a List of Officers, Fellows and Members, and An Address* (Boston, 1840). For an account of the formation of this group, see Walter F. Willcox, "Lemuel Shattuck, Statist, Founder of the American Statistical Assocation," *Journal of the American Statistical Association* 35 (1940): 224–35, and Barbara Gutmann Rosenkrantz, *Public Health and the State: Changing Views in Massachusetts, 1842–1936* (Cambridge, Mass.: Harvard University Press, 1972), pp. 14–23.

17. Walter F. Willcox, "Notes on the Chronology of Statistical Societies," *Journal of the American Statistical Association* 29 (1934): 442–43.

18. The town was Concord, Massachusetts; see Rosenkrantz, *Public Health,* pp. 16–17.

19. John Koren, "The American Statistical Association, 1839–1914," in Koren, ed., *The History of Statistics: Their Development and Progress in Many Countries* (1918) (reprint ed., New York: Burt Franklin, 1970), pp. 5–6.

20. For example, John P. Bigelow, on the council of the ASA, had written a survey of Massachusetts manufactures in 1837; Henry Colman had done a survey of Massachusetts agriculture; Henry Lee had published a collection of commercial statistics; Horace Mann had set the educational establishment of the state on a quantitative footing. Reformers included Robert Rantoul and Samuel Gridley Howe.

21. "The Approaching Census," *United States Magazine and Democratic Review* 5 (1839): 77–85.

22. The final act is published in *The Public Statutes at Large of the United States of America,* ed. Richard Peters, vol. 5: *Public Laws* (Boston: Charles C. Little & James Brown, 1848), pp. 330–36.

23. Russell, *Principles of Statistical Inquiry,* p. 209.

24. "Message from the President of the United States, recommending the return of the names and ages of pensioners, in the next general census," 25th Cong., 3d sess., 1839, Senate Report 282.

25. The representative was William Slade of Vermont, a staunch antislavery man, along with John Quincy Adams. The whole debate was published in the *Congressional Globe* 7 (February 28, 1839): 219, 286. For Russell on the age structure of the black population see his *Principles of Statistical Inquiry,* pp. 46–48.

26. See *National Cyclopedia of American Biography* and *Appleton's Cyclopedia of American Biography,* s.v. "William A. Weaver." The microfilmed *Letters of Application and Recommendation during the Administration of Andrew Jackson, 1829–1837* (Washington, D.C.: National Archives Microfilms, reel 26) contains nine letters about or by Weaver, detailing his continual quest for government patronage. For information from Weaver's confidential personnel file, also microfilmed by the National Archives, I am indebted to Professor Christopher McKee of Grinnell College, Iowa, who is researching the naval careers of the first officers of the U.S. Navy.

27. Edward Stubbs to Daniel Webster, May 5, 1842, in "Report" of the Committee on Claims on the petition of Thomas Allen, 28th Cong., 2d sess., 1844, House Report 2, pp. 24–26.

28. The original schedules of the 1840 census are available on microfilm from the National Archives. They are considerably more difficult to read than the final printed versions of the aggregate enumerations. What appears on the film is not what the enumerators carried from door to door; it is, instead, a neat copy of their original lists. Probably the assistant marshals were issued three sets of identical schedules: one for the rough draft and two for the final copies. Hence the schedules on film derive from the originals, which have presumably been lost.

29. The economic statistics were printed by Thomas Allen as *The Compendium of the Enumeration of the Inhabitants and Statistics of the United States, as Obtained at the Department of State* (Washington, D.C., 1841). The book was in fact published in 1842, but Allen predated it to cement his claim in the printing-contract dispute, discussed below.

30. From this it appears that it was the marshals, not the assistant marshals, who were legally responsible for doing the arithmetic; but in fact, in every case I examined, the assistant marshals added up the census, perhaps because their pay was based on the final total they returned and they were eager to see the result. Sometimes the marshal did the aggregate page, accepting the addition of the assistants; at other times the assistants themselves provided the aggregate

pages. Forsyth's report is contained in 26th Cong., 1st sess., 1839, Senate Document 13.

31. In this Forsyth appears to have been in error. The printed version of the 1830 census gives only one version, with the title "corrected at the Department of State"; the errata page at the end refers only to printing errors caught too late, not to errors made by the marshals and corrected at Washington.

32. *Statutes at Large,* vol. 5: *Public Laws,* p. 368.

33. This fact is noted in Weaver's personnel file (see n. 26, above).

34. Form letter, dated November 28, 1840, sent by Weaver to the census clerks, reprinted in "Errors in Sixth Census," 28th Cong., 2d sess., 1845, House Document 116, p. 119.

35. See "Report from the Secretary of State, showing, in compliance with a Resolution of the Senate, what progress has been made in the completion of the sixth census," 26th Cong., 2d sess., 1841, Senate Document 219, pp. 2–4.

36. See the "Report" of the Committee on Claims on the petition of Thomas Allen, 28th Cong., 2d sess., 1844, House Report 2, pp. 13–22, which repeats some of the testimony that Weaver and Webster had presented during the hearings in spring, 1842. Webster in particular had trouble in recalling the events of 1841.

37. The secretary of state filed an annual report in which he listed the clerks in his employ and their salaries. These reports did not include the full-time census clerks, which seems strange; it suggests that they were not seen as regular members of the department, on a par with the clerks, messengers, scribes, and box-handlers of the diplomatic section of State. One of the investigations, in 1842, required Webster to produce a list of all the Weaver relatives on the census payroll; this list appears in House Report 2, 28th Cong., 2d sess., pp. 23–25. The secretary's report on clerks for 1841 mentions that a total of seven clerks were employed on the census that year; they were paid wages, not salaries. Possibly these were extra hires, working on a short-term basis; they were not listed by name. A full list could be generated by consulting all the manuscript census returns for 1840; usually the correcting clerk put his or her signature on the front page of each district as it was checked over. See the reports titled "Persons Employed in the State Department" in 27th Cong., 2d sess., House Documents 30 and 177.

38. Adams to Webster, September 30, 1841, and Adams to Worcester, October 4, 1841, in *The Letterbook of John Quincy Adams,* in *The Adams Papers* (Boston: Massachusetts Historical Society, microfilm ed., 1955), part 2, reel 154. See also Worcester's remarks, *American Almanac* 8 (1842): iii.

39. Webster's private letters for these months show almost no concern over the census; see *The Papers of Daniel Webster,* ed. Charles M. Wiltse (Ann Arbor, Mich.: University Microfilms, 1971), reel 16.

40. "Report" on the claim of Thomas Allen, 28th Cong., 2d sess., 1844, House Report 2, pp. 13–22, 26–28.

41. The excellent recent biography by Gerald Grob, *Edward Jarvis,* (see n. 8, above), presents Jarvis in the context of the developing scientific and statistical ideas of the nineteenth century.

42. Edward Jarvis, "Statistics of Insanity in the United States," *Boston Medical and Surgical Journal* 27 (1842): 116–21.

43. Ibid., pp. 281–82.

44. George Tucker, "The Progress of Population and Wealth in the United States in Fifty Years, as Exhibited by the Decennial Census taken in the Period," *Hunt's*

Merchants' Magazine 7 (1842): 243. Tucker's articles appeared in several installments in 1842 and 1843 and were finally published as a book in 1855.

45. "Statistics of Population. Table of Lunacy in the United States," *Hunt's Merchants' Magazine* 8 (1843): 290, 460–61. The rejoinder might well have been authored by Tucker; he included it in his book in 1855.

46. "Reflections on the Census of 1840," *Southern Literary Messenger* 9 (1843): 340–52.

47. For example, see W. G. Brownlow and Abram Pryne, *Ought American Slavery to be Perpetuated? A Debate* (Philadelphia: Lippincott, 1858), pp. 142–47, 151–55, 173 ff.

48. Jarvis, "Insanity among the Coloured Population of the Free States," *American Journal of the Medical Sciences* n.s. 7 (1844): 71–83.

49. The memorial was written between January and May, 1844. It was reprinted several times; the most readily available version is in 28th Cong., 2d sess., 1844, Senate Document 5.

50. John Homans et al., "Report" of the Committee on the Subject of Insanity among the Colored Population of the State of Massachusetts, in *Medical Communications of the Massachusetts Medical Society* 7 (1845): 82–84, 90–95.

51. "Sixth Census, Letter from the Secretary of State, in answer to a resolution of the House," 28th Cong., 1st sess., 1844, House Document 245.

52. John Quincy Adams, *Memoirs*, ed. Charles Francis Adams, 12 vols. (Philadelphia: Lippincott, 1874–77), 11:520; 12:22–23, 27–29, 31, 61, 156.

53. Ibid., 12:27–29. See also Calhoun to Richard Pakenham, British envoy, April 18, 1844, regarding the annexation of Texas, in "Proceedings of the Senate and Documents Relative to Texas, From which the Injunction of Secrecy has been removed," 28th Cong., 1st sess., 1844, Senate Document 341.

54. "Statistics," 28th Cong., 2d sess., 1845, House Document 35.

55. "Report" of the Joint Committee on the Library, 28th Cong., 2d sess., 1845, Senate Document 146.

56. "Errors in the Sixth Census," 28th Cong., 2d sess., 1845, House Document 116.

57. Ibid., pp. 8–9.

58. Ibid., pp. 11–14.

59. Ibid., p. 19.

60. Ibid., pp. 25–30.

61. Ibid., p. 30. Weaver was wrong in saying that only Massachusetts citizens complained. The Congress had received a petition from Pennsylvania signed by Thomas Earle and twenty-four others; see "Last Census—Errors," report of the Select Committee on Statistics, 28th Cong., 1st sess., 1844, House Report 579.

62. Jarvis, "Insanity among the Colored Population of the Free States," *American Journal of Insanity* 8 (1852): 268–82. He was responding to "Startling Facts from the Census," *American Journal of Insanity* 8 (1851): 153–55.

63. "Errors in the Sixth Census," 28th Cong., 2d sess., 1845, House Document 116, pp. 19–20.

Conclusion

1. Joseph C. G. Kennedy, *The Progress of Statistics, read before the American Geographical and Statistical Society, at the annual meeting in New York, Dec. 1, 1859* (New York: J. F. Trow, 1861), p. 1.

2. *The Columbian Arithmetician, or a New System of Theoretical and Practical Arithmetic* (Haverhill, Mass.: William B. Allen, 1811), p. 5.

3. Hinton Rowan Helper, *The Impending Crisis of the South: How to Meet It* (New York: A. B. Burdick, 1857), p. 32.

4. *Advocate of Moral Reform* 1 (1835): 81–82.

5. Daniel Scott Smith and Michael Hindus, "Premarital Pregnancy in America, 1640–1971: An Overview and Interpretation," *Journal of Interdisciplinary History* 5 (1975): 537–70.

6. C. Brown, *Facts for the People: A Temperance Tract for Hartford County* (n.p., [185–]), p. 1.

7. *The Temperance Almanac for 1834* (Albany, N.Y.: New York State Temperance Society, 1833), pp. 34–36.

8. Helper, *The Impending Crisis*, p. vi.

9. Samuel Chipman, *Report of an Examination of Poor-Houses, Jails, &c., In the State of New-York, and in the Counties of Berkshire, Massachusetts, Litchfield, Connecticut, and Bennington, Vermont*, 4th ed. (Albany, N.Y.: New York State Temperance Society, 1836), p. 5.

10. William W. Sanger, *The History of Prostitution: Its Extent, Causes and Effects throughout the World* (New York: Harper & Bros., 1858), p. 457.

11. [Isaac Ray], "Statistics on Insanity in Massachusetts," *North American Review* 82 (1856): 79–80.

12. U.S. Congress, *House Reports*, 41st Cong., 2d sess., 1870, Report 3 (January 18), p. 48.

13. Stephen Jay Gould, *The Mismeasure of Man* (New York: Norton, 1981), pp. 50–69.

14. Sanger, *History of Prostitution*, p. 488.

15. Margo Conk, "Accuracy, Efficiency and Bias: The Interpretation of Women's Work in the U.S. Census of Occupations, 1890–1940," *Historical Methods* 14 (1981): 65–72.

16. Chipman, *Examination of Poor-Houses*, p. 7.

17. G. Thomann, *Real and Imaginary Effects of Intemperance: A Statistical Sketch* (New York: U.S. Brewers Association, 1884), pp. 40, 53.

18. George Tucker, "A General Statistical Society for the United States," *Hunt's Merchants' Magazine* 17 (1847): 571–72.

19. Helper, *The Impending Crisis*, p. 33.

20. Helper's faith in numbers was echoed in the work of Henry Chase and C. H. Sanborn, *The North and the South: Being a Statistical View of the Condition of the Free and Slave States* (1857) (reprint ed., Westport, Conn.: Negro Universities Press, 1970).

21. The four were Lemuel Shattuck, Edward Jarvis, Jesse Chickering, and Nahum Capen. See Edward Clark Lunt, "Key to the Publications of the United States Census, 1790–1887," American Statistical Association, *Publications* n.s. 1 (1888): 83–84.

22. J. D. B. DeBow, "Statistical Bureaus in the States," *DeBow's Commercial Review* 8 (1850): 441.

23. Helper, *The Impending Crisis*, p. 81.

24. DeBow, "The Southern States," *DeBow's Commercial Review* 8 (1850): 48–52.

25. Kennedy, *Progress of Statistics*, pp. 3, 4, 8.

Index

Abacus, 10, 18, 19
Abolition, 4, 193, 195
Accounting. *See* Bookkeeping
Adams, John Quincy, 185, 190, 197–98, 201, 203
Addison, Joseph, 89–90
Alcott, William, 3–4
Algebra, 7, 20; in colonial curriculum, 85, 122, 123, 124; on inductive plan, 134; and women, 142, 143, 144
Allen, Thomas, 190–91, 202
Almanacs, 126, 127; and mileage, 23; as personal notebooks, 111, 165; and political arithmetic, 83, 94; as statistical reference books, 151, 165, 179, 221, 257 n.37; and temperance, 171, 208, 210; as timepieces, 85, 176
American Almanac and Repository of Useful Knowledge, The (Worcester), 179, 190
American Annals of Education, 146–47
American Journal of Education, 135, 136
American Philosophical Society, 130, 161
American Statistical Association, 178; founding of, 181–82; involvement of, in 1850 census, 223; memorial of, to Congress, 196, 197, 198
Anglicans: church membership of, 79–80; ecclesiastical censuses of, 36, 38
Apprenticeship, 27, 125
Arabic numerals, 7; early usage of, 12, 16, 18–19, 28, 40; and mental

arithmetic, 135; and power of place notation, 10, 20, 25
Arbuthnot, John, 32; on mathematics and masculinity, 139; on national accounting, 28–29; on numeracy in America, 9, 118; on Petty, 33
Aristotle, 42, 44
Arithmetic: Alcott on, 3–4; as commercial subject in America, 118, 121–22, 129, 148–49; as commercial subject in England, 15–16, 24–28, 30, 39; Dennie on, 116–17; Franklin on, 81–82, 84, 114; Hamilton on, 4, 175; as inductive science, 8; as memory work, 8, 25–26, 121–22, 130–31, 134; and temperance, 210. *See also* Arithmetic instruction; Arithmetic textbooks; Mathematics; Mental arithmetic
Arithmetic instruction, 6, 7; in colonial America, 9, 118–25, 140–41; in the early republic, 130–38, 141–48, 165; and women, 139–48. *See also* Arithmetic; Arithmetic textbooks; Copybooks, arithmetic
Arithmetic upon the Inductive Method of Instruction (Colburn), 134
Arithmetic Simplified (Beecher), 145, 146
Arithmetic textbooks: commercial texts, 23, 24–27, 28, 82, 118, 130; earliest American, 119, 132; earliest English, 16, 17, 19–20; by a female author, 145–46; and mental arithmetic, 134–38; simplified, 133–34; using federal money, 128–30. *See also* Copybooks, arithmetic